D1707302

Succession in Saudi Arabia ⟋

Succession in Saudi Arabia ～

Joseph A. Kechichian

palgrave

First published 2001 by
PALGRAVE
175 Fifth Avenue, New York, N.Y.10010 and
Houndmills, Basingstoke, Hampshire RG21 6XS.
Companies and representatives throughout the world

PALGRAVE is the new global publishing imprint of St. Martin's Press LLC
Scholarly and Reference Division and Palgrave Publishers Ltd (formerly
Macmillan Press Ltd).

ISBN 0–312–23880–0 hardback

Library of Congress Cataloging-in-Publication Data
Kechichian, Joseph A.
Succession in Saudi Arabia / Joseph A. Kechichian
    p. cm.
  Includes bibliographical references and index.
  ISBN 0–312–23880–0 (cloth)
1. Saudi Arabia—Politics and government—20th century.   2. Saudi Arabia—Kings and
rulers—Succession.   I. Title.
DS244.52.K44   2000
953.8—dc21
    00–062607

A catalogue record for this book is available
from the British Library.

Design by Letra Libre, Inc.

First edition: June 2001
10 9 8 7 6 5 4 3 2 1

Printed in the United States of America.

For Angelica,
who gives meaning to it all

Saudi Arabia

Administrative Divisions

Province Boundary

There are no provincial captials. Administration of the
provinces is from Riyadh. Boundaries are approximate.

Al Qurayyat

Arar

Al Jawf

Al Hudud
ash
Shamaliyah

Rafha

KUWAIT

Al Muqata'ah
ash Shamaliyah

As Sharwrah
Tabuk

Ha'il

Tayma

Ha'il

Unadyzah

Ras Al Khafji
Ras Al Ghar
Al Jubayl
Ras Tannurah
Dammam
Dahran
Abdalq
Al Qatif
BAHRAIN
Al Hufuf

Al Wajh

Al Madinah

Al Qasim

Riyadh
Diriyah

QATAR

Yanbu Al Bahr

Madinah

Afif

Al Kharj

U.A.E.

Jiddah

Makkah

Al
Khasirah

Makkah
At Ta'if

Ranyah

Ar Riyad

Ash Sharqiyah

Al Bahah

Al Sulayyil

OMAN

Bishah

Khamis Mushayt

Asir

Najran

Jizan

Najran
Wudayah

Jizan

YEMEN

Contents

Acknowledgements

The publication of this book is the clearest indication that the Al Saud have reached a very high level of political maturity. Inasmuch as the subject is sensitive, the mere fact that so many Saudis—both from the ruling family as well as among the Kingdom's intellectual community—found merit in discussing it with an outsider demonstrates that what was once a taboo subject has become common. To an analyst, this is a solid sign of political emancipation, yet another indication of how strong the family's foundation is.

In the course of writing this book, as well as its companion volume on *The National Security of Saudi Arabia* (coauthored with Theodore W. Karasik, forthcoming), I visited the Kingdom on three separate occasions. Appendix 1 lists the individuals who were interviewed for both volumes and I thank them all. There are, nevertheless, several individuals who deserve special accolades. First, I wish to thank HRH Dr. Faysal bin Salman bin Abdul Aziz Al Saud, now a professor of political science at King Saud University in Riyadh. My genuine respect and affection for him is based on a firm belief that Prince Faysal is a true Al Saud. His intervention with the Ministry of Information opened several doors that, in turn, allowed me to exchange views with a slew of individuals. I hasten to add, however, that Prince Faysal is not responsible for my analysis. Dr. Fouad Al-Farsy, the Kingdom's affable minister of information, was equally generous with his time. I thank him for instructing his ministry to make the necessary arrangements during my visits to Riyadh and Jeddah. Finally, I owe a special debt of gratitude to Drs. Abdul Aziz Al-Fayez and Othman Y. Al-Rawaf, both of whom are now members of the Majlis al-Shura. My friendship with them is long-standing, ever since their tenures at King Saud University. Both have always welcomed me and entertained my fallacious opinions, even if we held different views on a variety of subjects.

Although the idea for this study first crossed my mind while I was at the RAND Corporation, it was Dr. Samantha Ravich, now with the Center for Strategic and International Studies in Washington, D.C., who ensured its realization. In her capacity as the international security and foreign policy program officer with the Smith Richardson Foundation (in Westport, Connecticut), Dr. Ravich encouraged me to apply for a grant that, fortunately, was approved in the fall of 1997. As I had just started my own consulting firm—after leaving the RAND Corporation under difficult circumstances—the opportunity was doubly satisfying. Drs. Marin Strmecki and Dale Stewart, also from the Smith Richardson Foundation, proved to be congenial colleagues, as they approved a timely extension to complete my work and coordinated the grant's various requirements at the University of California in Los Angeles (UCLA).

At UCLA, Drs. Irene Bierman and Afaf Lutfi al-Sayyid Marsot, respectively the director and the deputy director of the G. E. von Grunebaum Center for Near Eastern Studies, have hosted me between the fall of 1998 and the spring of 2001. Both encouraged this and other endeavors and—along with a number of UCLA students who attended my seminar on the subject—provided useful comments at an early stage. I am grateful to both for their support. It is a remarkable coincidence that my association with UCLA and especially Dr. al-Sayyid Marsot should move in the direction it is, given that she published my first scholarly work on Saudi Arabia in the *International Journal of Middle East Studies,* back in 1986. I have always cherished her confidence in my work. I also thank Jonathan Friedlander, Susan E. Sims, Natalie Jacob, Lisette Hurtado Mora, Diane James, and Tamika Merrick, all with the Center's administration.

Anthony Scardino, one of my students from Pepperdine University (where I taught a course on the Persian Gulf in the fall of 1998), and Theodore W. Karasik, my longtime research colleague, provided solid assistance and I thank both of them for their help.

Professor R. Hrair Dekmejian from the Department of Political Science at the University of Southern California was kind enough to read the manuscript in its draft from and offer various comments. I thank this accomplished scholar, who knows Saudi Arabia well, for both his time and his numerous recommendations.

Finally, the Palgrave team deserves special accolades for preparing the manuscript for publication. Karen Wolny, my editor, Ella Pearce, Sonia Wilson, and Rick Delaney all proved to be dedicated to this effort. Rodney Williams copyedited the text with skill. I thank each one for performing well beyond the call of duty.

A Note on Transliteration

A modified version of the Library of Congress transliteration system has been adopted throughout the book. In rendering Arabic words and names, however, I relied on the style used by the *International Journal of Middle East Studies*. Thus a name that is commonly rendered in English, for example Mohamed, becomes Muhammad, and Mecca becomes Makkah. Whenever known, I used the common English spellings for proper names, as well as for names of countries. Thus Fahd rather than Fahad (although the latter is used if the individual writes his name with that spelling) and Saudi Arabia rather than Su'udi Arabia. Because this study deals extensively with personalities, and since so many names sound identical, an effort has been made to identify individuals by their names, their fathers' first names, and, whenever possible, their grandfathers' first names—thus, Heir Apparent Prince Abdallah bin Abdul Aziz bin Abdul Rahman Al Saud, instead of Prince Abdallah. In a few cases, including with Heir Apparent Abdallah, the full name is not repeated each and every time, to avoid excessive verbiage. For practical purposes, all diacritical marks for long vowels and velarized consonants have been eliminated. Arabic speakers will know the correct reference for the transliterated words throughout the text.

Introduction

Although a medium-size power of longstanding, and a founding member of the United Nations, the Kingdom of Saudi Arabia was catapulted to the forefront of international affairs only in the aftermath of the 1973 energy crisis. At that time, decisions partially reached in Riyadh affected Western security interests and, for better or worse, have permanently altered the way Westerners perceive the Kingdom. To be sure, the Al Saud ruled Riyadh with skill and alleviated many apprehensions that the ruling family would follow the destiny of the Pahlavis in neighboring Iran, especially after the 1979 Islamic Revolution toppled the Peacock Throne. In fact, not only did the Al Saud survive the epoch-making crisis that rocked the entire Muslim world, but they opted to provide the Saudi people with a cradle-to-grave welfare system, to enhance their legitimacy and secure their rule. Still, as oil prices fluctuated, the ruling family came under strong pressure to continue its legitimizing policies and, equally important, faced a growing as well as increasingly educated population. By all accounts, Al Saud rulers fared well, given that senior members remained attuned to internal needs.

Yet, on June 6, 1999, Prince Talal bin Abdul Aziz, a brother of King Fahd of Saudi Arabia, called on Riyadh to "find a smooth way to pass the monarchy to the next generation, or face a power struggle after the era of old royals passes."[1] Prince Talal, who was the leader of the "Free Princes" movement—which called for democratic changes in the early 1960s—drew the ire of senior Al Saud family members in the late 1950s and early 1960s and may do so again as the Kingdom enters the twenty-first century. To be sure, Prince Talal was rehabilitated after several years in exile and, equally important, after pledging his undivided loyalty to the family. In 1962, Prince Abdallah bin Abdul Aziz bin Abdul Rahman (who became Heir Apparent in 1982 and was formally "decreed" as next in line in 1992) responded to the democratization call made by Prince Talal as follows:

> Talal alleges that there is no constitution in Saudia Arabia which safeguards democratic freedoms. But Talal knows full well that Saudi Arabia has a constitution inspired by God

and not drawn up by man. I do not believe there is any Arab who believes that the Koran contains a single loophole which would permit an injustice to be done. All laws and regulations in Saudi Arabia are inspired by the Koran and Saudi Arabia is proud to have such a constitution. . . . As for his statement about socialism, there is no such thing as rightist or leftist socialism; true socialism is the Arab socialism laid down by the Koran. Talal talked at length about democracy. He knows that if there is any truly democratic system in the world, it is the one now existing in Saudi Arabia.[2]

In his latest call, Prince Talal saw the need to further modernize the Kingdom, "including giving women more rights to work and allowing them to drive, . . . limit[ing] Riyadh's substantial military spending, and pass[ing] power to the next generation because," Talal further clarified, "our problems are with the grandsons," who will, presumably, require a new mechanism to ensure smooth successions.

Although Heir Apparent Abdallah bin Abdul Aziz did not publicly respond to these latest comments about modernization, social restructuring, and succession, these critical questions—certainly the most urgent and obvious facing the Kingdom—were well known to him. As Prince Talal noted in early June 1999, the ruling family faced certain inevitable challenges, to modernize and come to terms with the difficult succession question. Still, Prince Talal's frankness amply illustrated the dilemma for King Fahd and his successors, eager to maintain Saudi Arabia's traditions while engaging in a full-scale modernization program.

The purpose of this book is to assess the coming leadership changes in the Kingdom at a time when Saudi Arabia is growing in importance and increasingly affecting Western security interests.[3] It proposes to (1) identify individuals with the greatest leadership potential; (2) examine their political, social, and religious perceptions, including views of the United States and other key powers; and (3) assess the criteria for their endurance as a ruling family. In other words, the aim is to clarify for leading Saudi "leaders" what the "will to power" (the determinants to prevail against all odds) may be.[4] In doing so, the book will posit how succession is likely to develop during the next few years.

The Kingdom in the Twentieth Century

In 1999, Saudi Arabia held an estimated quarter of the world's proven reserves of petroleum in a space nearly one-third the surface area of the United States. Its geography occupies over 70 percent of the Arabian Peninsula, sharing borders with critical Middle Eastern states, including Jordan, Iraq, and Kuwait in the north; Bahrain, Qatar, and the United Arab Emirates to the east, and Oman and Yemen to the south. Two significant bodies of water, the Persian/Arabian Gulf[5] in the east and the Red Sea in the west, straddle the country. Given the strategic choke points at the Straits of Hormuz and Bab al-Mandeb, access to blue-water seas may be problematic. Divided into 18 provinces, its local leaders exercise substantial authority even as foreign, defense, and economic policies are made by the Al Saud ruling family in Riyadh.

In keeping with a traditional monarchy—in which the ruler remains supreme religious leader—the custodianship of the holy mosques at Makkah and Madinah confer on the Saudi ruler an unparalleled degree of legitimacy. Since 1932, when the tribes on the Arabian Peninsula were united by Abdul Aziz bin Abdul Rahman, the Al Saud ruled over the Kingdom with skill and perseverance. Not only were they successful in creating a modern state—where only tribal politics had dominated—they also developed a unique legitimizing framework for their rule.[6] To be sure, Abdul Aziz and senior members of the family aimed to preserve their power base. They also understood what their interests were and how to fend off threats. Yet, despite their perception of innate capabilities, the Al Saud operated in a vacuum for much of the past few centuries. In essence, they lacked a coherent political strategy that could shield the family from internal as well as external threats and ensure the family's continued dominion. The quest to rectify this lacuna led Abdul Aziz and his successors to create a unique political framework, equipped with a clear ideological basis that, ultimately, legitimized Al Saud rule. In the end, Riyadh developed a will to power that benefited from the family's strict adherence to Islamic values and, with oil wealth, transformed the desert into a modern country.

In addition to this will to power, a slew of ideological justifications were advanced to legitimate the elite's uninterrupted rule. These ideological claims generated a set of preconditions that enhanced regime stability. Certain institutional arrangements and political goals naturally arose out of the need to meet ideological preconditions. Indeed, most of the goals were political, military, and economic in nature and substance. For example, to attain doctrinal goals, a set of military, political, and economic strategies were devised. In turn, the purpose of these strategies was to minimize the threats to, and maximize the interests of, the ruling elite. Consequently, strategies were both feasible and credible when compared with the limitations upon the country's capabilities and influence.

The context within which Saudi elites operated for most of the past seven decades was one of general competition for power and influence within the country at large and over policymaking in particular. Taken together, the competition of elites and the process of policy formulation constituted national security decision making. In Saudi Arabia's case, the dominant elite was—and remains—the Al Saud.

Decision makers

In order to be able to rule effectively, the Al Saud maintained order within the ranks, chiefly by co-opting branches of the family that might otherwise mount a rival bid for the throne and challenge the succession process from within. The genealogically senior branch of the family, the Saud Al-Kabir (also known as the Araif) was a case in point. In the early 1900s this branch of the family mounted a challenge to the tribal succession system, basing their claim to rule on their seniority within the family. King Abdul Aziz thwarted this threat by marrying one of his sisters, Nura, to the leading contender from the senior family line, Saud bin Abdul Aziz bin Saud Al-Kabir.[7] By acting in this manner, Abdul Aziz co-opted the Saud Al-Kabir and gave them a continuing stake in the rule of his branch of the family.[8]

Co-optation of this kind proved useful in the case of another branch of the family that could have—but has not—mounted a rival bid for power, the Jiluwi. Since the inception of the Kingdom, the Jiluwi have been given the responsibility of holding governorships in key provinces. Until King Fahd's ascent to the throne, the Jiluwi controlled the governorship of the important oil-producing province of Al-Hasa.[9] King Fahd's son Muhammad was entrusted the governorship of Al-Hasa in 1985, but Prince Muhammad bin Fahd bin Jiluwi continued to govern two of the province's major cities: Hofuf and Ahsa. Prince Abdallah bin Abdul Aziz bin Musaid bin Jiluwi, governor of the Northern Province, was another example of a senior member of the family who was entrusted with a position of authority. In short, the Jiluwi support, by means of appointments to key posts, was carefully tailored to suit the needs of the ruling family.

Similarly, the Thunayan branch of the family has never mounted a threat to the succession process within the ruling line of the family. Yet, this line of the family was fortuitously brought into the mainstream, although in this instance it was "the result of romance rather than arrangement." King Faysal married Iffat bint Ahmad Al Thunayan, thus establishing an important connection between the Thunayan and the ruling line.[10] The appointments of Shaykh Abdul Aziz Al Thunayan as deputy minister of foreign affairs and Prince Saud bin Abdallah Al Thunayan as deputy minister in the Ministry of Municipal and Rural Affairs have given this branch of the family additional interest in maintaining the ruling line in power.

These examples do not begin to decipher the complexity of the ruling family's well-crafted system of rule, as intermarriages are not limited to "rival" cadet branches. The power of cadet branches within the family, especially in the decision-making process, is not only demonstrated by the powerful positions that the "co-opted" cadets hold, but is also shown by the behavior of powerful cadets such as King Abdul Aziz's brothers Muhammad and Abdallah bin Abdul Rahman. Together with King Fahd, these two senior cadets were instrumental in building the consensus required within the family to depose King Saud (in 1964) in favor of then Heir Apparent Prince Faysal, persuading the Saudi ulama to label the former incompetent to rule after a series of policy blunders. Without a doubt, this was one of the most important decisions the family made this century.[11] Nevertheless, and although such "arrangements" were practiced on a regular basis in the past, the exponential growth of the family is forcing changes in the way succession is practiced and how senior leaders are stacking their offspring against each other.

Succession and Heir Apparent Abdallah

Succession has—with minor exceptions—passed to the sons of Abdul Aziz in order of seniority since the death of the dynasty's founder. Understanding the interrelationships and precedence within this ruling family line is therefore important in identifying how the pattern may change.[12] In a break with long-standing tradition, the ruling family published an explicit order of succession for the first time in 1992. In addition to existing "understandings" regarding the identity of the Heir Apparent, a royal decree now explicitly states that Abdallah is first in line for the throne, while it is understood that Prince Sultan stands second in line—both are sons of the Kingdom's founder.[13] In addition to the King, these two princes naturally remain key present and future decision makers in Saudi Arabia.

Until recently, Heir Apparent Abdallah maintained a rather cool attitude toward Western powers in general, and the United States in particular. This outlook underwent considerable change once the prince saw Washington make good on its promise to support the monarchy by intervening successfully after Baghdad's 1990 invasion of Kuwait.[14] Heir Apparent Abdallah's connection to internal political affairs comes by virtue of his leadership of the Kingdom's internal security force, the National Guard. Unlike the regular army, which is stationed on the country's periphery, this force is situated at key facilities. Raised from tribal levies and thus a unique instrument by which to maintain tribal loyalty to the ruling family, the Guard is also a tested tool by which to maintain internal security. Under the circumstances, the National Guard can easily be used to enforce Prince Abdallah's claim to succession after King Fahd's rule, should there be any challenges.

Still, and despite the fact that Prince Abdallah controls the National Guard, the Heir Apparent is relatively weak because of his overall position within the family. Prince Abdallah is the son of a Shammar bride whom Abdul Aziz married in order to suborn and co-opt the support of the rival Al Rashid dynasty of Hail after he defeated them in battle.[15] As such, Heir Apparent Abdallah does not enjoy the gaggle of full princely brothers that other Saudi leaders possess—he is a relative outsider. Furthermore, Prince Abdallah has a limited number of well-situated male progeny. Perhaps because of his lack of broad family ties, those three sons whose positions are known remain employed exclusively within the Heir Apparent's National Guard fief. The consequence is that Abdallah lacks a strong network of supporters within the broader government bureaucracy—an asset that other princes managed to fashion by placing their sons and relatives widely throughout the government.

Heir Apparent Abdallah's genealogical ties within the ruling house are thus weak, and his ability to place his men within the government limited. As Prince Abdallah prepares himself to assume the throne, this has to change if the Heir Apparent is to gain effective control of the Kingdom and its government. Such change could come only at the expense of other powerful princes who participate in the decision-making process. How will Prince Abdallah accomplish this, and who will he dismiss? Will he succeed in pushing his offspring to the forefront? Will he enter into specific new alliances and/or encourage his sons to do likewise? Once in power, how will he rearrange the succession process, and at whose expense? Ultimately—and this is the key question with Heir Apparent Abdallah—will he feel free to dismiss his own Heir Apparent (allowed him under the 1992 Royal Decree) if the family imposes Defense Minister Sultan, or any other candidate, on him?

These questions deserve careful scrutiny given that so much of the decision-making process in Saudi Arabia is driven by personalities.

Prince Sultan and the Sudayri Seven

The second in line for the throne, Sultan bin Abdul Aziz, enjoys strong family ties because he shares a mother, Hassa bint Ahmad Al Sudayri, with six other full princes. Much has been made of the influence of the

"Sudayri Seven" within the Al Saud—and with good reason.[16] King Fahd is monarch, Prince Sultan is minister of defense and civil aviation and second in line for the throne, Prince Nayif is the minister of the interior, Prince Ahmad is deputy minister of the interior, Prince Salman governs Riyadh, Prince Turki is Prince Sultan's deputy at the defense ministry, while Abdul Rahman represents an important business conglomerate. The influence of the Sudayris within the ruling family extends beyond the seven full brothers, however, to five more full princes of the blood and a further five Sudayris who are entrusted key gubernatorial and ministerial posts.

By dint of his connection to the Sudayri clan, Prince Sultan can thus call upon a strong base of support within the family. Moreover, Defense Minister Sultan's relatives are well situated in key posts throughout the government. One Sudayri offspring, Badr, serves as deputy commander in chief of the National Guard to Heir Apparent Abdallah. Such a presence and influence within the principal political asset by which Prince Abdallah bin Abdul Aziz is expected to enforce his claim to the throne is nonnegligible.

Prince Sultan's sons are also well positioned within the government to act as proponents of his eventual candidacy for the highest office in the land. Until recently, the elder son, Khaled, was well known to Westerners as the Saudi army commander of the Arab coalition force that successfully participated in Operations Desert Shield and Desert Storm.[17] In fact Prince Khaled's success generated so much political capital and commercial opportunity for him that he saw fit to resign his army commission prematurely—an event in which the influence of the King and the opprobrium of other princes concerned with Khaled's growing power were likely to have played significant roles.[18] Nonetheless, Prince Khaled bin Sultan is still a political force within the Kingdom by virtue of the political platform that his ownership of two influential London-based periodicals grants him and his father.[19]

Sultan's second son, Prince Bandar, is better known in the West than Prince Khaled largely because his post as Saudi Arabia's ambassador to the United States creates numerous public opportunities. Prince Bandar, who is reportedly close to the monarch, implements the Kingdom's deliberate political and military strategy of codependency with the United States, designed to ensure that Washington has a continuing stake in supporting the ruling family in power. The success of this policy is an integral part of Saudi security initiatives. For this reason, any political capital that Prince Bandar builds because of his close ties with Western, especially American, political and business elites is as much a credit to his own and his father's political standing within the ruling family as it is a bonus to the country's long-term security. Indeed, given the Sudayri command of this liaison post to a key ally, one may wonder how it is that Heir Apparent Abdallah makes his voice heard in Washington independent of Sudayri mediation and what Prince Bandar's long-term prospects may be in his current post as Prince Abdallah moves closer to assuming the throne.

Sultan bin Abdul Aziz thus enjoys a strong base of power within the government thanks to the superior positioning of his sons and relatives. He also enjoys a strong base of support within the ruling family because of his connections to his extended Sudayri family. Still, it would be a mistake to assume that Prince Sultan can automatically rely on the support of monolithic ranks of the Sudayris within the ruling family in his bid to influence policy. While he remains alive and secure on his throne, King Fahd is not only the senior member of the Al Saud, but also the senior male member of the Sudayri faction within the family. King Fahd has first claim to Sudayri loyalties and it is for this reason that another Sudayri, Muhammad bin Turki, is entrusted the governorship of Baha Province. Earlier, Turki Al Sudayri and Fahd bin Khalid Al Sudayri controlled the key southern provinces of Asir and Najran. This whole area of the Kingdom was wrested from Yemen as recently as the early 1930s. It was the scene of extended border skirmishes financed by Egypt in the 1950s and is a likely future source of discord between the Kingdom and unified Yemen.[20]

King Fahd's Outlook

The King too has positioned his male offspring in key decision-making positions. He is grooming the young Abdul Aziz for responsibility and allows his sons Khalid and Saud to maintain ties with the business community. But most importantly, the ruler has altered the traditional power balance within the Kingdom and displaced the traditional Jiluwi governor in order to give his son Muhammad control over the oil-rich Eastern Province (Al-Hasa), from which Saudi Arabia derives its wealth. In doing so, not only has King Fahd placed someone of unquestionable loyalty to him in a strategically sensitive province of the Kingdom, the monarch has also offered one of his sons an unparalleled opportunity to prove himself—in a position requiring the utmost judgment and sensitivity. Should Prince Muhammad bin Fahd continue to prove himself in this position (following his success in winning over a majority of the Shia opposition leaders there), he will be well positioned to claim even greater responsibilities further down the road.

King Faysal's Offspring

In addition to this set of principal actors, two other princes from a branch of the family that is no longer in line for the throne deserve mention as key players in succession matters. They are Princes Saud and Turki, the sons of the late King Faysal. With his marriage to Jauhara bint Faysal bin Abdallah bin Abdul Rahman, Minister of Foreign Affairs Saud has attempted to secure his future by marrying into the family of the future monarch's extended family. Prince Turki's influence derives from his responsibilities as director of Saudi intelligence.

Pressures on Succession

Given the above discussion, the fact that the principle of succession within the Kingdom is under pressure is a matter of some concern to observers of Saudi Arabia. To be sure, the principle of succession is not under attack by any one individual or group, but rather by time. The sons of Abdul Aziz are advancing in age. Indeed, the passage of time will inexorably exhaust the Kingdom's supply of qualified successors and may generate a rate of turnover among rulers that could become destabilizing in itself. While the number of senior princes declines, five thousand hopefuls from the second and third generations wait in the wings, with no agreed criteria for choosing among them. This familywide competition is crucial, even if less than ten princes have any chance of acceding to the throne over the next few decades. Nevertheless, the future composition and stability of the decision-making elite are subject to dramatic change, because of complex interfamily realignments. How will these alliances evolve? Who will come to dominate the system? What will it take to earn the support of those who are not chosen?

Undoubtedly, certain family factions will negotiate the winnowing that must take place amongst the second and third generations better than others. If history is a guide, one may expect the family to present the outside world with a solution to the succession question in a manner that appears sensible and expeditious. Such a move would remove uncertainty and end opportunities for open speculation on intrafamily contentions. Nevertheless, the prospect that behind-the-scenes resolution of the succession question may be more extended, and that a solution may not come quickly or for that matter felicitously, should be carefully assessed.

While the ruling family will probably always try to avoid allowing events to reach the scale of an unseemly public dispute, differences of view among its members are not unprecedented in Saudi history. A repeat of past questioning of the monarchy's ideological or doctrinal legitimacy would be particularly destabilizing.[21] There is a chance that the resolution of the succession issue could turn into a significant and bitter behind-the-scenes skirmish. Players may well act early, promoting their sons to positions in which they can build the internal or external political capital needed for a credible bid for the throne or attempting to broaden their relatives' base within both family and government at the expense of other princes. Any attempt by a faction of the ruling family to build a rival power base within the Saudi religious or tribal establishment would be indicative of such behind-the-scenes struggles. Past clashes for power within Saudi Arabia have not been without violence either.

Moreover, a full-blown succession contest could literally polarize the Al Saud. Indeed, the prospect of stalemate, extreme rivalry, and instability within the family would remain of concern for both Riyadh and its Western allies. The implications of any such development for major Western powers would be serious, as family strife could hinder the monarchy's efforts to meet growing internal and external challenges to its continued rule and, potentially, destabilize the regime.

The Influences of Religion and Tribal Behavior on Succession

Succession issues are problematic in hereditary monarchies because of ingrained power skirmishes that, for better or worse, determine how the mighty rule. In Europe, where dynasties flourished, succession was once determined by a show of strength among a ruler's sons. In time, however, it reverted to primogeniture, in which a ruler's oldest male descendant acceded to the throne.[22] For a variety of reasons, chiefly because of religious and tribal traditions, primogeniture has not developed among Arabian dynasties in quite the same way, because under Shariah law, all sons of a man are equal and legitimate, even if they were born from illegitimate marriages. Moreover, in pre-Islamic tribal norms, while the throne could have passed from one generation to the next within a particular family, it was not necessarily passed from father to son. Rather, authority also fell to a ruler's brother, uncle, or cousin, depending on which of these oldest male relatives was seen to possess "the qualities of nobility; skill in arbitration; *hazz* or 'good fortune'; and leadership."[23]

The major difficulty of this tradition lies in the determination of ability, or disability, in ambiguous situations, particularly since the pool of potential heirs is expanded to include both the ruler's lineal relatives (sons) and his lateral relatives (brothers), as well as other members of a ruling family. Since there are several potential rulers and no means—either observed or formal—to finally arbitrate among various claimants, the traditional Saudi political system has tended to foster succession struggles. Although the system has the advantage, at least in principle, of determining the most able ruler—that is, the succession of the fittest—in practice the struggle can be extremely destructive and can expose the Kingdom to a number of internal and external foes.

To some extent, the inherent fragility of the succession principle on the Arabian Peninsula is mitigated by the traditional prerogative of rulers to designate their successors, and even the heir to the Heir Apparent. This is particularly the case for strong rulers of long tenure, who have typically attempted to establish a lineal line of succession, usually to their oldest son. While this designation helps to ensure a smooth continuation, it has not prevented a struggle for succession in the face of problems and failures.

Similarly, the maintenance of a ruler's position is inherently tenuous, since the basis of his legitimacy depends on a continued demonstration of ability. Evidence of failure, or disability, thus weakens the ruler's position and opens opportunities for rivals to challenge him with the entirely legitimate claim that they can rule the realm better. It is for this reason that crises facing Saudi dynasties have tended to aggravate family rivalries, to the extent that a ruler could be held accountable for causing a particular crisis, or fail to resolve it. In fact, the most able ruler was often challenged by other family members, or even rival families, when rule by consensus diminished.

Historically, the lack of an institutionalized state structure also tended to complicate succession problems. Without a central state apparatus, it was more difficult for a designated heir to guarantee his succession and deter challenges, or to maintain his position once he became ruler. Similarly, there were no government positions independent of a ruler's household that the ruler could use to reward supporters and conciliate opponents. Rather, the power of a ruler on the Arabian Peninsula stemmed from his complicated, but highly effective, personal loyalties from relatives and advisers. To be sure, the absence of formal state institutions on the Arabian Peninsula did not mean that dynastic rulers operated in a vacuum, but, despite the rich tribal traditions that ensured the survival of a particular dynasty, Arabian rulers inherited the complications that resulted after the advent of Islam.

The Legacy of Islamic Succession. Whether the process for legitimate and orderly succession was ever envisaged by the Prophet Muhammad, the absence of a male heir ensured that there would be no dynasty for the first Islamic State.[24] The first four caliphs who succeeded the Prophet—

Abu Bakr (632–634), Umar (634–644), Uthman (644–656), and Ali (656–661)—not only were related to him through marriage, but were members of the Quraysh tribe. Indeed, the first three successors were chosen by tribal acclamation, and even though the struggle did not culminate until 656 with Ali's rule, major differences arose almost from the beginning. Uthman was challenged by Ali and was assassinated in 656 by the latter's supporters. Ali himself was challenged by Mu'awiya, the Umayyad governor of Syria, who demanded vengeance for the murder of Uthman. What unfolded in the major sectarian division in Islam, between Sunnis and Shias (followers of Ali), was a genuine struggle for legitimate authority.[25]

In 661, the caliph Ali was assassinated by a disgruntled follower in yet another struggle for succession. Mu'awiya then founded the Sunni Umayyad dynasty (661–749) in Damascus, which, in turn was succeeded by the Sunni Abbasid dynasty (750–1258) in Baghdad.[26] For their part, the followers of Ali established their own realm in Cairo in what has become known as the Fatimid dynasty (909–1171).[27] The Abbasids, who claimed descent from the Prophet's uncle of the Hashim clan within the Quraysh tribe, rose against the Umayyads in a classic dynastic clash. In the event, the victorious Abbasids slaughtered most of the Umayyad leadership, with the exception of Abdul Rahman, who managed to escape to Spain, where he founded a new Umayyad dynasty (755–1031). What followed was relative peace and a unique awakening period in the Muslim realm.

In the tenth century, the Abbasid caliphate lost its secular power to warlords in Baghdad, and in 1258 the Abbasid dynasty was eradicated altogether by the Mongol invasion.[28] Various military powers then emerged whose leaders were astute enough to rule in the name of Islam and, ostensibly, by applying Shariah law. Over time, Sunni jurists started to interpret that rule seized by force was legitimate, provided that rulers declared their support for the Shariah.[29] Such interpretations, while expedient and, perhaps, even necessary, certainly hindered the development of proper succession mechanisms in the Muslim world in general and the Arabian Peninsula in particular.

The Legacy of the Ottoman Empire.   For the next 600 years, succession patterns within most of the Muslim world were set by the behavior of Ottoman rulers, who, more often than not, were innovative and bloody.

From the thirteenth to the sixteenth century, 12 sultans ruled the Ottoman Empire following a lineal setup, with authoritative governance passing from a ruler to his eldest son.[30] Despite this seemingly orderly pattern, there was no clearly defined system of primogeniture, and the strongest male offspring routinely eliminated rival siblings. Under the rule of Mahmud I (1413–1421), a "law of fratricide" was introduced, which gave the conqueror the right to execute any surviving brothers to eliminate potential uprisings.[31] This approach was violently followed by Muhammad III, who acceded to the throne in 1595 and, conveniently, had 19 surviving brothers executed. His own children were not spared, allegedly for court conspiracies; that left prospects for succession rather dim. Muhammad III died in 1603 with two minor heirs, Ahmad and Mustafa, and, fittingly, both ruled, but more as the result of a winnowing of ranks than through any merit in their intrinsic capabilities. In 1617, Sultan Ahmad instituted a new mechanism, known as the *Khafes* (cage), to further isolate his own sons and nephews from the seat of authority in Constantinople.[32] The *Khafes* were isolated courts—often spread in remote parts of the empire—serviced by deaf-mutes and sterilized concubines to further control the production of undesired offspring. If and when the services of a particular eligible "successor" were required, the sultan would fetch one, but naturally the practice weakened whatever institutions the empire could support. Moreover, isolation often resulted in nurturing mediocrity, which in time affected the quality of successors. Several sultans subjected to the *Khafes* treatment in their youths suffered from personality disorders and other psychological problems that affected their putative rules. Of course, the loss of quality did not escape shrewd rulers, and in the case of Sultan Abdul Hamid (1774–1789), the suspension of the *Khafes* system was necessary because his own son was not particularly promising. Abdul Hamid retrieved his nephew Selim III (1789–1807) because the latter was allegedly bright. Sultan Selim III, although responsible for the organization of military institutions, proved to be less enlightened than his uncle because, once in power, he reinstituted the system, ostensibly to limit palace intrigues.[33]

To their credit, none of the tribes on the Arabian Peninsula instituted fratricide or cage methods, although most were aware of such practices. Even if tribal traditions—steeped in family honor and the survival of the entire community—prevented behavior similar to the ones practiced by Ottoman sultans, succession struggles were not eliminated. Largely because of widespread poverty, the struggle for survival on the Peninsula meant that intrigues and clashes were not only meant to retain power, but to literally ensure that a strong leader would safeguard tribal members from harm. This was certainly the case with the Rashid dynasty that ruled Hail in Saudi Arabia from 1835 to 1921.

The Legacy of the Rashid Dynasty.   When Abdallah bin Ali bin Rashid
came to power in 1835 as ruler of the Jabal Shammar, he was rewarded
by Faysal bin Turki bin Abdallah bin Muhammad bin Saud (1824–1834)
for helping the latter defeat Mish'al bin Abdul Rahman, who was responsible for the assassination of Faysal bin Turki's father.[34] Upon his
death in 1847, Abdallah bin Ali bin Rashid was succeeded by his son
Talal (1847–1867), who, although able, died in a mysterious accident.[35]
In turn, Talal was succeeded by his brother Mit'ab, who was assassinated
by his nephew Bandar in 1869. Bandar did not rule for long and he too
was assassinated by his uncle Muhammad during a caravan journey.[36]
Muhammad bin Abdallah, also known as Muhammad the Great, had earlier moved to Riyadh, where he established a successful trading enterprise.
He was an exceptional fighter and ruler, responsible for a vast expansion
of the Rashidi realm and, in 1891, the expulsion of the Al Saud from
Riyadh. When he died in 1897, after 25 years in power, he left no male
offspring. Although a quarter century of relative tranquillity had de-
scended on and around Hail, the struggle for succession was once again
open to contention.

Muhammad was succeeded by his nephew Abdul Aziz bin Mit'ab
(1897–1906), who died in a fierce battle with Abdul Aziz bin Abdul Rahman Al Saud. He was succeeded by his son Mit'ab, who was murdered in
1907 by his second cousin, Sultan bin Hammud—a rising member of the
Obaid branch of the tribe—after he failed to gather the consensus of the
family. Sultan, who declared himself ruler without even the consent of his
own father—ostensibly for having violated unwritten family agreements—was murdered by two of his brothers, Saud and Faysal, in 1908
because he was unable to prevent the plundering of several settlements by
Al Saud forces.[37] Saud, the new governor, was himself assassinated in
1919 by members of the Subhan family of Hail, a distant collateral
branch of the Rashid. In 1920, Saud bin Rashid was murdered by his
cousin Abdallah bin Talal, who was in turn immediately killed by Saud's
slaves. Abdallah bin Mit'ab was then announced the eleventh ruler of
Hail and immediately imprisoned the murderer's brother, Muhammad
bin Talal, fearing vengeance. In 1921, Abdul Aziz bin Abdul Rahman Al
Saud finally defeated the Al Rashids, already weakened by their constant
internecine struggles.[38]

In the case of the Al Rashid, a series of weak leaders failed to maintain
order, than plunged the dynasty into chaos. To be sure, vengeance fueled
the successive murders, but underlying weaknesses were equally important. Tribal customs, especially the contest over meager landholdings, determined the extent to which the strife evolved. Moreover, the belief that

all were "equal," even when that was not the case, prompted those who possessed military resources to challenge rulers, in search for legitimizing authority. Equally important were the influences of outside forces, especially the Ottoman and British Empires, that slowly aligned themselves with several Arabian Peninsula tribes. To be sure, the Al Rashid failed because several rulers were too narrowly concerned with internal disagreements, and because they slowly lost the ability to compromise and govern through consensus. This was a major lesson to the equally ambitious Al Saud leaders.

Lessons Learned

Long before Abdul Aziz bin Abdul Rahman reconquered Dir'iyah and unified central Arabia, the pattern of succession and intrafamily politics determined, to a large extent, his preferences and behavior. The problems inherent in the Saudi pattern of succession and maintenance were very evident to the future monarch as he contemplated the history of the first (1744–1818) and second (1822–1891) Saudi Kingdoms.[39] Abdul Aziz realized that different branches of the family struggled to fill vacuums in the line of succession when foreign powers interfered and disrupted the relative tranquillity within the Peninsula.[40] Even without external influences, the balance of power among rivals for the throne frequently broke into open fighting, because self-preservation required family leaders to protect and provide for their members. Out of a total of 14 successions between 1744 and 1891, only 3 were uncontested. The 11 contested successions included assassination, civil war, and, in a few cases, bloodless revolution.

The first great Saudi leader was Muhammad bin Saud (1742–1765). Having joined forces with Muhammad bin Abdul Wahhab (the founder of the unitarian movement pejoratively known as Wahhabism) in 1744, Muhammad bin Saud expanded the Al Saud power base to control most of central Arabia in about two decades.[41] The Al Saud secured the land, and the Al Shaykh, as the family of Muhammad bin Abdul Wahhab came to be known, provided religious legitimacy. Not only was the combination an effective tool to retain power but, equally important, it guaranteed political stability for several generations.

After Muhammad bin Saud, the first two successions went unchallenged, as power passed from ruler to eldest son. In addition, these two successors, Abdul Aziz bin Muhammad (1765–1803) and Saud bin Abdul Aziz (1803–1814), confirmed their tenure by further expanding Saudi landholdings. Potential claimants from either the lineal or lateral lines were either too young or too undistinguished in battle to challenge the two leaders, although several established family branches that would appear in later family politics. Saud bin Abdul Aziz was a fierce warrior who won several key battles in Najd, which naturally enhanced his credibility as leader. In 1788, his father appointed him Heir Apparent—with Shaykh Muhammad bin Abdul Wahhab's full consent—and, most importantly, without any known objections from any member of the extended family. To be sure, Saud's prowess in battle, especially in absorbing the difficult provinces of Al-Hasa in 1793, Karbala in 1802, and Makkah in 1803, endeared him to all. Thus, when a revenge-minded Shia from Karbala assassinated Abdul Aziz bin Muhammad, Saud was proclaimed leader without opposition.[42]

A victim of his own successes, Saud bin Abdul Aziz (1803–1814) was quickly challenged by the Ottoman Empire, which directed its viceroy in Egypt, Muhammad Ali, to invade the Hijaz and defeat the unitarian movement. Like his father and grandfather, Saud bin Abdul Aziz groomed his eldest son, Abdallah, for the throne. At first, Abdallah proved successful in defeating the invading Egyptians, but in 1812 he lost the Hijaz. When Saud died of fever in May 1814, Abdallah became ruler but faced internal challenges, in part because of his poor performance on the battlefield. The emerging family rivalry was resolved by the Egyptian invasion when the Saudi capital in Dir'iyah fell (1818). Several senior Al Saud members were captured and carted off to Cairo, where many simply disappeared. Abdallah, who was also arrested and taken to Egypt, was beheaded in 1819 in Constantinople. Without a doubt, the Porte was after the Al Saud—as well as the Al Shaykh—and aimed at the total elimination of the unitarian movement on the Arabian Peninsula. In the event, Turki bin Abdallah successfully escaped the Ottoman Empire's net, hiding in the harsh environment of the Najd, where few Ottoman or Egyptian levies survived.[43] Within a few years, occupying Egyptian forces lost interest and had withdrawn from most of central Arabia by 1822. The Al Saud entered a period of intense internal rivalry in the absence of a single recognized leader or dominant branch of the family. With the collapse of family order, several rivals sought the support of Egypt against their brothers, clearly abandoning the fundamental consensus principle that had seen them through difficult times. This too was not lost on Abdul Aziz bin Abdul Rahman Al Saud.

By August 1824, the Al Saud power base was restored when Turki bin Abdallah (a grandson of Muhammad bin Saud and uncle of the beheaded Abdallah bin Saud bin Abdul Aziz) returned to Riyadh, captured it, and claimed it as a new capital. He appointed Mishari bin Nasir (from the collateral Mishari branch) as governor of Riyadh. Importantly, he was the first leader of the Abdallah bin Muhammad line to assume leadership, thereby introducing an alternative to the Abdul Aziz line.[44] In time, several captured Al Saud leaders managed to escape from Egypt, and returned to Arabia. Among these was Faysal bin Turki, who quickly rose to prominence and became his father's designated successor. Still, the Al Saud were boxed in central Arabia because, by this time, the British Empire had appeared over the horizon. In the absence of additional landholdings, the instinct to survive aggravated dynastic rivalries, as the Al Saud, once again, fell prey to internecine conflict. Turki bin Abdallah survived a challenge from his cousin Mishari bin Abdul Rahman in 1831 but was finally assassinated by Mishari's agents in 1834.[45] This was the first political murder recorded since the 1744 alliance established the first Saudi state. As fate would have it, Mishari's tenure on the throne was very short, since he too was assassinated, by Turki's son, Faysal, who captured Riyadh in 1834 and proclaimed himself ruler.[46]

Faysal's rule was cut short in 1838 by the return of agitated Egyptian forces who were concerned with the rising influence of the British in and around the Peninsula. The Egyptians expelled and replaced Faysal bin Turki with a puppet ruler, Khalid bin Saud, who, at least theoretically, restored the original dominant branch of the family to power. As alluded to above, the British soon pressured Muhammad Ali to withdraw his forces in 1840, and soon after, Khalid was overthrown by a distant cousin, Abdallah bin Thunayan bin Ibrahim.[47] This was the first time that a member of the Al Thunayan branch of the family assumed power. Abdallah bin Thunayan was deposed in 1843 by Faysal bin Turki, who had escaped Egyptian captivity and returned to Riyadh. This was Faysal bin Turki's second reign and, by far, the most stable period in the history of the Peninsula up to that time. What Faysal bin Turki did—which was carefully studied by Abdul Aziz bin Abdul Rahman Al Saud several decades later—was legendary.[48]

First, the ulama—who tended to recognize whichever prince won the secular struggle for power during these byzantine and bloody family struggles—were gently persuaded to preach faith and conciliation.

Second, Faysal bin Turki succeeded in establishing a more cohesive though smaller Saudi realm, satisfied with the Najd, Hasa, and Jabal Shammar. He accepted Ottoman control over the Hijaz—at least temporarily—because he simply could not rule it with meager resources.

Third, and perhaps as important as any measure ever taken by a leading official, Faysal bin Turki restored order within the family. Loyalties were fostered through appointments, marriages among various young and promising princes, and financial concessions for burgeoning trade efforts—all of which enhanced internal stability.[49]

With Faysal's death in 1865, however, the ruling family was again plunged into a long period of struggle and civil war. Unlike the previous period of family strife, which had stemmed from the vacuum created by foreign invasion, the struggles after Faysal's death were the result of a failure to share power among Faysal's heirs. Following the pattern of other strong rulers, Faysal had designated his eldest son, Abdallah, as Heir Apparent, but Abdallah was challenged by his younger half brother Saud. The consequence was more than a decade of civil war that included attempts by rival princes to make alliances with external powers, this time with the Ottoman Empire, against each other. By 1871, Saud bin Faysal had succeeded in deposing Abdallah bin Faysal. At Saud's death in 1875, his younger full brother, Abdul Rahman, ascended the throne, only to be deposed that same year by Abdallah bin Faysal, who returned to power with Ottoman support. With Abdallah bin Faysal's death in 1889, his younger half brother Abdul Rahman bin Faysal again ascended the throne. By this time, however, the Al Saud dynasty was so weakened by internal fighting that Riyadh was captured by a rival Najdi family, the Rashids.[50] After leading an unsuccessful revolt against the Rashids in 1890, Abdul Rahman, the last surviving son of Faysal bin Turki, along with his immediate family, was forced to seek exile in Kuwait. It was one of Abdul Rahman's sons, Abdul Aziz bin Abdul Rahman Al Saud, who recaptured the family seat and founded the third Saudi state.

Beginning from exile in Kuwait in 1902, Abdul Aziz captured Riyadh and expelled the Rashids. Over the next three decades, Abdul Aziz defeated a host of enemies—including the Ottoman Turks, rival Arabian families, rebellious tribes, and even rival princes from the Al Saud family—to establish the present Kingdom of Saudi Arabia in 1932. What Abdul Aziz bin Abdul Rahman concluded was that constant challenges to the dominant branch within the family substantially weakened the ruler, and that rivalries from collateral branches, although limited, were equally harmful. Simply stated, there were too many claimants to power who, literally, could not be sustained. Moreover, the founder of the third state realized that lineal challenges were detrimental to the survival of the family, and partly to address this problem, he reintroduced an additional mechanism to support his own Heir Apparent, namely the *bay'ah* (oath of loyalty). Faithful to the 1744 alliance between the Al Saud and Al Shaykh, the *bay'ah* to his designated heir by the *Ahl al-Aqd wal-Hall* ("the council that ties and binds," composed of senior family members and religious notables) ensured a modicum of stability. Much like the first Saudi state, which had been achieved through a combination of religious fervor and tribal ethos, Arabia would be reconquered by Abdul Aziz bin Abdul Rahman using the same methods. The alliance with the ulama, neglected when expediency gave way to principles, would be restored in full. Only by adhering to such values, reasoned Abdul Aziz bin Abdul Rahman, could the Al Saud transcend intertribal feuding. Although personal authority and demonstrated prowess were helpful, internal unity was absolutely necessary to successfully challenge outside foes. Finally, the Najdi also noted that both states that had preceded his own failed to create basic institutions that would assume the burden of governance and, in a real sense, create a buffer between the population and the leadership on one level, and among leaders on the other. He set out to address all of these concerns systematically even before 1932 to ensure that his own successors did not engage in fraternal struggles.

Methodological Approach

Although much has been written on Saudi Arabia, the bulk of what is available is on the economy, largely because access to primary sources is extremely difficult.[51] The state of the literature on succession is scant at best. Simply stated, and perhaps understandably, Saudis have not encouraged the study of internal political developments. Consequently, this effort embarks upon a seldom charted course, by relying on as many primary sources—interviews—as possible. Given the sensitivity of the subject, as well as the reluctance of many interviewees to discuss some of the issues raised herein in an open way, an attempt has been made to ask questions tactfully. An effort was also made to canvass the available literature to draw on earlier analyses of the subject.

As discussed above, what we know about succession in the Kingdom of Saudi Arabia is incorporated in larger studies, dealing with political and economic developments. Irrespective of the topic, references to succession appear with some regularity, even if the authors barely scratch the surface.[52] More often than not, these discussions skirt the issue, simply because few writers have secured the necessary access required for a more detailed assessment. To date, the exception to this rule has been Simon Henderson, who ventured into the field to produce an enlightened recent study.[53] It is critical to note that Henderson's monograph focused on King Fahd and the succession dilemma that may arise immediately after his rule. This study explores succession from a generational perspective, identifying a slew of younger leaders who may accede to the throne or influence those who will.

This study aims high. Indeed, the goal is to produce an original essay that will withstand the test of time. Still, it will not operate in a vacuum, given the existence of seminal theoretical work by a number of leading academics. The book relies on Majid Khadduri's legacy of leadership research that, for the past two generations, has stood unchallenged.[54] Khadduri's early efforts—to discuss internal political developments through the leadership prism—is the prototype used for this effort. It must be emphasized that Khadduri emphasized nation building as well as the crucial role that Arab leaders played in that process. This volume updates and enlarges the scope of Khadduri's research by emphasizing future leaders' perceptions of secularism and religious objectives.

The study also relies on Marwan R. Buheiry's unique methodologies in deciphering domestic political challenges.[55] Buheiry studied the interactions of key Western leaders (Alfred T. Mahan, Anthony Eden, Harry Truman, Henry Kissinger, and others) with Arab decision makers to better understand how the latter made policy or reacted to political developments. An effort has been made to draw on this rich theoretical material to build a solid analytical foundation and to better identify emerging patterns that influence internal Saudi policies.

Toward that end, the book is divided into four sections.

Chapter 1 examines the current generation and provides a thorough analysis of the succession issue before King Fahd. The reigns of Kings Saud, Faysal, and Khalid are analyzed briefly before turning to the 1982 succession of King Fahd. The chapter closes with an elaboration of succession for Heir Apparent Abdallah, Defense Minister Sultan, and King Fahd's sons. The chapter also provides some background on past and present succession issues. Although the first two sections of the chapter cover the Saud, Faysal, Khalid, and Fahd reigns, the bulk of the discussion here highlights current Saudi leaders' perceptions of authority. Equally important, the analysis delves into the three most senior officials' views of power and how each may be positioning himself—as well as his offspring—to benefit from future developments.

Chapter 2 examines the next generation by deciphering the key 1992 edict and identifying new leaders (and their perceptions of secularism, religiosity, and political participation), the formation of potential alliances within the family, and the ties between the Al Saud and cadet branches of the family.

Because so much of what is included in this chapter identifies up-and-coming Saudi leaders' views, an effort has been made to classify as many princes as possible within the family political structure (what roles they played), to decipher their views on a number of concerns. This proved invaluable in establishing future internal family alliances as well as the roles of those who will support future monarchs.[56]

Chapter 3 focuses on perceptions of security concerns, emphasizing both religious and secular opposition movements against the Al Saud. In this instance as well, evaluating Al Saud family members' views of key security concerns and how members of the ruling family saw opposition within the Kingdom proved essential. A special effort was made to provide detailed views of the Committee for the Defense of Legitimate Rights (CDLR) and the role that it, as well as the three splinter groups that emerged from the London-based organization, plays in the Kingdom. Finally, the chapter also evaluates the Al Saud's perceptions of both the Iraqi and Iranian threats to their power.[57]

Chapter 4 homes in on the order of the family by examining two potential crisis scenarios to better assess how the Al Saud might fare. This chapter places the analysis of security concerns (provided in the previous chapter) in the framework of imminent changes within the family. In the first instance, how senior family members managed an internal uprising, and in the second case, how they reacted to a family-instigated military takeover were deemed to be useful exercises to test various assumptions about the family's capabilities. Again, the purpose of the chapter is to assess whether the Al Saud could withstand the wind of change and, in the affirmative, how well. Ultimately, this is the real test of succession given that the "management" of crisis situations will surely determine who will emerge on top and govern the Kingdom.

Finally, chapter 5 provides an overall assessment of the new alliances emerging in the Kingdom, and the leaders that could rule. Past alliances proved highly effective because the number of actors was rather limited. Today, Saudi Arabia faces the dilemma of several thousand male princes competing for high office. Although less than a handful will eventually rule, many will have a distinct voice in the decision-making process, which is reached by consensus after thorough consultations. Because the alliances that emerge from such a mechanism are poorly understood, this concluding chapter attempts to clarify—as best as possible—what may be inferred in a scholarly way.

Saudi succession is an important question because it defines the Al Saud and the kind of government they enjoy. Although this volume relies on an unparalleled series of interviews, to date, my "conversations" with Saudi leaders—especially those in the younger generation—yielded several valuable insights.[58] In the end, and irrespective of current developments, the Al Saud are far more secure than generally assumed.

Chapter 1 ⌐

The Current Generation

The stability of Saudi Arabia is largely determined by the nature of its political system, which is, in large part, centered on the ruling Al Saud family. While ruling family politics in the Kingdom share many characteristics with other hereditary monarchies, it is unique in a number of aspects. The family's sheer size and complexity, in terms of both its internal structure and composition and its connections to Saudi society, make the Saudi political system markedly different from other past and present monarchies.[1] In addition, family politics have developed in the context of vast wealth and profound transformations that have altered the face of Saudi Arabia, perhaps permanently. Thus, it is on this basis that family politics is analyzed with an emphasis on determining the interplay between politics and policy on the one hand, and the balance between cohesive and disintegrative forces within the family on the other. These implications for Saudi behavior have a direct bearing on Saudi stability.

Indeed, to assess the legacy of King Abdul Aziz bin Abdul Rahman—certainly the leading Al Saud figure in the twentieth century, who branded the country into his image—and to better understand the many changes that occurred within the ruling family, a careful look at the latter is necessary. Abdul Aziz's progeny institutionalized the Kingdom's political features, ranging from governance to succession, and, despite serious challenges, managed to preserve the dynasty's authority. Four of his sons succeeded him into power. In less than a century, these successors further legitimized the founder's—as well as their own—power bases, adding value to both country and family against some odds. Even if Abdul Aziz's successors were relatively ensured of their positions, all had to distinguish themselves and come to terms with the many limitations that the complex Al Saud entity represented.

The Al Saud Family:
Size and Structure

The ruling Al Saud family is notable for its sheer size, diverse composition, and complex internal structure. Because these features directly influence the political dynamics of the family, it is useful to examine them in some detail. The exact size of the family is not known to any outsider, although educated estimates range between five thousand and eight thousand adults.[2] A more useful breakdown is to consider three politically relevant groupings from which all current and future leaders will probably emerge: (a) descendants of King Abdul Aziz, (b) descendants of Abdul Aziz's brothers, and (c) cadet branches of the Al Saud dynasty. These three groupings must, in turn, be broken down into several subgroupings, to better identify rising leaders. Whether the founder had a clear idea of what his succession should look like, or what patterns it should follow, is difficult to determine. Suffice it to say that challenges from several cousins (also known as the Saud Al-Kabir line) as well as from the Araif and Jiluwi branches of the family all influenced the founder's preferences.[3] If anything, King Abdul Aziz was determined to avoid disputes that had dominated 200 years of family discord, weakened it, and allowed outside powers to interfere in the country's internal affairs.

The Legacy of King Abdul Aziz

Abdul Aziz bin Abdul Rahman founded the third Saudi Kingdom in 1932 and ruled as monarch for 21 years until his death in 1953. In many respects, he was the "father" of modern Saudi Arabia, although his rule was carefully balanced with a reinvigorated alliance with members of the Al Shaykh clan.[4] Moreover, and because his campaign to unify the many tribes on the Arabian Peninsula required it, Abdul Aziz married a large number of women from important tribes, who gave him 36 sons.

The sons of Abdul Aziz form the core of the ruling family (see appendix 6). His four successors—Saud (1953–1964), Faysal (1964–1975), Khalid (1975–1982), and Fahd (1982-present), along with the rest of his surviving sons, occupied the most important political positions in the country. Still, it would be a mistake to assume that King Abdul Aziz's sons either formed a unified bloc in the past or can claim to have established such an "institution" since 1953. Apart from each individual's personal attributes, which may be issue driven within family politics, several topics determined the direction many followed. These ranged from ideological preferences to business interests, and helped form the pattern of whatever factions emerged over the years. Nevertheless, seniority, maternal descent, and the availability of full brothers enhanced one's standing within the exclusive grouping that, by and large, remained a valid illustration of family cohesiveness and the establishment of subgroupings.

Seniority.   As a first criterion, seniority emerged as a key political requirement for succession. To date, the four monarchs of Saudi Arabia since Abdul Aziz have been from amongst the oldest sons. Prince Muhammad voluntarily stepped aside in 1975 in favor of his younger brother Khalid, and both Princes Nasir and Saad were skipped by the family council that acclaimed King Fahd monarch in 1982. To some extent this pattern may be explained by both traditional and practical factors. While the Saudi system of succession is not based on primogeniture, seniority denotes a respected claim to political primacy. Indeed, any political system based on bloodlines provides for elder heirs to have a special relationship with their father. In practical terms as well, elder sons are more likely to get the first taste of power and responsibility, especially in a tribal setting like Saudi Arabia, where several young princes fought alongside the founder in physically unifying the country. Both Saud and Faysal, for example, led armies in the conquests and, subsequently, served as first viceroys of Najd and the Hijaz, respectively.[5] Several other sons received their first opportunities to lead after the seniority succession pattern was set in motion. Given this fundamental characteristic, younger sons of Abdul Aziz, once they matured, challenged the positions of their older brothers. This was demonstrated during the period of struggle between King Saud and Heir Apparent Faysal, when policy differences accelerated their feud. At the time, a group of "middle sons," known as the free princes, supported Saud against Faysal when the Heir Apparent represented the more established—and older—generation, whereas King Saud garnered the support of the younger ones.[6]

While seniority is an important characteristic of succession, it is but one of several features that determine family politics. To be sure, seniority has helped, but it has not—and probably will not—guarantee political prominence. As stated above, Princes Muhammad, Nasir, and Saad were passed over in the line of succession for various reasons, some that are probably next to impossible to decipher. What role family elders played in anointing an Heir Apparent, and how they exercised their persuasive skills to encourage three senior princes to renounce their claims—on the basis of seniority—are undocumented. Suffice it to say that family political alliances are influenced by several factors, aside from seniority, including maternal lineage and the availability of full brothers.

Maternal Lineage.   As important as seniority, the social standing of mothers and their tribal connections often determine the prominence of individual princes. In general terms, sons with mothers from prominent families, such as the Jiluwi or Sudayri, or important tribes, such as the Shammar, have stronger political credentials. Moreover, the influence of maternal lineage must be examined along with the seniority factor, because Abdul Aziz's early marriages were of greater political significance. Given the fact that King Abdul Aziz produced 36 sons, maternal lineage shaped political and social alliances.[7]

Prince Abdallah, Heir Apparent and commander of the National Guard, is widely thought to have strong ties to tribal elements in Najd Province because his mother, Fahda, was from the Shammar tribe. Equally key is the undeniable fact that the Shammar contributed—and continue to do so—to the tribal levies that constitute the National Guard, in significant numbers.[8] King Khalid's mother, Jauhara, was of the Jiluwi family, while King Fahd's mother, Hassa, was a Sudayri. Both families have a long history of association with the Al Saud and played prominent roles in Saudi politics. On such a basis, one is able to infer that Khalid and Fahd represented different factions, and called on members of the prominent Jiluwi and Sudayri families for support when needed. Perhaps the best example of the maternal seniority linkage may be found with the late King Faysal, whose mother, Tarfah, was from the Al Shaykh family. Indeed, Faysal benefited from this lineage because the Saudi religious establishment supported him against King Saud (whose mother, Wadhba, was from the small Bani Khalid tribe) in 1964.

To be sure, there is an element of truth in the argument that maternal descent and seniority are complementary and useful, but the complexity of the family structure does not allow for a simple confluence. The Jiluwi, Sudayri, and several other subfamilies intermarried with the Sauds, as well as with each other. King Khalid's maternal grandmother was of the Sudayri family, for example, even if his mother was born into the Bani Khalid. For their part, the Jiluwis and the Sudayris, like the Sauds, have so many internal divisions that it may be misleading to conclude that they represent unified "groups." As a case in point, and aside from King Fahd and his six full brothers, there are two additional sets of Abdul Aziz's sons born of two other Sudayri women, who have not supported the current monarch.[9] In 2000, it is next to impossible to draw clear lines for blood-tie connections, even if the exercise may shed some light on family intricacies.

Full Brothers.   Perhaps the major factor in family alliances is the role of full brother divisions. Although neither Kings Saud nor Faysal had full brothers, the characteristic has gained prominence in recent years, as King Fahd and his full brothers formed a distinctive political association that merits careful analysis.

The seven sons of the Hassa bint Ahmad Al Sudayri family, led by King Fahd, form a formidable alliance within the Al Saud dynasty. Following the eldest are Sultan (minister of defense); Abdul Rahman, who reportedly handles family finances; Nayif (minister of the interior); Turki, another leading businessman;[10] Salman (governor of Riyadh); and Ahmad (deputy minister of the interior). Whether by luck or by design, the political fortunes of the "Sudayri Seven" or, as they are sometimes known, the "Al Fahd," have been closely linked. For example, as minister of defense, Prince Sultan welcomed—perhaps even encouraged—his younger brother Turki to be appointed as his deputy in July 1969. Similarly, when King Fahd was minister of the interior (1963–1975), he promoted Nayif as his deputy (June 1970). Not surprisingly, when Nayif became minister of the interior in 1975, the youngest of the full brothers, Ahmad, was advanced to the deputy post.

Although it may be a mistake to think of the "Sudayri Seven" as a cohesive unit—because factions have emerged within it in recent years—the sheer presence of these senior princes in positions of authority considerably adds to their overall power. More important, several sons of the seven full brothers have joined the alliance on specific issues, thus forming a power nexus second to none.[11] King Khalid and his older full brother, Prince Muhammad, were united on virtually all political and policy issues. Similarly, King Fahd and Prince Sultan seem to have a long-standing political partnership that extends back to the late 1950s, when both supported Heir Apparent Faysal against King Saud. Under Faysal, Fahd and Sultan were also partners in various family skirmishes that, for better or worse, sealed their alliance.[12] Fahd and Sultan cooperated together, starting during King Khalid's rule, to further limit the influence of other senior princes, especially that of Abdallah bin Abdul Aziz.[13] There is no doubt that the "partnership" of full brothers is to be acknowledged as a leading factor in Saudi succession.

Lest one is to conclude that this phenomenon is exclusive to the Sudayri Seven, the fortunes of Princes Mansur, Mish'al, and Mit'ab—sons of Shahida (an Armenian woman who was a favorite of Abdul Aziz bin Abdul Rahman)—provide another interesting example of linkage between maternal lineage and seniority. When Prince Mansur, the first Saudi minister of defense, died in 1951, he was replaced by his younger full brother Mish'al, who had been his deputy. In turn, the youngest of the brothers, Mit'ab, was then appointed to the deputy position. Both

Mish'al and Mit'ab were ousted from office under King Saud, but they were returned to power in 1963 by King Faysal, who entrusted them the key governorship and deputy governorship, respectively, of Makkah. Interestingly, both left office in 1971, for reasons that are not entirely clear. Mit'ab was finally appointed minister of public works and housing in October 1975.[14]

These examples notwithstanding, the association of full brothers is by no means an inviolable rule, as the case of Princes Talal and Nawwaf illustrate. Talal and Nawwaf were born to Munaiyir, another Armenian concubine who became a favorite wife. Surprisingly, the two brothers became bitter enemies during King Saud's reign, even to the point of contesting their inheritances.[15]

Grandsons of Abdul Aziz.　If the sons of Abdul Aziz constitute the active political core of the ruling family, it is their sons—the grandsons of Abdul Aziz—who are the emerging political leadership in Saudi Arabia. While the exact size of this group is not known, it may include an estimated 200 males and an equal number of females. A number of these princes have been entrusted with important administrative positions in the state bureaucracy as well as the armed forces.

Because of their relative advantages, especially in terms of education and exposure to Western ideas, several "grandsons" may well be identified as a distinct faction within the family. Still, this rising group—with distinct political interests—is not a homogeneous entity either. In fact, the grandsons, much like their fathers, are divided into several factions. Connections between fathers and sons, against other fathers and sons, seem to be present as well. In certain instances too, there are connections between some of Abdul Aziz's sons and some of his grandsons.[16] Nevertheless, the political fortunes of many of the grandsons are heavily influenced by the successes or failures of their fathers, thus keeping the founder's traditions alive. Just as Abdul Aziz passed power on to his sons, rather than his equally qualified nephews, this pattern among grandsons may well persist unless significant changes are introduced by royal decree. There are several examples of this trend, most notably the divergent fortunes of the sons of Kings Saud and Faysal, as well as those of King Fahd.

When Saud was King, he appointed some of his estimated 53 sons to a number of prominent positions, including the Ministry of Defense (Fahd and Muhammad), commander of the National Guard (Saad), commander of the Royal Guard (Bandar and Mansur), governor of Riyadh (Badr), governor of Makkah (Abdallah), and several other posts.[17] The influence of these sons, then known as the "little kings," became so prevalent that Saud's brothers feared he intended to establish a lineal line of succession, and this accounted, in part, for the support Heir Apparent Faysal received against the monarch in the early 1960s.[18] In turn, when Saud was deposed in 1964, his sons were quickly distanced from power. In despair, several followed their father into exile, and although most were rehabilitated, none of them is any longer a contender for the highest position. Likewise, the sons of King Faysal, who succeeded Saud, were quickly promoted after 1964, and two continue to play significant roles in contemporary Saudi affairs (Saud and Turki). By contrast, King Fahd's sons, including the young Abdul Aziz, emerged as the rising stars of the next generation, although another change at the head of the family will surely witness agitations on this score as well.

Still, and unlike the sons of Kings Saud and Fahd—who rose to prominence at the expense of their uncles—King Faysal's sons tended to start at more junior positions and work their way up the ranks. Prince Saud, for example, spent five years as deputy director of Petromin, deputy minister of petroleum and mineral resources, and executive director of the Supreme Petroleum Council before becoming foreign minister at his father's death in 1975.[19] Prince Turki, who earned a doctorate from a British university, spent five years as deputy director of the Directorate General of Royal Intelligence before moving to the director's spot. In 1979, he commanded the Saudi forces at Makkah to help diffuse the Mosque takeover.[20]

As these two examples illustrate, bureaucratic stints have tended to give several princes greater administrative experience and, not a negligible point, the distance necessary to rise above petty family disputes. These work experiences further allowed many to observe intricate internal developments and, perhaps, appreciate the necessity to form alliances, because the relative success of a father did not always ensure prominence for his progeny. As a case in point, the three sons of King Khalid did not play any discernible roles while their father was monarch, and most relinquished any claims after his death in 1982. By contrast, King Fahd's six sons assumed identifiable and very public positions. The eldest, Faysal, was the director-general of youth welfare starting in 1971, and a director-general at the Ministry of Planning starting in 1977. Faysal bin Fahd, who held the rank of minister of state after 1977, was also a private "emissary to Iraq." He died of a heart attack in 1999. His younger brother Khalid, a prominent businessman, replaced him as head of youth welfare, a significant visible post that earned King Fahd and his progeny legitimacy. Another son, Muhammad bin Fahd, was entrusted the critical Eastern Province governorship in 1985 (replacing a key Jiluwi ally). Saud bin Fahd, who was elevated to minister rank in September 1997, has occupied the deputy headship of External Intelligence since 1985. Sultan bin Fahd, a career army officer, was also elevated to minister rank in November 1997. Abdul Aziz bin Fahd, allegedly the monarch's favorite son, was carefully groomed as well. He "represented" his father at most public ceremonies and, in 1999, was elevated to minister rank.

All of these examples depict that paternal success is important because it guarantees a visible platform and instant notoriety. Other cases abound throughout the ruling family. The sons of Princes Abdallah and Sultan bin Abdul Aziz are perfect illustrations. Two of Prince Abdallah's six sons—Mit'ab and Turki—serve in the National Guard, and two of Prince Sultan's seven sons—Khaled and Bandar—were once attached to their father's ministry. Although Abdallah's children are not in the army or the air force, Sultan's sons are also absent from the ranks of the National Guard. At least in these two cases, the grandsons reflect and reinforce divisions that have emerged in the earlier generation.[21]

Characteristics.   Seniority, maternal lineage, and full brother status that apply to the sons also apply to the grandsons of the founder even if no single factor is decisive. To discuss the complexities involved, the examples from the sons of King Faysal, who were once considered among the most important of the third generation, will clarify these contentions. King Faysal's eldest son, Prince Abdallah bin Faysal (1921-), started his political career in 1945 when he disputed his uncle Mansur's appointment as acting viceroy of the Hijaz, and actually assumed the office a year later.[22] Between 1951 and 1959, Abdallah served as minister of the interior, but retired in the early 1960s to extensive business interests. His public career amply depicts the extent to which there is a generational overlap between the sons and grandsons of Abdul Aziz. Having been born in 1921, Abdallah is older than the majority of Abdul Aziz's sons, and even one of Abdul Aziz's brothers. Similarly, many of Abdul Aziz's great-grandsons are older than his grandsons, and consequently the pool of potentially active princes contains elements of four generations that are of roughly similar ages. This pattern tends to blur generational distinctions and complicates the entire seniority characteristic.

As for maternal lineage, all of King Faysal's sons received a solid start because their mothers came from either the established Sudayri or Jiluwi families. Even the full brother characteristic played a part among Faysal's sons. In order of age, Muhammad, Saud, Abdul Rahman, Bandar, and Turki are full brothers, sons of Iffat bint Ahmad Al Thunayan. Given the critical role that the Thunayan played—as an important cadet branch of the Al Saud family—and given that Queen Iffat was the monarch's favorite wife, this characteristic becomes important.[23]

When this single line is multiplied by the progeny of all 36 sons of King Abdul Aziz, it becomes amply evident that the direct descendants constitute a prolific and powerful group. They include approximately 300 princes—36 sons and an estimated 260 grandsons and great-grandsons— as well as a similar number of princesses.[24] Their absolute size is more than matched by the concentration of power within the group as a whole, especially when compared with other units in the ruling family and with clusters of power within the rapidly evolving Saudi society. Within the primary nexus of power, however, there is no even distribution. Personal attributes, seniority, paternal and maternal lineage, and full brother subgroups all help create an internal hierarchy of power that is simultaneously complex and fluid. These same characteristics tend to divide descendants of King Abdul Aziz into dozens of factions that cut within and across generations. If this were not complicated enough, at least two other broad groupings within the ruling family—the descendants of the founder's brothers and several key cadet branches—hold significance because of their intrinsic capabilities to form or influence political alliances.

Descendants of Abdul Aziz's Brothers

If the direct descendants of Abdul Aziz, as a whole, constitute the inner political core of the ruling family, it is the brothers of Abdul Aziz, and their descendants, that make up the outer circle of family politics. Much less is known about these clusters, but available sources suggest that similar rules apply, including the complexity of internal divisions. Intermarriages, both within these subgroups and between them and the bin Abdul Aziz, have been extensive.[25] Though larger, this group has had less direct political influence than Abdul Aziz's descendants. Nonetheless, several of Abdul Aziz's brothers have played critical roles in family politics in the past, and some of their descendants currently hold sensitive government positions.[26]

Abdul Aziz's father, Abdul Rahman bin Faysal bin Turki, had a total of ten sons, including Faysal (1870–1890), Abdul Aziz (1880–1953), Muhammad (1880–1943), Saad (d. 1916), Saud (1890–1965), Abdallah (1900–1976), Ahmad (1899–), Musaid (1922–), and Saad (1924–1955).[27] Muhammad, Abdallah, and Musaid have played the most important political roles, aside from Abdul Aziz. Indeed, at one point, Muhammad and Abdallah presented potential challenges to Abdul Aziz's attempt to establish a lineal line of succession.[28] Later, Abdallah and Musaid played a pivotal role in the struggle between Abdul Aziz's sons, Saud and Faysal, attempting to mediate the conflict as "neutrals" and finally throwing their weight behind Faysal.[29] Following Faysal's assassination, Abdallah was the first name listed in the official communication proclaiming Khalid as King; the others were Khalid's brothers listed in order of age—Muhammad, Nasir, Saad, and Fahd.

To be sure, the influence of Abdul Aziz's brothers has declined, as age and infirmity has taken its toll. The last to hold office, Musaid, resigned as minister of finance in September 1975, and the eldest, Abdallah, died in 1977. The youngest, Ahmad, has never played an active political role and little is known about him. At the same time, the surviving brothers (Musaid and Ahmad) of Abdul Aziz are respected as senior family members whose advice on family matters carries the weight of tradition.[30]

If Abdul Aziz's brothers are dying out, their sons, grandsons, and great grandsons are playing an increasingly active role in politics. Not surprisingly, these princes tend to be the descendants of Abdul Aziz's most prominent brothers. Abdallah's sons, for example, include Fahd (naval officer), Bandar (director-general for districts in the Ministry of the Interior), Saud (in charge of Arab affairs at the foreign ministry), and Khalid (a leading businessman with close ties to the Ministry of Defense through Northrop, Lockheed, and Raytheon). The fourth generation is also active. For example, two of Muhammad's great-grandsons, Bandar and Khalid, are an army officer and deputy minister of education, respectively. Inasmuch as these descendants are successful in their myriad endeavors, their political influence is further enhanced by extensive intermarriages with the direct descendants of Abdul Aziz. Abdallah's children, for example, have married into the "Sudayri Seven," the children of Abdul Aziz and Hassa bint Ahmad Al Sudayri. Abdallah's daughter, Nuri, is married to Turki bin Abdul Aziz, and one of Turki's sisters is married to Abdallah's son Khalid. Although marital ties do not necessarily explain political alliances, in the case of Khalid bin Abdallah, it probably accounted for his close ties to the minister of defense. In some instances, marital ties help explain political prominence. For example, the mother of Muhammad bin Abdul Rahman's great-grandson Khalid, who is deputy minister of education, is Anud, a daughter of former King Faysal. One of Khalid's sisters is in turn married to Turki bin Faysal, who is chief of Royal Intelligence.

Still, despite several key linkages, the positions held by the descendants of Abdul Aziz's brothers are less impressive than those held by Abdul Aziz's own descendants. In fact, Abdul Aziz's descendants have priority, since his heirs have almost always replaced his brother's progeny in various government positions. The reverse is almost never true. For example, in 1971, Khalid bin Faysal bin Abdul Aziz replaced Fahd bin Saad bin Abdul Rahman as governor of Asir Province. More recently, Abdul Illah bin Abdul Aziz replaced Fahd bin Abdallah bin Abdul Rahman as governor of Qasim Province. When the reverse occurred, it was almost exclusively at times of feuding among Abdul Aziz's descendants, when his brothers or their descendants were turned to as compromise or neutral candidates.[31] It is in this regard that the political significance of this group of princes is noteworthy, as they represent both a pool of potential supporters outside the inner circle and a potential challenge to princes of the inner circle. In neither capacity, however, do the descendants of Abdul Aziz's brothers appear to act as a "bloc," since all the factors that make for inherent divisions among the founder's descendants also apply to them.

Cadet Branches.   A third broad grouping of political significance within the ruling family are some of the cadet or collateral branches, descendants of more distant relatives of Abdul Aziz.[32] Cadet branches are normally named after the oldest male who established a distinct bloodline. For example, Abdul Aziz belonged to the Al Faysal branch, named after his grandfather, Faysal, who ruled Saudi Arabia in 1834–1837 and 1843–1865. Aside from this branch, there are five other recognized branches of the Saud family; the Al Saud Al-Kabir, Al Jiluwi, Al Turki, Al Thunayan, and Al Farhan.[33] The relationship of these branches to the descendants of Abdul Aziz's father, Abdul Rahman, are sketchy, and relatively little is known about the size and genealogies of the various branches. For the most part, their political importance stems directly from alliances and intermarriages with Abdul Aziz and his descendants.

This can be seen in the difference between the Al Farhan and Al Thunayan branches. Members of both branches are equally distant relatives of Abdul Aziz (the founders of each branch were two of Abdul Aziz's great-great-great-great-great-granduncles), but the Thunayan are more prominent because a relatively senior member of the branch, Adham, was a close political adviser of King Faysal and managed the monarch's personal finances.[34] Another Thunayan, Abdul Aziz, married Faysal's daughter, Latifa, and served in important posts.[35] By contrast, no members of the Farhan branch presently occupy political office, although some members may be serving in the armed forces.

Unlike the Thunayan, who have been somewhat influential, the Al Turki branch—descendants of another brother of Abdul Aziz's grandfather, Faysal bin Turki—has seen its influence erode. The Turki branch have not married extensively with Abdul Aziz's descendants nor did they play an important role in helping Abdul Aziz establish the present Saudi state. As a consequence, their political prominence is paltry. Two possible members of the branch in current Saudi political life are Abdul Aziz Al Turki, deputy minister of petroleum, and Mansur Al Turki, the deputy minister of finance.

The Jiluwi, on the other hand, are a large and politically important branch. One of Jiluwi's sons, Abdallah, was an early supporter of Abdul Aziz and was appointed the first governor of the Eastern Province in 1913.[36] Since then, the Jiluwi have enjoyed semihereditary control of the governorship in the oil-rich Eastern Province, relishing considerable autonomy in dealing with the internal affairs of the region. When Abdallah bin Jiluwi died in 1938, his son Saud became governor, and when Saud died in 1967, another son, Abdul Muhsin, was promoted in turn.[37] As stated above, in 1985, King Fahd appointed his third son, Muhammad, to the governorship but, importantly, kept a Jiluwi as his deputy to assist the young prince with sensitive issues facing the governorate. Younger members of the branch served as mayors of towns in the Eastern Province as well, given their widespread influence there. In the early 1950s, Jiluwis served as governors in other provinces of Saudi Arabia, including Hail, Qasim, and the Northern Frontiers. Over time, however, they were gradually replaced by descendants of Abdul Aziz, and now only Abdallah bin Abdul Aziz bin Musaid bin Jiluwi remains as governor of the Northern Frontiers Province. As far as can be ascertained, no Jiluwis serve in the central government apparatus, but it is likely that some may be found in the ranks of the armed forces, National Guard, and internal security forces.

As discussed above, the main collateral branch of the Al Saud family—the Al Saud Al-Kabir line—descend from one of Abdul Aziz's uncles, Saud, who had six sons and at least 14 grandsons.[38] One of these grandsons, Saud, challenged Abdul Aziz's early efforts to lead the Saud family. He was finally defeated in 1912 and married Abdul Aziz's favorite sister, Nura.[39] The most prominent member of the Al Saud Al-Kabir branch in present politics—Fahd bin Abdallah bin Muhammad—is a great-grandson of this Saud. He is a full colonel and was in charge of the Saudi air force before replacing Turki bin Abdul Aziz as assistant to the minister of defense. Reportedly, other members of the branch serve in the armed forces as well, although a full listing is next to impossible.

Aristocratic Families

As in any monarchical system, there are a number of aristocratic families in Saudi Arabia that are connected to the ruling family through intermarriages. In general, descendants of Abdul Aziz married women of aristocratic and tribal families, and continue on the same path. Of the major aristocratic families, two stand out: the Al Shaykh and the Al Sudayri.[40]

The Al Shaykh are descendants of Muhammad bin Abdul Wahhab, the founder of the unitarian doctrine (Wahhabism). As such, the Al Shaykh branch have traditionally provided the ulama, learned religious officials who are influential in law and education.[41] Since the 1960s, members of the family have also headed various ministries. In the June 1999 government, Saleh bin Abdul Aziz Muhammad bin Ibrahim Al Shaykh is minister of Islamic endowments, Dawa, Awqaf and guidance affairs; Abdallah bin Muhammad Al Shaykh is minister of justice; and Muhammad bin Abdul Aziz Al Shaykh is a minister of state.[42] The family is also present in the armed forces. General Abdallah bin Abdul Rahman Al Shaykh is director-general of public security, and Lt. General Muhammad Al Shaykh is a senior commander in the Royal Saudi Army.

Whereas Al Shaykh family members are heavily concentrated in the legal, educational, and religious establishments, the Al Sudayris are prominent as governors. The most important Sudayris descend from Ahmad bin Muhammad Al Sudayri (1869–1936), who was an early political supporter of King Abdul Aziz.[43] Of Ahmad's sons, Khalid was governor of Najran, and Turki was governor of Jizan Province. Turki's son, Muhammad bin Turki Al Sudayri, was appointed to the critical Jizan governorship in 1989. Other Sudayri governors (sons of Ahmad's brothers) included Abdul Aziz and Saud. The next generation of Sudayris are also present as officials in the central and provincial government bureaucracies and they continue to play important unifying roles.

Aside from their early control over governorships, the Sudayris have probably provided more women for royal matrimony than any other single family in Saudi Arabia.[44] King Abdul Aziz's mother was a Sudayri, and Abdul Aziz himself married three Sudayri women. One of them, a daughter of Ahmad, Hassa, gave the founder the current monarch and his six full brothers (the "Sudayri Seven").[45] As for the two other women: Jauhara bint Saad gave Abdul Aziz Princes Saad, Musaid, and Abdul Muhsin, whereas her sister, Haya bint Saad, gave him Badr, Abdul Illah, and Abdul Majid.[46] At one time or another, all of these sons have played, and continue to play, important political roles. It is also important to note that, in turn, several of Abdul Aziz's sons married Sudayri women. For example, King Faysal married Sultana bint Ahmad Al Sudayri, who gave the monarch his eldest son Abdallah.[47] Still another daughter of Ahmad, Mudhi, married Nasir bin Abdul Aziz and, in turn, produced five sons: Khalid, Abdallah, Fahd, Turki, and Ahmad, two of whom are officers in the armed forces.[48]

The Succession Issue Before King Fahd

Like his predecessors during the first two Saudi "states," Abdul Aziz bin Abdul Rahman attempted to establish a lineal line of succession and, in the process, distributed power and responsibility among his oldest sons. A year after the Kingdom of Saudi Arabia was officially established, the founder nominated his eldest surviving son, Saud, as Heir Apparent—making sure that his decision was firmly supported within the family by both senior members as well as key religious figures. Previously, Abdul Aziz had divided regional responsibilities between his two oldest sons, appointing Saud as viceroy of the Najd and Faysal as viceroy of the Hijaz. What the founder did not foresee, however, were a number of fundamental changes in the Saudi political system that substantially complicated the process.

More than any other factor, the tremendous growth in size that started under the founder's rule, substantially complicated dynastic affairs. Unlike two of his predecessors, King Abdul Aziz was personally responsible for the tremendous growth that the family experienced. Muhammad bin Saud, who founded the first Saudi "state" in 1747, fathered 5 sons, and only 2 survived the fierce battles that ensued. Faysal bin Turki, the second great Saudi leader, fathered 4 sons, including Abdul Rahman, who in turn had a total of 9 sons.[49] As discussed above, King Abdul Aziz fathered 36 sons, and his successor's progeny stood at 53 sons. The result of these permutations was a significant growth in the number of "royal princes." Naturally, the larger pool of available talent meant that the number of potential heirs, coupled with politically ambitious princes, further confounded family politics. Other changes, including the overlap of generations, as well as the diversity of maternal connections, further tied the Gordian knot. Of course, this factor has grown in importance even more so since the younger sons, grandsons, and great-grandsons of Abdul Aziz assumed key positions in the bureaucracy and the military.

Equally crucial was the linkage between succession and the distribution of power within the family. At first, Abdul Aziz attempted to ensure smooth succession and yet divided responsibility among his top progeny through the rudiments of a national bureaucratic structure. Thus, in October 1953, barely a month before his death, the founder decreed the formation of a Council of Ministers and appointed Heir Apparent Saud as prime minister. Saud immediately appointed Faysal as deputy prime minister. Both decisions reinforced Saud's claim to the throne and cemented Faysal's standing as second in line.[50] The solution meant that a nexus of power existed between top government positions and family politics. Of course, it served the dual purpose of strengthening the authority of the Heir Apparent while consolidating the line of succession among potential challengers. Ironically, it was this practice that complicated matters, as the number of potential contenders to the throne increased because the theoretical lines of succession—from among other qualified individuals—were neatly blocked. To further solidify their respective claims, and starting in 1954, all Saudi monarchs decided to be their own prime ministers, whereas the position of deputy prime minister (except for the brief period 1962–1965) was either left vacant or occupied by an Heir Apparent. It was only in 1967 that the position of second deputy prime minister was added for the apparent heir to the Heir. Thus, King Fahd is also prime minister, whereas Heir Apparent Abdallah bin Abdul Aziz is deputy prime minister, and the apparent heir to the Heir, Prince Sultan bin Abdul Aziz, is the second deputy prime minister.[51]

To be sure, this innovation fell short of a complete "rationalization" of succession procedures, as senior positions did not guarantee priority in the succession order. Nevertheless, they served to evince the underlying balance of power, especially since whatever "rules" existed were tacit rather than formal. Even as mutual understandings, these rules are relatively recent and subject to periodic jolts. Still, the establishment of a national council contributed to sharing power and dividing responsibility between Saud and Faysal.

After Abdul Aziz's death, King Saud concentrated his power among members of the family, whereas Heir Apparent Faysal, who became prime minister in August 1954, exercised greater influence in the Council of Ministers. As with the government-succession nexus, however, the division of authority and responsibility between the family and the Council of Ministers remained fluid and informal. It proved cumbersome at best, and destructive at worst, when, for example, Saud and Faysal used their institutional positions to challenge each other.[52]

Irrespective of how the two leaders fared, the emergence of a formal state structure affected the distribution of power among princes not in the immediate line of succession. Prior to this, senior princes had held traditional positions as the King's advisers, or served as governors in various cities. As such, their power had remained extremely dependent on the personalized basis of a patrimonial system, encouraged by the monarch to best serve his intrinsic interests. The creation of national ministries, in contrast, provided for a more independent power base for princes controlling these ministries. As a result, the central government was strengthened, which in turn expanded the power in the hands of astute princes.

Within a very short period of time, an additional balance of power mechanism was established within the family—to conciliate rivals—even if the risk for internal struggles increased. Various divisions within the defense and security fields (Royal Guard, National Guard, regular armed forces, public security, Royal Intelligence, etc.) were all entrusted to princes who, in most cases, were involved in opposing factions. Given the fact that several factions had access to the use of force, the multiplicity of these ensembles imposed a certain restraint on family rivalries. Conversely, when antagonisms escalated beyond the point of reconciliation, force proved to be necessary to neutralize opposing force, as in the early 1960s and during the 1979 Makkah Mosque takeover.

The active involvement of Al Saud princes in state affairs further complicated family ties because bureaucratic politics were interjected into traditional rivalries. For example, Defense Minister Sultan had an interest in emphasizing external military threats to Saudi Arabia—which his ministry was best able to meet—and cultivating ties with major Western powers, which could provide training and equipment for a modern army. By contrast, the commander of the National Guard, Heir Apparent Abdallah, had an institutional interest in stressing internal threats to the regime, which the Guard was designed to check. This feature was considerably amplified because ministers, who enjoyed a very large degree of autonomy, ran their organizations as personal power bases.

Over the years, the emerging state structure complicated family ties in yet another way, as the political process for determining control of individual ministries paralleled the succession process. A weak or incompetent minister, like a weak or incompetent ruler, could disqualify himself from office and invite specific challenges. Conversely, a strong incumbent minister could designate his successor, just as a strong monarch frequently groomed his own heir. As a case in point, after the 1979 Makkah Mosque takeover, the governor of the province, Fawwaz, was forced to resign.[53] Of course, the appointment of princes to key ministries became entangled with underlying rivalries for succession, as contenders for the throne attempted to place their followers in important ministries or replace perceived allies of opponents. These maneuvers increased opportunities for accommodation and compromise but, simultaneously, expanded tensions within family ranks.

A third development that complicated family politics was the emergence of new social groups seeking access to political power. Family politics had always been tied to the tribal structure and traditional oligarchy, but the diversity of Abdul Aziz's realm and the effects of Saudi Arabia's oil wealth in the 1970s created several new classes within both the country as well as the family. One consequence was for the family to be divided between members closer to traditional or modernizing groups. For example, as viceroy of the Hijaz, Faysal built a base of support among important merchant families and the educated elite of the province. Saud, on the other hand, as viceroy of the Najd, was responsible for tribal affairs, including the distribution of subsidies to key shaykhs. The manner in which these divergent ties interacted with family politics has varied. When the rivalry between Faysal and Saud was latent, the impact of different social bases was contained within family circles. As the rivalry escalated, however, both Saud and Faysal attempted to rally supporters outside of the ruling family, specifically to undercut each other's political base. In general, when family unity was maintained, the destabilizing effects of oil wealth were mitigated, but when unity collapsed, these effects were accelerated. Still, the impact of oil wealth tended to strain family unity, because it divided Saudi society into opposing social groups with different interests and ideologies.[54] Oil wealth tended to disrupt the balance of power within the family, and altered the institutional and social bases of different subgroups. As a case in point, and for many years, modernization benefited the regular armed forces far more than it did the tribal levies of the National Guard.

As these developments complicated family politics, a number of factors tended to increase the complexity of issues facing the Saudi leadership. In particular, the impact of oil wealth on Saudi society and the emergence of the Kingdom as a key regional and international actor confronted the Al Saud with an unprecedented number of challenges and difficult choices. In fact, several of these challenges turned into persistent dilemmas for Riyadh, which, for better or worse, was faced with intractable choices. In foreign policy, for example, the dilemma centered on the need to balance Saudi-American relations with the Kingdom's positions in the Arab and Islamic worlds. In domestic affairs, dilemmas centered on balancing political reforms with the preservation of the traditional political system, while combining economic development and modernization with traditional tribal and religious norms.

Given the complexities that emerged, the Al Saud family environment turned into an arena for political contests. Internal balances were created based on shifting coalitions. Within this arena, policies and politics became closely interconnected. Ties were further strained since family affairs remained without explicit rules—for determining political outcomes. Indeed, no institutionalized structures for arbitrating disagreements were created, save for the informal family council.[55] The informal rules that existed, and which persist—comprised of traditions and tacit understandings—were ambiguous at best. Moreover, most were fragile because any contestant that felt strong enough to violate them could do so with impunity. In other words, the informal and personalized nature of the Saudi political system meant that the pattern of family politics (and the balance of power that underlies this pattern) appeared in sharply different forms. This was best illustrated in the contrasting pattern of family politics under the last four rulers. Under Saud, family politics were marked by an ungovernable division of power and escalating feuds, with a variety of deleterious consequences for the country's stability. Under Faysal, there was a centralization of power that controlled the feuding—which tended to enhance the effectiveness of Saudi policy and strengthen its stability—but at a very high price for the monarch. Under Khalid, an intermediate pattern of multiple power centers emerged—which managed feuding—with ambiguous implications for stability. And under Fahd, family feuding was accelerated, as senior princes positioned themselves and their offspring for coming changes.

King Saud bin Abdul Aziz

Ruling family politics under King Saud (1953–1964) was marked by a sharp division of power between the King and the Heir Apparent Faysal that escalated into a bitter feud over political and policy differences.[56] In the prolonged struggle that ensued, the balance between Saud and Faysal shifted back and forth several times, as the ruling family was split apart in innovative alignments. The contest was finally resolved in Faysal's favor nearly at the point of bloodshed. In the event, Saudi domestic and foreign policy suffered from confusion and reversals because the ruling family was not united.

Saud bin Abdul Aziz succeeded his father in 1953 during a smooth transfer of power. Prince Faysal became Heir Apparent, and during the following few years the founder's eldest sons shared both power and responsibility. With some exceptions, Saud strengthened his power base within the family, while Faysal concentrated his efforts in the Council of Ministers. Although the nascent monarchy was fully engaged in state-building efforts, the pattern of appointments indicated internal schisms. For example, Faysal's supporters included his son, Abdallah (minister of the interior), and his half brothers, Fahd (Education) and Sultan (Communications), while Saud installed his sons as commander of both the National and Royal Guards, chief of the Diwan, minister of defense, and governor of Riyadh. Whatever arrangements existed began to break down under the strain of two developments. Internally, the Kingdom's finances deteriorated amidst charges of corruption and extravagance.[57] Externally, the rise of Gamal Abdel Nasser in Egypt—on a wave of Arab socialist ideology—confronted the conservative Saudi establishment with an unprecedented foreign threat.[58] By early 1958, the monarch's capricious fiscal policies, coupled with his impulsive foreign adventures, had resulted in a head-on family collision.[59]

Senior members of the ruling family were both concerned and embarrassed at Saud's tendency to appoint his inexperienced young sons to major governmental positions, rather than older and more seasoned uncles and nephews. Many feared that such appointments signaled that Saud was planning to transfer succession to his offspring. Such concerns, coupled with their observations of Saud's lavish spending habits, increased overall dissatisfaction, to the point that senior family members urged Saud to relinquish power to Faysal. On March 24, 1958, and under much duress, Saud issued a royal decree transferring to Faysal executive powers. The Heir Apparent turned the embarrassing financial situation around, although reductions in family expenditures infuriated Saud. Gradually, the monarch usurped Faysal's privileges that, not surprisingly, limited the prime minister's authority. The monarch opposed his Heir Apparent's systematic appointments within the Council of Ministers, especially after Faysal gained personal control over the Ministries of Foreign Affairs, Interior, Commerce, and Finance.[60]

The very success of Faysal's efforts—to meet the financial and foreign policy crises facing Saudi Arabia—created opportunities for Saud to reclaim full power. For example, because strict financial restrictions were necessary to restore Saudi fiscal standing, Saud relied on tribal and commercial circles (the two groups that paid dearly), promising fundamental changes. It was typical that most would support him against Faysal. The Heir Apparent's concentration of power also created a faction of disgruntled younger princes who advocated constitutional reforms. King Saud endorsed the "free princes," not because he believed in their advocacy, but because they posed as natural allies against the power and authority of his half brother. By late 1960, Saud had engineered a complete reversal in concert with the free princes, as Faysal and his supporters were swept from the Council of Ministers. The monarch appointed himself prime minister and replaced several cabinet officials with some of his sons. Key supporters, including Princes Talal, Abdul Muhsin, and Fawwaz bin Abdul Aziz, were brought in as well.[61] Faysal and his Council of Ministers tendered their resignations.

Family politics then entered an extraordinarily complex period, with three sets of main competitors: King Saud and his sons (the "little kings"), the free princes, and Heir Apparent Faysal and his supporters.[62] Yet, because King Saud was conservative at heart, tensions quickly developed between him and Prince Talal, especially over the latter's calls for constitutional reforms.[63] The growing influence of Saud's sons, as well as the division of power between members of the family and the Council of Ministers, amplified the overall anxiety. Sensing an opportunity to further weaken Prince Faysal, King Saud played off Talal against the Heir Apparent. In September 1961, he managed to remove the most troublesome of the free princes, including Talal, yet denied Faysal and his supporters any positions in government. By fragmenting the free princes and frustrating Faysal, Saud was strengthening the power of his sons—especially Minister of Defense Muhammad, who was being discussed as a possible successor.

At the height of his power, however, Saud's health deteriorated, and in December 1961 the monarch flew to the United States to receive medical care. This marked the beginning of Faysal's return to power.[64] About the same time, civil war broke out in Yemen, and Egyptian forces arrived to support revolutionary elements there against Saudi-supported royalists. Steeped in international politics, Faysal perceived the inherent advantages of the Egyptian intervention to secure and strengthen his authority. With Saud indecisive, Faysal seized the crisis to assume full executive powers and, in a foresightful move, appointed a new Council of Ministers composed of loyal princes. These included confirmed supporters such as Fahd (Interior) and Sultan (Defense), but also a key new ally, Prince Khalid, as deputy prime minister.[65] Given Khalid's ties to the critical Jiluwi tribe, his alliance with Faysal severely undercut Saud's traditional power base. In 1963, Faysal appointed Abdallah bin Abdul Aziz as commander of the National Guard (in place of Saud's son Saad), and Salman bin Abdul Aziz as governor of Riyadh (in place of Saud's son Badr).[66]

Armed with emergency powers, Faysal fortified his position by implementing a number of foreign and domestic policies (including a ten-point reform program) to meet the Yemen crisis.[67] Saud, however, made one last effort to recover his powers. In January 1964, the monarch met with Egyptian President Nasser over the Yemen situation, and arranged for the return of the free princes (who had fled to Cairo) to Saudi Arabia to prepare yet another comeback. By doing so, however, he brought the ideological struggle that had boiled within family circles for almost half a decade to a head, when he ordered that all his executive powers be restored. To achieve this aim, he appealed to the ulama for a decision on March 13, 1964. In response, and literally at the end of his patience, Faysal mounted a palace coup by inviting the leading religious figures and princes to convene in Riyadh and consider a formal settlement of the persistent feud.[68] His supporters arrested a group of Saud's men, including his son Sultan bin Saud, commander of the Royal Guard, thereby eliminating the King's access to military force.

Faysal's victory was sealed by a series of proclamations from the ulama and the Council of Ministers following the March 25 meeting at Prince Muhammad bin Abdul Aziz's palace. On March 26, a delegation composed of religious leaders—including Muhammad bin Ibrahim Al Shaykh, Abdul Malik bin Ibrahim Al Shaykh, Abdul Aziz bin Baz, and Muhammad bin Harakan—confronted King Saud at his Nasiriyah palace. Four specific demands were made: (1) attach the Royal Guard to the armed forces, (2) attach the monarch's personal guards (the Khuwiyah) to the Ministry of the Interior, (3) abolish the Royal Diwan, and (4) reduce royal expenses "to reasonable amounts and investment of saved funds in development projects."[69] Not surprisingly, King Saud rejected these demands and immediately mobilized the Royal Guard around the palace. What followed was a classic *coup de tête* because Defense Minister Sultan and National Guard Commander Abdallah had surrounded both the palace as well as the Royal Guard, with their respective forces. King Saud was, perhaps, expecting support from his traditional tribal allies, but none was forthcoming. In the event, Faysal stood still and, in the melee that followed, had Sultan bin Saud arrested and placed under house arrest. The Royal Guard yielded within 24 hours, declaring their allegiance to the Heir Apparent. Saud still refused to abdicate. On November 2, 1964, the Council of Ministers, under Deputy Prime Minister Khalid bin Abdul Aziz, "asked the Kingdom's Ulama to examine the 28 October 1964 letter from the ruling family—deposing King Saud and proclaiming Faysal monarch—from a canonical point of view, and to issue a suitable fatwa [religious decree]."[70] A fatwa confirming the latter was issued on the same day, and made public—along with the Council of Ministers' decision as well as King Faysal's first royal decree—on November 3, 1964. Faysal immediately became King, and Saud, along with some of his sons, went into exile.

Assessment. Saud's truncated rule confirmed several emerging trends in family politics:

First, succession was a persistent source of tension within the family. Although the rivalry between Saud and Faysal prevented the designation of an heir to the Heir, as the rivalry escalated, the King sought to establish a lineal succession. The Heir Apparent—Prince Faysal—opted to establish critical political alliances by appointing Khalid as his deputy prime minister (which implied priority in the succession line), and several of his loyal brothers to senior bureaucratic and military posts. In 1965 Faysal persuaded his brothers to observe the principle of birth order among them to regulate succession, although the next eldest brother, Muhammad, voluntarily stepped down in favor of Khalid.[71]

Second, another source of tension was the attempt to divide power and share responsibility between the ruling family and the Council of Ministers. Not only did this arrangement prove inadequate for effective policy-making, it also aggravated family rivalries, as Saud and Faysal used their respective positions to challenge each other. At different times, both leaders found it difficult to maintain their respective positions, as any attempt to concentrate power tended to arouse the opposition of other princes. Associations with unsuccessful or unpopular policies, including fiscal difficulties as well as foreign entanglements, opened the way for challenges.

Third, the shifting fortunes of Saud and Faysal were also reflected in the unstable distribution of power among other princes. In all, four major government reshuffles occurred in less than five years, with the composition of each government corresponding to the existing balance of power between the King and his Heir Apparent.

Fourth, control over the Kingdom's different armed forces was a critical element in the balance. Although Saud controlled the National and Royal Guards, as well as the Ministries of Defense and Interior, his defeat was the result of defections. Miscalculations about tribal loyalties contributed to his undoing. Of course, the ultimate resolution of the Saud-Faysal struggle was bloodless, but the threat of force was necessary to depose the King.

Fifth, as family unity broke down, all of the major contenders for power appealed to groups outside the ruling family, attempting to undercut each other's power bases as required. For example, Saud's alliance with the free princes was designed to woo Faysal's base in the Hijaz, and it was Faysal's strategic alliance with Princes Khalid and Abdallah that severed King Saud's links to the tribes.

Sixth, and finally, the escalation of family rivalries led to the involvement of foreign actors in internal struggles. All of the major contenders—Faysal, Saud, and Talal—used (and were used by) Egypt's Nasser to strengthen their internal positions. In the end, the orientation of Saudi foreign policy, the pace of internal developments, and the implementation of political reforms all became enmeshed in the power struggle. As the rivalry escalated, policy positions became polarized and Saudi behavior fluctuated as the political balance changed.

King Faysal bin Abdul Aziz

Under King Faysal, Al Saud family politics developed in a fundamentally different way, though the transformation was gradual and not without setbacks. Altogether, Faysal's rule was marked by increased centralization of power, greater internal stability, and clearer policy direction, all of which were in sharp contrast to the 1953–1964 period. These developments had a direct bearing on succession and the distribution of power within the family.

As discussed above, the division of power between the ruling family and the Council of Ministers under King Saud proved to be a source of dispute, with the position of prime minister shifting back and forth between King Saud and Heir Apparent Faysal, and with the powers of the deputy prime minister remaining undefined until 1962. By contrast, King Faysal combined the powers of his throne with formal control over the Council of Ministers for the entire period of his reign.[72] Although this fusion of power enhanced his intrinsic capabilities, it also stalled the strengthening of the cabinet to balance the King's immense prerogatives. This was particularly the case since the deputy prime minister, Khalid, was not active in daily affairs, serving instead as Faysal's representative during the King's absences.

Resolution of the succession issue, like the division of power between the Al Saud and the Council of Ministers, also remained unresolved during the Saud period. Indeed, King Saud's numerous attempts to promote his own sons to succeed him were a significant political issue in the struggle between the founder's two eldest. Still, under Faysal, the basis for a smooth succession—from brother to brother—was gradually established. Whether the discerning Faysal had any aspirations for his own progeny is difficult to verify. On the other hand, the formation of an *alliance* with Princes Muhammad, Khalid, and Abdallah—officials with close ties to influential tribal groups—indicated that the monarch preferred family consensus over expediency. Given that his calculated maneuvers ended his predecessor's reign, a different succession formula would have, at the very least, appeared in the eyes of all Al Saud princes as being disingenuous. To cement his alliance, Khalid was appointed deputy prime minister in 1962, a position that implied priority in the line of succession. Even if Khalid was not officially decreed Heir Apparent until 1965, the delay probably reflected Faysal's desire to consolidate his position and avoid provoking family rivalries at a time when Saudi Arabia was beset by internal and external threats stemming from the civil war in neighboring Yemen.

Another early supporter of Faysal was Prince Fahd, who had worked with his half brother from the very beginning of the dispute.[73] In October 1967, Fahd was appointed second deputy prime minister, in addition to holding the interior ministry portfolio, which he had held since 1962. Much like the earlier designation of Khalid in the same post, Prince Fahd's new position implied priority in the line of succession, after the Heir Apparent. Therefore, Faysal, like his father, attempted to establish a line of succession for the next two kings, and in this respect, accomplished his objectives.

In addition to temporarily resolving the succession issue, Faysal carefully distributed several key positions to his closest allies and, in the process, ensured a modicum of internal stability within the family. The Council of Ministers that was first appointed in 1962, which had included Princes Fahd (Interior) and Sultan (Defense), and Ahmad Zaki Yamani (a trusted commoner who would run the petroleum ministry for over two decades), remained virtually unchanged. Other important positions, such as commander of the National Guard (Abdallah) and governor of Riyadh (Salman), were also mobilized.

Ironically, the long tenure of these princes in such visible posts would become a critical factor in the pattern of family politics after Faysal's death, as each developed his own office into a personal power base. Sophisticated patron-client networks were created and nepotism ensued.[74] For example, Prince Sultan's younger full brother, Prince Turki, was appointed deputy defense minister in July 1969, and another full brother, Prince Nayif, was made deputy interior minister in June 1970. To be sure, King Faysal's political supporters were not the only ones benefiting from such appointments. Even some of the free princes were incorporated into the new family equation. These included Badr (deputy commander of the National Guard, 1965), Abdul Muhsin (governor of Madinah, 1965), Nawwaf (adviser to the King, 1968), and Fawwaz (governor of Makkah, 1971). To some extent, these appointments served to conciliate political discontents, but they also balanced other princely factions, especially since the majority were deeply indebted to King Faysal.

Still, neither Talal bin Abdul Aziz nor any of King Saud's sons were rehabilitated by Faysal. Indeed, several of Saud's sons, including Khalid, Mansur, Badr, and Sultan, joined their father in exile and supported his efforts to regain the throne.[75] The deposed monarch was most active from 1964 to 1967, when President Gamal Abdel Nasser gave him refuge in Egypt and even allowed him propaganda time on Radio Cairo.[76] After the June 1967 Arab-Israeli war, however, King Saud lost Egyptian support, finally settling in Greece, where he died in 1969.[77]

A final significant political development during Faysal's reign was the introduction of several previously uninitiated princes into politics. These included some of Abdul Aziz's younger sons, such as Sattam (deputy governor of Riyadh, 1968) and Ahmad (deputy governor of Makkah, 1971). In addition, a number of Abdul Aziz's grandsons were entrusted with their first assignments, including sons of Faysal, Fahd, Sultan, and Abdallah.

Assessment. Because of his supremacy, and the general success of his policies, there is little evidence to suggest that King Faysal faced serious opposition from within the family, especially after the initial purges distanced many of his foes. Still, Faysal's rule was distinguished by several trends:

First, he established a secure line of lateral succession, as a strong presence muted whatever tensions existed among the diverse group of princes serving under him. Although rumors of opposition abounded, particularly in the early years, Faysal ruled with justice.[78] Moreover, preparations for succession after Faysal were in the works for several years, and as early as 1972 it was clear that Heir Apparent Khalid would become King, while his younger half brother, Fahd, would follow. Hours after Faysal's death, a group of senior princes met in Riyadh and proclaimed Khalid King. The official announcement identified the family "leaders" as Abdallah bin Abdul Rahman (Abdul Aziz's eldest surviving brother) and Princes Muhammad, Nasir, Saad, and Fahd (Abdul Aziz's oldest sons in order of age). Immediately following his ascension, Khalid nominated Fahd as his Heir Apparent; and two older half brothers, Nasir and Saad, who were passed over in the line of succession, formally renounced their claims to the throne.

Second, collective leadership ended even if multiple power centers existed. Compared with Saud's rule, the pattern of family politics was sharply different under Faysal, and the connection between politics and policy became blurred. Under Saud, the inherent dilemmas facing Saudi Arabia in domestic and foreign policy issues were polarized as the power struggle escalated. Consequently, Saudi behavior was often erratic and contradictory. Under Faysal, on the other hand, these same dilemmas were balanced under his central control. Economic development, for example, had received scant attention throughout the 1950s, whereas long-range development plans were adopted by Faysal. If promises of political reforms had been inflammatory in the 1950s and early 1960s, under Faysal, they were carefully handled after the mid-1960s. Similarly, in foreign policy, the inconsistency of Saud's reign was replaced with a strategy that effectively combined Saudi Arabia's Arab and American connections.[79] In the later years of his reign, Faysal's many successes in both the domestic and foreign policy arenas greatly strengthened his political influence in family affairs. Without a doubt, Faysal's overshadowing presence helped to smooth the transition when, on March 25, 1975, the monarch was assassinated by a "deranged" nephew, Faysal bin Musaid bin Abdul Aziz.[80]

Third, technocrats emerged within the Al Saud ruling family. As grandsons and great-grandsons of the founder reached political maturity, Faysal harnessed their talent. The advent of King Faysal's own sons, followed by the progeny of the Al Fahd, meant that new alliances could be established. Naturally, this exponential increase of talented and ambitious young princes also meant that rivalries would emerge, fueled by powerful fathers who positioned their offspring as needed. This was not just nepotism but a case in which genuinely talented individuals would be recruited to reinforce existing or emerging alliances. Not only did King Faysal's policies encourage such promotions but, to better serve both family and country, many were encouraged to assume additional responsibilities.

King Khalid bin Abdul Aziz

Al Saud family politics under King Khalid (1975–1982) represented yet a third distinct pattern, namely the reinforcement of multiple centers of influence. Consequently, internal discourse was marked by more fluid coalitions and complex alignments, in contrast to the polarization under King Saud and the relative unity under King Faysal. Indeed, while putative family rivalries were more apparent between 1975 and 1982, they were far less pronounced than in the Saud period. Three specific factors empowered the multiple centers of power that emerged.

First, the division of power between King Khalid and Heir Apparent Fahd tended to be more fluid than the division that had existed between King Faysal and Heir Apparent Khalid. Though Khalid, following in Faysal's tradition, became prime minister as well as King, he delegated much of his ministerial duties to the Heir Apparent. Yet, this arrangement varied depending on the issue at hand, the condition of Khalid's health, and the state of Fahd's political standing. The monarch played a more assertive role in early 1979, following Fahd's temporary eclipse, but after his health started deteriorating later that year, he relinquished a major part of his official duties to his half brother.[81]

King Khalid's frequent illnesses notwithstanding, he remained a check on Heir Apparent Fahd's growing authority.[82] According to one observer of the Kingdom, "Fahd's attempt to act as *de facto* Prime Minister has failed, and the ministers have refused to inform him regularly of their activity."[83] Against the growing influence of the Heir Apparent, other power centers, such as the National Guard and Royal Intelligence, reported directly to the King. The proliferation of supraministerial supreme councils, such as the Supreme Petroleum Council, further fragmented responsibilities within the Council of Ministers.

A second factor that strengthened the multiple power centers was the continuation in office of princes who had built up entrenched bureaucratic fiefdoms during Faysal's reign. Prince Sultan, defense minister since 1962, for example, and Prince Abdallah, commander of the National Guard since 1963, retained and advanced their positions during Khalid's reign. While the autonomy of these princes had been checked by Faysal's strong leadership qualities, the division of power between Khalid and Fahd tended to expand their prerogatives and independence.[84]

Third, the pattern of promoting younger princes to government positions accelerated, as several older players retired. The impact of these younger princes on family politics further complicated internal maneuvers by adding new factions and diversifying old ones.

A new Council of Ministers was announced four days after Faysal's assassination. The cabinet represented a stopgap measure to consolidate the new regime and convey continuity at a time when Saudi leaders feared that Faysal's death would lead to domestic instability. Yet, and following the pattern set by Faysal, Khalid became prime minister and foreign minister, though one of Faysal's sons, Saud, was appointed minister of state for foreign affairs.[85] Heir Apparent Fahd was appointed first deputy prime minister and minister of the interior. Other measures included pay hikes for the defense and security forces, a general amnesty for political prisoners, and numerous public statements promising popular steps. Fahd pushed for the appointment of his younger full brother, Nayif, to become minister of state for internal affairs (in effect the deputy minister). This device of appointing Saud bin Faysal and Nayif bin Abdul Aziz as ministers of state, rather than full ministers, indicated an attempt to ensure government operations in the absence of complete agreement on the allocation of positions. Finally, the commander of the National Guard, Prince Abdallah, was appointed as second deputy prime minister, a position that implied, as under King Faysal, rights as heir to the Heir. The other Al Saud ministers—Sultan at Defense and Musaid bin Abdul Rahman at Finance and Economy—remained in place, as did the nine commoners.

If the March 1975 Council represented a stopgap measure, the major reshuffle announced on October 13, 1975, reflected the new balance of power within the family, which had been worked out in the intervening months. While rumors of a reshuffle had circulated for several months, two specific developments accelerated the changes: (1) the second five-year plan for 1975–1980 (announced on May 18, 1975), required some government reorganization for effective implementation; and (2) the re-tirement of Finance Minister Musaid bin Abdul Rahman (the last brother of King Abdul Aziz to hold office) for health reasons on September 6, 1975, altered the political composition of the March Council.[86] There-fore, the October reshuffle reflected an attempt to both reorganize gov-ernment and reapportion political power. As for the first objective, six new ministries were created: Industry and Power; Public Works and Housing; Municipal and Rural Affairs; Higher Education; Planning; and Posts, Telegraphs, and Telecommunications.[87] Some of these were carved out of existing ministries, for example, Industry and Power was detached from the Ministry of Commerce. Others were created simply by promot-ing existing bodies to ministerial status. The Ministry of Planning had been the quasi-independent Central Planning Organization before being elevated to cabinet rank.[88]

Accompanying this reorganization was an extensive reshuffle of tech-nocrats and commoners in the Council. At the ministerial level, four commoners were removed altogether, three were shifted to different min-istries, six were promoted to minister rank from junior positions within the same ministry, and four were recruited from outside the government, especially from academic positions.[89] In fact, the only technocrat unaf-fected by the reshuffle was Ahmad Zaki Yamani, who remained as minis-ter of petroleum, a position he had held since 1962.[90]

In political terms, these new commoners fell into two broad categories: (1) "pure technocrats," (Saudis from relatively humble backgrounds who had acquired higher education and technical training) and (2) "techno-cratic aristocrats" (who supplemented their expertise with their own fam-ily connections). The three Al Shaykhs in the new Council, Hasan bin Abdallah (Higher Education), Ibrahim bin Muhammad (Justice), and Abdul Rahman bin Abdul Aziz (Agriculture), enjoyed a certain level of independent political authority on the basis of lineage. Another candidate in the second group was Ghazi bin Abdul Rahman Al Ghosaibi (Indus-try), who was from the influential Al Ghosaibi business family.[91]

In terms of family politics, the significance of this full-scale reshuffle was difficult to unravel. During periods of open family quarrels, such as the Saud-Faysal struggle, technocrats associated with chief rivals were swept in and out of office like pawns as the political balance shifted back and forth. In the October 1975 reshuffle, however, family rivalries were relatively latent. Perhaps, with Faysal dead, King Khalid and Heir Apparent Fahd wished to make a clean sweep of Faysal's protégés and place their favorites in key administrative positions. Some evidence for this interpretation emerged a few years later as different technocrats began to advocate positions associated with their royal patrons. Several of the new technocrats, for example, argued for cautiously paced development, while others stressed the need to push ahead with modernization.[92] Still, the most important political shifts in the new Council were reflected in the changes concerning princes at the ministerial level.

At first, Saud bin Faysal and Nayif bin Abdul Aziz were promoted from ministers of state to full ministers for their respective posts, Foreign Affairs and Interior. In effect, this change meant that King Khalid was relinquishing Foreign Affairs and Heir Apparent Fahd was relinquishing the Ministry of the Interior to their respective allies within the ruling family. Moreover, the move codified a de facto arrangement, because both Saud and Nayif had actually been running their respective ministries ever since their promotions to ministers of state in March 1975. Prince Sultan remained as minister of defense, and Prince Abdallah continued as commander of the National Guard and second deputy prime minister. Two additional sons of King Abdul Aziz were added to the Council to head two of the newly created ministries. Mit'ab bin Abdul Aziz was named minister of public works and housing, and Majid bin Abdul Aziz became minister of municipal and rural affairs. Since both princes were known as supporters of Abdallah, Fahd's chief rival, these appointments were widely seen as part of an effort to balance the influence of Fahd and his supporters in the new regime.[93] Both Mit'ab and Majid came from politically active full brother factions. Mit'ab's eldest brother, Mansur, had served as the first minister of defense until his death in 1951, and the next eldest brother, Mish'al, had served as minister of defense from 1951 to 1955 (as well as governor of Makkah Province from 1963 to 1971). Mit'ab himself, the youngest of the three, had also served in various capacities. Under his older brother Mish'al, Mit'ab had been deputy defense minister (1951–1956) and vice-governor of Makkah (1963–1971). Interestingly, he had been replaced in this last position by Ahmad, Heir Apparent Fahd's youngest full brother. Though Majid bin Abdul Aziz had a less active career, his only full brother, Sattam, has served as vice-governor of Riyadh Province since 1968.[94]

On one level, the October 1975 Council reflected a rough balance between the two main factions of Abdul Aziz's sons. With respect to political issues, Fahd could count on his full brothers Sultan and Nayif, while two of Abdallah's supporters, Majid and Mit'ab, had entered the Council.

The role of King Khalid varied. Although he was frequently associated with Abdallah, he also appeared to be a mediator, the result of his extended absences. The position of Saud bin Faysal, the only grandson of Abdul Aziz serving as minister, was more difficult to ascertain.[95]

A new family balance was thus created before the end of 1975, which translated into relative stability for about half a decade, though several changes in the positions of individual princes occurred. First, some of the next generation of princes began to move up the political ladder. One of Fahd's sons, Faysal, chief of the Youth Welfare Department since 1972, became a minister of state in July 1977. In September 1977, Turki bin Faysal, a brother of Foreign Minister Saud, was appointed minister of state and chief of Royal Intelligence, where he had been deputy chief since 1968. At the same time, several current-generation princes dropped out of politics, at least in an official capacity. The most important departure was that of Turki bin Abdul Aziz (a member of the "Sudayri Seven"), who resigned as deputy defense minister and chief of military intelligence in May 1979.[96] Another resignation was that of Fawwaz bin Abdul Aziz, who was forced to relinquish the Makkah governorship after his disastrous handling of the Holy Mosque takeover. Whether or not Fawwaz was partly responsible for the lapse in security that made the Mosque takeover possible is impossible to verify, but he served as a convenient scapegoat.[97]

Although it is difficult to ascertain whether these individual appointments and resignations were the direct result of family rivalries, they certainly contained implications for underlying family politics. Indeed, personnel changes strengthened or weakened princely factions and opened up positions that could become the focus of fresh family maneuvers. Fawwaz's "retirement," for example, along with Riyadh's desire to strengthen internal security after the 1979 Mosque incident, led to a major governorship reshuffle on March 19, 1980. In all, four younger sons of Abdul Aziz were appointed to new posts as governors. Majid bin Abdul Aziz resigned as minister of municipal and rural affairs and took over the position of governor of Makkah. Though Majid's resignation removed one of Prince Abdallah's supporters from the Council of Ministers, his promotion to governor of Makkah placed him in a relatively more important position. Another new governor, Miqrin bin Abdul Aziz, retired as a major in the air force and took over Hail Province, replacing Nasir Al Shaykh, acting governor since the death of Fahd bin Saad bin Abdul Rahman in 1972. Abdul Illah bin Abdul Aziz was appointed governor of Qasim, replacing Fahd bin Abdallah bin Abdul Rahman, and Abdul Majid bin Abdul Aziz became governor of Tabuk, replacing Sulayman bin Turki.[98]

At the time these appointments were announced, it was impossible to identify the loyalties of these last three princes with any certainty. Miqrin's career at the Ministry of Defense meant that he was probably inclined to support Sultan and Fahd, while the close ties of Abdul Illah and Abdul Majid to Prince Abdallah placed them closer to the latter. Of course, particularly in the wake of the Makkah incident, the common family interest in strengthening control over provincial bureaucracies outweighed all efforts by Fahd and/or Abdallah to place their supporters in government, at least in any overt way.[99] Nonetheless, periodic governor and cabinet reshuffles represented a "balanced" package of family factions, although group and individual reshuffles between 1975 and 1982 were the only episodes that clarified family affairs.

One set of issues concerned the problem of determining who would succeed King Khalid, who periodically appeared to be on the verge of abdication or retirement. These rumors were particularly intense through 1977 and 1978, when Khalid underwent a series of operations and suffered prolonged periods of illness. While it was generally agreed that Heir Apparent Fahd would assume the throne in the event that Khalid abdicated, there was apparent disagreement over who would then become Heir Apparent, despite the fact that Abdallah, as second deputy prime minister, had a certain claim on the position. A secondary point of disagreement was who would inherit control over the National Guard in the event Abdallah was designated Heir Apparent.

Over the years, several versions of internal family discussions of these issues emerged, all agreeing that Fahd, supported principally by his full brothers Sultan and Salman, was at odds with Abdallah. In turn, Abdallah was allegedly supported by Khalid and the King's elder full brother Muhammad. In one version, Fahd was said to back Sultan's desire to become Heir Apparent, cutting out Abdallah entirely. In another version, Fahd and Sultan agreed to support Abdallah's claim, but only on the condition that he relinquish control over the National Guard, which would then be integrated into the regular armed forces controlled by Sultan. In yet a third version, the price of accepting Abdallah as Heir Apparent was that Salman would take over control of the National Guard.[100]

At the time, the underlying balance within the family prevented any one faction from imposing a solution to the succession problem, and furthermore the "terms" offered—if accurate—would have upset this balance. In particular, Abdallah's primary power base resided in control over the National Guard, and its loss, either by absorbing the Guard into the regular armed forces or by transferring control to one of Fahd's full brothers, would have placed all of the country's instruments of defense and security in the hands of one faction. Finally, since King Khalid's health recovered after his open-heart surgery in 1978, there was no need to visit the issue.

Internal family squabbles continued, and in mid-1979 the focus was on Fahd's weakened position in the context of Saudi Arabia's reaction to the Camp David agreements.[101] Several sources reported that Fahd favored a policy of minimum sanctions against President Anwar Sadat, so as to retain Egypt's services as a counterweight against so-called radical Arab states and revolutionary Iran and to avoid strains in American-Saudi relations.[102] Prince Abdallah, on the other hand, reportedly advocated cooperation with key Arab states, including Syria and Iraq, to punish Sadat, in part to avoid placing Saudi Arabia in an exposed position on the Palestinian issue. In the event, Abdallah was (allegedly) supported by King Khalid, Muhammad bin Abdul Rahman, Saud bin Faysal, and perhaps even some of Heir Apparent Fahd's full brothers. Whether a disagreement emerged over the Camp David Accords is impossible to verify, but Heir Apparent Fahd left Saudi Arabia in late March 1979 for an extended European vacation, and no official explanation was given for his sudden departure. A source close to Fahd reported that the Heir Apparent had left in disgust after the United States rejected a last-minute compromise plan proposed by Fahd to Zbigniew Brzezinski during the latter's visit to Saudi Arabia on March 17, 1979. The plan, supposedly coordinated with President Anwar Sadat, intended to neutralize Arab hardliners and preserve Saudi-Egyptian relations by sending a delegation of foreign ministers from Islamic countries to Washington, to lobby for the Palestinian cause.[103] Other sources claimed that Fahd's departure was a consequence of being overruled by Abdallah and his supporters.[104] On March 25, an official statement was issued, announcing that Heir Apparent Fahd had entered a Spanish hospital for routine medical examination.[105] *The Washington Post* reported that Fahd had returned to heavy drinking and suffered from being overweight, stomach ulcers, and diabetes.[106] King Khalid, for his part, declared that Fahd's absence was not due to ulcers or diabetes, but a "weight increase due to official duties which prevented him from taking exercise and walking."[107]

In any event, Heir Apparent Fahd's departure had several political consequences. First, Prince Abdallah began to chair meetings of the Council of Ministers, and took a more active role in Saudi diplomatic affairs. Though Riyadh resisted extreme Arab demands at the Baghdad Rejectionist Front Conference, including the imposition of an oil embargo against the United States, the Saudis quickly acquiesced to the full set of sanctions against Egypt after Cairo signed the Camp David Accords and, accordingly, broke diplomatic relations. Kamal Adham, a protégé of Fahd and a long-standing adviser who was known to advocate cooperation with Egypt, was dismissed. There was even a discussion to reshuffle the cabinet, replacing other Fahd protégés like Ahmad Zaki Yamani and Defense Minister Sultan, but no changes occurred. The only change that may have been connected to a shift in family politics was the resignation of Turki as deputy minister of defense in May 1979. Nonetheless, it was widely felt that Abdallah's claim to become Heir Apparent, once Fahd ascended to the throne, was now secure. Even when Fahd returned to Saudi Arabia in late May, he maintained a low profile, and both Khalid and Abdallah continued in more active roles, especially in regard to domestic policy toward the tribes and foreign policy on Arab matters. Heir Apparent Fahd accepted the new direction of Saudi foreign policy, especially after Egyptian President Anwar Sadat launched a series of public attacks on the Saudi leadership, including Fahd, in May 1979.[108]

Irrespective of what was said and how often it was repeated, reports of Fahd's demise were greatly exaggerated, because the Heir Apparent reemerged as a key decision maker—particularly with respect to Saudi Arabia's oil policy and relations with the West—after the monarch's health deteriorated. It was the governor of Riyadh, Prince Salman bin Abdul Aziz, who mediated the dispute between Fahd and Abdallah, especially after the Makkah Mosque takeover, which had raised a common threat to the ruling family. In this regard, the March 1980 governorship reshuffle represented a correction to the "balance" within family factions.[109]

The pattern of reshuffles between 1975 and 1982 indicated two main factions among the sons of Abdul Aziz and possibly a third faction emerging from among some of his grandsons. Details about each group's composition and internal structure, as well as their relationship to each other, tended to be inconsistent, but this reflected the obscurity and secrecy of Saudi family politics.

Perhaps the most cohesive and structured faction in late 1970s and early 1980s family politics were the "Sudayris," who consolidated their power base with some success. Presumably, some of their sons, including Faysal bin Fahd (director of youth welfare) and Bandar bin Sultan (air force major, later ambassador to the United States), were also part of this faction. The second faction grouped several sets of full brothers and a few "only sons." In addition to Commander of the National Guard Abdallah, these included King Khalid and his elder full brother Muhammad, Deputy Commander of the National Guard Badr and his full brothers Abdul Illah (governor of Qasim) and Abdul Majid (governor of Tabuk), as well as Majid bin Abdul Aziz (governor of Makkah) and his full brother Sattam (deputy governor of Riyadh). Minister of Public Works and Housing Mit'ab was also a member of this grouping. Some of their sons, including Turki and Mit'ab bin Abdallah, who served in the National Guard, were also included. Unlike the Sudayri Seven, the second group was far more diverse, but still strong. Finally, the third faction, which emerged in early 1981, included the sons of King Faysal, led by Foreign Minister Saud. In addition to Saud, his brothers Muhammad (formerly deputy minister of agriculture), Khalid (governor of Asir), Saad (deputy governor of Petromin), Bandar (air force officer), and Turki (chief of Royal Intelligence) were influential within it. Since their political prominence was relatively recent, at the time their influence was somewhat limited, but the relative balance between the more established Fahd and Abdallah factions presumably provided members of the third group distinct opportunities for maneuver. There is little doubt that Saud bin Faysal, for example, benefited from the 1979 Fahd-Abdallah discord by siding with Abdallah.

Assessment. The consequence of these multiple power centers existing within the ruling family under King Khalid's reign was that no single individual or faction was able to dominate central issues related to succession and the distribution of power. Two specific trends emerged as well:

First, in the absence of consensus, basic issues remained unresolved. This was reflected in the inability to agree on a line of succession in 1975. Moreover, whatever agreements were reached, they tended to reflect a pattern of compromise and trade-offs, rather than conviction. Even the apparent establishment of Abdallah's place in the line of succession involved securing another claim, that of Defense Minister Sultan, as third in line for the throne. Of course, later developments added several twists to this particular issue, but in 1979 it was the product of effective compromise.

Second, the legacy of King Khalid was to increase the level of consensus, certainly on basic political issues, to ensure family interests. Khalid worked to avoid the establishment of permanent fissures in the family, and, in this regard, he succeeded. Khalid remembered how internal and external foes had manipulated family feuds during the reign of King Saud. Still, when Khalid seemed on the verge of resignation due to ill health or when Heir Apparent Fahd's political fortunes were temporarily on the wane, the management of family politics was strained. This much was certain. As the dynamics of family politics corresponded to the relationship between politics and policy, latent political rivalries within the family overlapped with differences on basic policy issues. Consequently, the orientation of Saudi foreign policy, the pace of internal development and political reforms, and the direction of Saudi oil policy all polarized senior members of the family into clusters of power. These differences reflected, and reinforced, political rivalries. Yet, just as the need for consensus and compromise on political issues—a product of the underlying balance in the family—prevailed, the same approach was also applied to policy disputes. Similarly, just as political rivalries were alleviated by common political interests, policy differences were tempered by a basic set of shared policies. At the same time, the policymaking process, like the family's internal political balance, was most strained during periods of crisis and challenge.

King Fahd bin Abdul Aziz

King Khalid bin Abdul Aziz died from heart failure on June 13, 1982, in the midst of several foreign policy crises. The consensus monarch, who had been the most acceptable candidate in 1975, lived up to his billing as he fulfilled the task of reconciling various factions. Over a period of seven years, Saudi leaders collaborated, even if shifting alliances and consensus building were in full swing. The result was the establishment of clusters of power.

Because the monarch had gone through a prolonged illness, his death did not come as a surprise, and elaborate succession arrangements were already in place. Within minutes of the death, an official court statement declared that "Royal family members, led by Prince Muhammad bin Abdul Aziz, have pledged allegiance to Heir Apparent Fahd bin Abdul Aziz as King of the country."[110] The same statement further declared that King Fahd had nominated Prince Abdallah as Heir Apparent, a decision that was wholeheartedly accepted by the majority "to maintain the Saudi principle of collective leadership."[111] For his part, a perceptive Heir Apparent stated that King Khalid's death was a huge tragedy, although, specified Abdallah, "our consolation is that God has compensated us well in His Majesty the great King Fahd," adding, "we must unite our efforts and grow together, government and people, behind my lord, His Majesty King Fahd."[112] Before the end of the day, a slight cabinet shuffle was also announced, with Defense Minister Sultan appointed as second deputy prime minister. His place in the ruling hierarchy as heir to the Heir Apparent was thus secured, at least in 1982.

Not only was the transfer of power smooth—strongly suggesting that a family agreement had been reached days if not months ahead of time—but neither Abdallah nor Sultan relinquished their traditional power bases. The Heir Apparent retained full control over the National Guard, and Defense Minister Sultan was in full charge of the regular armed forces, even if all three senior figures displayed remarkable unity. Whether this unity was genuine or the result of convenience following several years of regional and international crises was difficult to determine. True to Al Saud traditions, it was not unusual for all members of the extended family to unite in times of crisis, but what could be accomplished in the presence of a unifier was quite different during the absence of such a figure.

For the balance of the 1980s, King Fahd and Heir Apparent Abdallah shared governing responsibilities, the former concentrating on international concerns and the latter on regional, especially Arab, affairs. To a certain degree, this pattern of specialization reinforced underlying differences in orientation, with Fahd and Abdallah viewing foreign policy issues from the perspective of their different capabilities. As a result, Fahd's was labeled "pro-American" and Abdallah's "pro-Arab."[113] In reality, these labels were greatly exaggerated because Abdallah was never "anti-American" and Fahd was seldom "anti-Arab." Both agreed with the vast majority of the Al Saud family on the strategic necessity of good relations with major powers, including the United States and key Arab states like Egypt and Syria. Moreover, this conviction did not mean that periodic disagreements did not exist, as in the aftermath of the Camp David Accords, when then Heir Apparent Fahd had argued for milder sanctions against Egypt while Prince Abdallah had been inclined to support the Arab consensus against Egypt. At other times, both Fahd and Abdallah agreed, as in 1987, for example, when Riyadh requested that Washington recall Ambassador Hume Horan after a rather ugly incident that had infuriated both men.[114]

However, the division of labor, at least for most of the 1980s and 1990s, was not fluid. Defense Minister Sultan, for example, had the specific responsibility of dealing with Yemen. To be sure, Sultan's prominence in Yemeni affairs indicated the extent to which the Saudis considered Yemen a military threat.[115] Likewise, Interior Minister Nayif was particularly active in relations with the Gulf states, including his successful September 1979 agreement with Iraq on internal security cooperation. Interestingly, the foreign policy orientations of several other princes correspond to those of their major political allies. Sultan and Nayif are generally said to agree with Fahd's line, though perhaps with a French twist. Over the years, both cooperated with their French counterparts, attempting to create a balance among the Kingdom's foreign suppliers. Saud bin Faysal was usually more inclined toward Heir Apparent Abdallah's views. The foreign minister was often associated with those advocating a more "nationalist" Saudi foreign policy. Still, these differences, like those between Fahd and Abdallah on foreign policy, were mitigated by a common set of strategic interests.

In contrast to foreign policy concerns, differences between Fahd and Abdallah on domestic issues, especially in the 1980s, appeared to be greater. Both agreed on maintaining the dominance of the ruling family in internal affairs but shared different perspectives on how this could be achieved. These differences, in turn, were directly related to their corresponding political bases. With close ties to key tribes and conservative religious leaders, Abdallah favored a more cautious pace of economic development, arguing that overtly rapid development posed a threat to Saudi values and stability. While it was unlikely that he wished to turn back the clock, modernization presented a major challenge to the Kingdom, especially after oil prices collapsed in the mid-1980s. Reduced income immediately translated into a weakening of his traditional base, as the recruiting process in the National Guard shrank. By contrast, King Fahd favored a more "progressive" approach, seeking a rapid rate of development and implementation of social reforms. As minister of education in the 1950s, for example, Fahd had pushed for the education of women. Both as Heir Apparent and as monarch, he also favored the adoption of ambitious development strategies. In this perspective, he was joined by his full brothers Sultan and Nayif, who reportedly believed that failure to provide material benefits to their constituency presented the greatest threat to internal stability. Naturally, additional expenditures for military and internal security operations translated into strengthened power bases for both.

These permutations notwithstanding, the superlative source of disagreement between Fahd and Abdallah throughout the 1980s centered on the question of political reforms. King Fahd repeatedly announced his intentions to establish a Basic Law and a Majlis al-Shura (Consultative Council),[116] and entrusted Interior Minister Nayif to coordinate the drafting of the basic statutes. Abdallah, on the other hand, seldom made any public statements in favor of such a proposal in the period before 1990. Of course, promises of basic political reforms were almost always associated with internal events that rocked the stability of the ruling family, including the epoch-making 1979 Makkah Mosque takeover. From King Fahd's perspectives, these pronouncements could well have been designed to appease internal opposition. Nonetheless, the monarch's endorsement of such reforms appealed to loyalties of various disenfranchised groups, while Heir Apparent Abdallah's lukewarm position alienated others. Yet, one of the most serious obstacles to the establishment of a Basic Law in the 1980s was the proposed solution to the succession issue.[117]

Another point of disagreement between Fahd and Abdallah in the 1980s concerned the overall organization of Saudi Arabia's defense and security establishment. Aside from a variety of police, frontier, and internal security forces, and as is widely known, the Saudi defense and security establishment is divided into two separate and distinct forces, the regular armed forces and the National Guard. King Fahd and Prince Sultan made a number of efforts to undercut Prince Abdallah's institutional base, either with proposals to merge the two forces under army command or restrict the National Guard to light weapons that would reduce it to a police force rather than the paramilitary organization it really is. For his part, Defense Minister Sultan frequently advocated the establishment of a national conscription program, which, in reality, would deprive Abdallah of bedu recruits for the Guard. Throughout the 1980s, Abdallah resisted these efforts, and the advance in his political standing in the 1990s corresponded with new plans to increase the size and strength of the Guard.

Although the division between the National Guard and the Royal Saudi Army (RSA) implied different perspectives on the threats facing Saudi security and stability, the RSA was better equipped to handle external threats to Saudi Arabia, while the National Guard was more suited to meeting internal challenges. Thus, and as stated above, Defense Minister Sultan's institutional interests implied an emphasis on external attacks, while Abdallah was more inclined to stress internal dangers, including the danger of a military coup. These differences further corresponded to foreign policy preferences, since, on balance, key Western powers, led by the United States, offered greater protection against external attacks, while cordial relations with the Arab world were more essential for internal tranquillity. Both of these variables took on concrete forms in the aftermath of the 1990 Iraqi invasion of Kuwait and the ensuing 1991 war to liberate the shaykhdom.

Following the War for Kuwait, the Al Saud ruling family became sensitive to both domestic and international pressures, calling for liberalizing reforms. For the first time in decades, dynastic succession in Saudi Arabia turned into a topic of discussion and analysis, due in large part to the vast influx of foreigners into the country. The world's media focused on the cultural and ideological peculiarities of a closed society, encouraging Saudi traditionalists and more liberal elements alike to voice their opinions. Although King Fahd had spoken of reforms in the 1980s—even funding the construction of a building to house a consultative body (which has remained empty)—no changes had been introduced by early 1992. Against a new trend of open challenges,[118] however, the monarch hinted that he was ready to nominate 60 leading citizens to a Majlis al-Shura, although even this minor pledge was delayed. In this endeavor, Fahd was supported by his Heir Apparent, who, true to Al Saud traditions, rallied behind his monarch to ward off opposition.

Succession and Heir Apparent Abdallah

Despite the fact that Abdallah controls the National Guard, the Heir Apparent remains relatively weak because of his position within the family. As discussed above, Abdallah is the son of a Shammar bride whom Abdul Aziz married to suborn and co-opt the support of the rival Rashid dynasty of Hail after he had defeated them in battle.[119] As such, Abdallah does not enjoy the gaggle of full princely brothers that other princes have.[120] Furthermore, Abdallah has a limited number of well-situated male progeny. Perhaps because of Abdallah's lack of broad family ties, those three sons whose positions are known are employed exclusively within the Heir Apparent's National Guard fief.[121] The consequence is that Abdallah lacks a strong network of supporters within the broader government bureaucracy—an asset that other princes have managed to fashion by placing their sons and relatives widely throughout the government.

Still, despite these inherent weaknesses, Prince Abdallah cultivated close relationships with half brothers and nephews who, in turn, lacked family allies and needed the political support of a senior leader. In recent years, the Heir Apparent has adopted a sharply different strategy, namely that of enhancing his public legitimacy. In October 1999, he strolled through a Riyadh mall, chatting with shoppers and indulging in fast-food items.[122] In a country where leaders are traditionally aloof, Abdallah is increasingly perceived as "a man of the people," almost as if he were running for office.[123] Long hampered by a stuttering problem, the Heir Apparent welcomed the care of a speech therapist who helped him overcome this severe handicap. In fact, Abdallah was widely praised for speaking honestly about the country's economic difficulties, vocalizing his opposition to corruption, and expressing his many concerns to bureaucrats about complaints from citizens. In fact, one observer concluded that Abdallah had become the "people's King" because he had "a common touch" and "people felt close to him." The political analyst concluded that Saudis believed that their Heir Apparent was "concerned with their problems and [wa]s personally trying to do something for them."[124] Another observer posited that despite his age, Abdallah was galvanized by the challenge of ruling the Kingdom, and was determined to "turn Saudi Arabia into a modern nation able to compete in the next century."[125]

To his credit, the Heir Apparent confronted Saudis with stark realities when he declared, for example, that "the days of the oil boom were over." In 1998, Abdallah *asked* Saudis to cut down on unnecessary spending, all to help reduce the substantial subsidies on various products. It remained to be determined, of course, whether he would be able to impose similar discipline on family members. Confidential reports attributed to the Heir Apparent reveal that Abdallah goaded his own sons to pay for telephone, electricity, and service flights on the national airline. His cautionary remarks were extended to eliminating commissions paid on various construction projects, which, if confirmed, would indeed be revolutionary. He even openly discussed the possibility that Saudis should rely less on government and more on themselves.

To be sure, Abdallah's efforts to enhance his public legitimacy may be rewarding, but, without a doubt, support within the family remains far more important. Prince Talal bin Abdul Aziz echoed this sentiment when, speaking about succession, he reportedly declared: "We are grateful that King Fahd drew up two clauses in the Basic Regulations. What he said was the king must be the oldest and the most fit to rule. So it is not enough to be only the oldest, you must also be the most fit to rule."[126] Prince Talal recognized that there were "two legal leaders" in Saudi Arabia—the monarch and his Heir Apparent—and that, in turn, the sons of Abdul Aziz will choose their successors.[127]

Prince Sultan and the Sudayri Seven

The second in line for the throne, Sultan bin Abdul Aziz, enjoys strong family ties because he shares a mother, Hassa bint Ahmad Al Sudayri, with six other full princes.[128] Much has been made of the influence of the "Sudayri Seven" within the House of Saud—and with good reason. Moreover, Prince Sultan's sons have been well positioned within the government to act as proponents of his eventual candidacy for the highest office in the land. In late 1996, for example, Prince Bandar bin Sultan, Saudi ambassador to the United States, warned of government paralysis in Riyadh, suggesting that two deputy prime ministers should be appointed, to govern the Kingdom more effectively. According to one report, Bandar "was extremely generous in his praise of the crown prince, which indicated to Saudi-watchers that the succession issue ha[d] been decided and that Prince Abdallah ha[d] secured the support of his half brothers, the Sudayris."[129]

Irrespective of whatever arrangements may have been reached, Defense Minister Sultan bin Abdul Aziz enjoys a strong base of power within the government, thanks to the superior positioning of his sons and relatives. He further enjoys a strong base of support within the ruling family because of connections to his extended Sudayri clan. Still, it would be a mistake to assume that Sultan can automatically rely on the support of monolithic ranks of the Sudayris within the ruling family in his bid to influence policy. It may be worth repeating that while he remains alive and secure on his throne, King Fahd is not only the senior member of the ruling house, but also the senior male member of the Sudayri faction within it. Fahd has, therefore, first claim to Sudayri loyalties.

King Fahd's Outlook

Even if the monarch's inclination were to support his full brothers, several key developments created a noticeable wedge between them, notably after Muhammad bin Fahd was appointed governor of the Eastern Province in 1985. This sensitive move triggered demands of King Fahd, chiefly by Defense Minister Sultan, to designate Fahd bin Sultan governor of Tabuk. The ruler complied with his brother's wish but did not stop there. Within a very short time, Muhammad bin Saud was appointed governor of Baha, Mish'al bin Saud went to Najran, Faysal bin Bandar was entrusted the sensitive governorship of Qasim, and Khalid bin Faysal was trusted with the post in Asir. These selections meant that Defense Minister Sultan was dealt a further "complication" by King Fahd, as the former tried to check Muhammad bin Fahd's growing influence. Sultan's own alliance was balanced by these various promotions while Muhammad bin Fahd was building up his reputation in the troubled Eastern Province. King Fahd boosted his son's chances within the family, adding several junior princes—King Saud's offspring no less—to his ledger, as allies. In fact, almost all such appointments were geared to advance one's interests, promote the designator's credentials, and secure the designee's loyalty. Moreover, all designations were also meant to deny one's competitor any potential gains.

After his late-1995 stroke, King Fahd transferred power to Heir Apparent Abdallah for a period of six weeks, but then announced he was resuming his duties in full, although he has never really done so.[130] He remained bedridden and in some pain from various health ailments. More alarming, his mental capabilities were failing, and his physicians did not believe he would ever recover in full. "His behavior has been stubborn, bizarre and unpredictable," argued one diplomat.[131] "There has been a decline to the point where essentially most of the time he is in a state of dementia," the diplomat continued, "and basically, he has no short-term memory." Various other sources confirmed this general condition, although, miraculously, the monarch has managed to perform selected public duties from time to time.

The Succession Dilemma

Since the death of the current dynasty's founder, and with minor exceptions, succession has passed among the sons of Abdul Aziz (1932–1953) in order of seniority. Understanding the interrelationships and precedence within this ruling family line is therefore important in identifying the country's decision makers and how they have promoted their offspring. In a break with long-standing tradition, the ruling family published an explicit order of succession for the first time in 1992. In addition to existing "understandings" regarding the identity of the Heir Apparent, the royal decree explicitly stated that Abdallah was first in line for the throne, while Prince Sultan stood second in line—both are sons of the Kingdom's founder.[132] Obviously, this decree placed the next succession in high gear, pitting against each other two powerful princes who have disagreed far more than they have agreed and whose personal ambitions may yet get in the way of governance. As stated earlier, the issue has not been whether Abdallah will become King, but (1) whether that rule will be strife free, and (2) whether senior members will take precautionary measures to strengthen their offspring.

As discussed throughout this chapter, the ruling family occupies a central position in the political, economic, and social systems of Saudi Arabia. Although the size, diversity, and complex structure of the family have tended to promote internal divisions, these factors have also served to centralize power in the family's hands.

The centrality of the ruling family is particularly evident in the Saudi political system. In principle, the King serves as head of state, tribal and religious leader, and commander of the armed forces. Al Saud princes occupy key positions within the government apparatus and in the Council of Ministers. The positions of prime minister, deputy prime minister, and second deputy prime minister are always held by senior figures. The family also maintains a monopoly over the main instruments of defense and security—the Ministry of Defense and Aviation, the Ministry of the Interior, and the National Guard. In addition to senior Al Saud officials, "technocratic princes" have emerged to control various technical offices. This trend may well grow in the future as more Western-educated princes become politically active. Below the cabinet level, and as will be discussed in the following chapters, a large number of younger princes hold important administrative posts. Interestingly, their influence is not in the formal bureaucratic authority attached to their posts, but rather in their abilities to form and/or join existing political alliances. Outside the central government, the governorships are also directly controlled by the Al Saud. The governors and deputy governors, both direct descendants of Abdul Aziz bin Abdul Rahman and members of cadet branches, yield substantial power.[133] Finally, beyond the formal government apparatus, a web of patron-client networks and intermarriages link Al Saud members with important social groups throughout the country that, without a doubt, strengthen and legitimize the current generation.

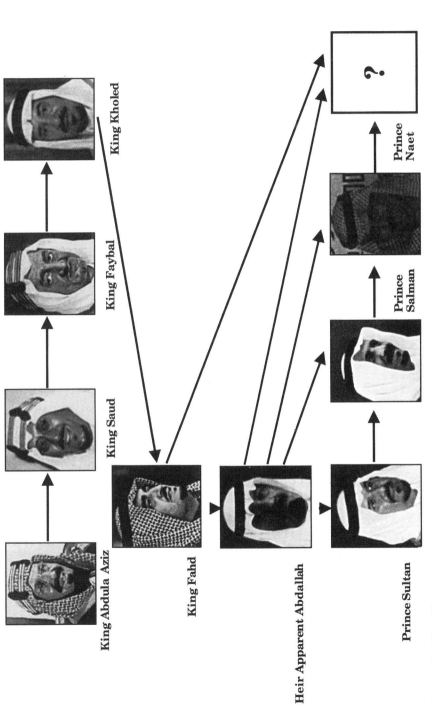

King Abdula Aziz

King Saud

King Faybal

King Kholed

King Fahd

Heir Apparent Abdallah

Prince Sultan

Prince Salman

Prince Naet

?

Succession Line-Up

Abdulaziz bin Fahd [behind King]   **Muhammad bin Fahd**

King Fahd's Progeny

Heir Apparent Abdallah

Mitab bin Abdallah   **Sultan bin Abdallah**

Crown Prince Abdallah's Progeny

Prince Sultan

Khalid bin Sultan

Bandar bin Sultan

Defense Minister Sultan's Progeny

Saud bin Faysal

Khalid bin Faysal

Other Contenders to Rule

Chapter 2 ⌒

The Next Generation

The whole world should know that this is our tradition and not a new thing. There is no power struggle between any of the brothers over the throne, because as I said this matter has been laid down in the two clauses in the Saudi Basic Regulations.

Prince Talal bin Abdul Aziz[1]

Although succession had been handled within inner family circles for most of the century, the 1992 royal decree portended to resolve whatever contradictions existed in the Kingdom's rule. The decree aimed to accomplish far-reaching solutions. Quite possibly, it also threatened to be the harbinger of serious clashes in the not too distant future, as a generation of young and ambitious Al Saud princes rose through the ranks. Despite Prince Talal's optimism, the decrees made matters far more ambiguous than heretofore recognized. No matter how specific these edicts appeared, the impetus for maneuvers increased, as the complicated process of selecting from among the hundreds of eligible and qualified candidates remained ill-defined. In the event, eager candidates readied themselves to assume responsibilities, although many were puzzled by what the decree specified. Who are the-up-and coming Saudi leaders of the next generation?

The purpose of this chapter is to classify several Al Saud princes within the family political structure—focusing on the roles they play individually and in concert with either their fathers, siblings, or other relatives—and, once that is accomplished, to decipher their views on a number of policy issues. The discussion will then move into the creation of internal family alliances as well as the roles of those who will support future monarchs.

The 1992 Edict

On March 1, 1992, King Fahd addressed his subjects on television and issued several key documents, including the Basic Law of Government, the statutes governing the newly created Majlis al-Shura (Consultative Council), and the *Law of the Provinces.*[2] This was, by any measure, a momentous step forward because an institutionalization process was clearly established. Even if the monarch's decision was propelled by the rising tide of internal opposition, as well as the repercussions of the War for Kuwait, significant and permanent changes were under way.

The Basic Law of Government was divided into nine main sections, dealing with the general principles of the state, the law of government, the values of Saudi society, the country's economic principles, the various rights and duties of citizens, the authority of the state, financial affairs, auditing authorities, and general provisions.

It was the second section of the Basic Law "that was of greatest interest and proved to be a bombshell both within and outside the Al Saud."[3] In fact, just two subsections of the second chapter contained the most controversial, and undefined, lines. Article 5, section (b), stated that "rulers of the country shall be from amongst the sons of the founder, King Abdul Aziz bin Abdul Rahman Al Saud, and their descendants," and that "the most upright among them shall receive allegiance according to the Holy Quran and the Sunnah of the Prophet (Peace be upon him)."[4] The last line, imposing a qualification—"the most upright"—was telling. One interpretation was that seniority was no longer the primary qualification for succession and that other considerations, including being upright, strengthened a candidate's eligibility. Another interpretation alluded to the fact that all direct descendants of the founder, that is, grandsons as well as sons, could now be eligible to rule the Kingdom.

Just as enigmatic, Article 5, section (c), further stated that "the King shall choose the Heir Apparent and relieve him by a Royal Decree."[5] Without a doubt, this last line threatened the entire balance of power that existed in the Kingdom, foreshadowing the authority of Heir Apparent Abdallah bin Abdul Aziz.

King Fahd's bold declarations by royal decree—which had the power of law—that a Saudi monarch could name and remove his Heir Apparent, and that the latter would not automatically succeed, have established new procedures for succession. First, a prerogative to choose and withdraw approval of an Heir Apparent was firmly grounded in law. Second, an acknowledgment that the more than 80 grandsons of Abdul Aziz were legitimate claimants to the throne was also confirmed. By declaring that successors could be chosen from the most suitable of Abdul Aziz's progeny, King Fahd implied that Heir Apparent Abdallah was not necessarily the presumed heir to the throne. Finally, the decision to include grandsons in the process proved that some senior members were indeed committed to the younger generation. This was the turning point in the current succession issue, for the decree clearly broke away from a time-tested tradition.

At the time these edicts were announced, Heir Apparent Abdallah "was said to have been 'outraged,' that his position . . . was defined as being at the whim of King Fahd, rather than as his right as the next in line."[6] Even if Abdallah was advanced in age, he was in good health and certainly considered himself to be eminently qualified for the post. The monarch, ever so aware of such nuances, issued another decree on March 1, 1992, confirming Heir Apparent Abdallah's command of the National Guard.[7] Defense Minister Sultan, for his part, apparently was equally concerned. After several years as second deputy prime minister, and presumed heir to the Heir Apparent, Sultan would now have to lobby much harder within the family to step up the succession ladder. Moreover, he could—at least theoretically—face stiff competition from some of his younger brothers, sons, and nephews. Indeed, after 1992 nothing prevented the ruling family from settling on a younger son or grandson of Abdul Aziz, to provide both continuity and change. Given that the succession line was not agreed upon, and that it had formerly moved from brother to brother through the sons of the founder, the 1992 edict further ensured that a fundamental change may now be acceptable.[8]

In late 2000, there were 25 surviving sons of Abdul Aziz bin Abdul Rahman, even if several never expressed an interest to rule. Others lacked the backing of their brothers. A few, perhaps not surprising in such a large family, were ill-equipped to fulfill the taxing requirements of rule. Diplomatic observers of Saudi Arabia maintained that the most able grandsons were the sons of the late King Faysal, but several also noted that other family members resented their rise to prominence. Seasoned observers insisted that the problems of lineal succession would eventually fall on the governor of Riyadh, Prince Salman bin Abdul Aziz, who is slightly older than his nephew, Foreign Minister Saud bin Faysal. Such a move would effectively skip a generation within the present rank of brothers, because Salman, born in 1936, is only sixty-three years old. He has charm and ability, and most importantly, he has great respect among members of the family.

Salman bin Abdul Aziz

By establishing permanent institutions, the King's edicts enhanced the country's political stability. The Al Saud were further secure in the knowledge that succession was legitimized, even if the identity of the putative successor remained murky. At the time of Fahd's accession to the throne, "the designation of Abdallah and then Sultan reflected a balance of family factions and a continuing adherence to principles of seniority," although the order remained vulnerable to the untimely death of one of the successors or an escalation of family rivalries.[9] No matter how unpalatable Fahd's 1992 decisions were—since he was not known for bold political moves—they, at the very least, guaranteed Al Saud rule.[10] He was also confident that the family contained several leading candidates who could maneuver through difficult times. The leading candidate acceptable to all major princes is Salman bin Abdul Aziz.

Usually mentioned as the reconciliator between Fahd and Abdallah, the governor of Riyadh combines modernizing and traditional qualities. Attuned to the country's critical tribal constituents—and their various needs—Salman is also surrounded by a slew of young and well-qualified technocrats, mostly recruited from King Saud University. Were he to be elevated, however, a dozen older princes would be passed over, and that clearly would be an unprecedented move. Even if a majority of Abdul Aziz's surviving sons did not have strong claims to the throne, seniority remains an issue. Irrespective of how the majority felt, four princes would pose credible claims to priority, including Abdul Muhsin, Badr, Mit'ab, and Nayif. The first two were once part of the so-called free princes movement, but they were rehabilitated and, in all fairness, have reestablished their credentials. Both are closely tied to Heir Apparent Abdallah. Mit'ab's political career has been somewhat erratic, but his loyalty cannot be questioned. Nayif, for his part, clearly emerged as a powerful minister of the interior, though, unlike Salman, there have been various hints of friction between Nayif and Abdallah.[11]

Prince Salman's potential nomination and elevation would not be without its drawbacks. Were he to succeed Sultan, for example, certain family members could be concerned that the "Al Fahd" would be "establishing a lateral line of succession among themselves and, in the process, violating the tradition of interspersing half brothers in between full brothers."[12] On the other hand, if King Fahd, Heir Apparent Abdallah, and heir to the Heir Apparent Sultan agreed on a single candidate, namely Salman, then it would be doubtful that the objections of bypassed brothers or ambitious nephews would carry much weight, especially since the ruling princes would inevitably seek to console the disappointed. Moreover, whenever the triumvirate was united, their abilities to apportion power among themselves, deputize responsibility to junior princes, and reconcile policy differences avoided disruptions.[13] Salman's elevation could indeed avoid such disruptions, but even his putative candidacy was subject to the two sections of Article 5 in the Basic Law described above. In any event, King Fahd maintained the delicate family balance for almost a decade, but ill health and his forced transfer of power to Heir Apparent Abdallah—starting in 1996, before the latter was named regent (in 1999)—essentially meant that momentous decisions would be made in the near future. Whether the Kingdom's leadership would remain in the hands of the founder's sons or pass to the next generation was the key question facing Saudis.

New Leaders

In addition to several grandsons mentioned earlier, including Khaled and Bandar bin Sultan, as well as Muhammad and Abdul Aziz bin Fahd, a number of important young princes are making significant inroads in the Saudi decision-making process. To this short list must be added Abdul Aziz and Sultan bin Salman, Saud and Turki bin Faysal, Mit'ab bin Abdallah, and Fahad bin Abdallah bin Saud Al-Kabir (see chart 2.1). Potentially, the latter four are allies of Crown Prince Abdallah, who has, over the years, established important links with each one. Other prominent figures dominate the political scene, but most of those in the second generation are reflections of their fathers' fortunes within the family.[14]

What do we know about these ten men, particularly in respect to their views on secularism, religious questions, and political participation? What do they think of each other and how do they see family politics evolving? Do they have any alliances amongst themselves, or are they first and foremost rivals? Do they see the need to extend a hand to cadet branches that played such a crucial role with their fathers and grandfathers? In short, do they have the skills needed for the Al Saud to sustain their authority? Although much is known about all ten, especially their education and career backgrounds, little is known of their views on important issues. Even less is known about their alliances. To some extent this is the result of conservative norms and the general Saudi trait for utter privacy.

Chart 2.1 Ten Rising Al Saud Leaders

Muhammed bin Fahd	Abdul Aziz bin Salman
Abdul Aziz bin Fahd	Sultan bin Salman
Mit 'ab bin Abdallah	Saud bin Faysal
Khaled bin Sultan	Turki bin Faysal
Bandar bin Sultan	Fahad bin Abdallah bin Saud Al-Kabir

Biographical Details[15]

Muhammad bin Fahd, Governor, Eastern Province. One of the King's favorite sons and certainly the most visible of his brothers, Muhammad bin Fahd is, in addition to his important political duties, heavily involved in various business enterprises. He is a partner in the huge Al-Bilad Trading Company—a conglomerate involved in importing and construction. Another of his companies managed the $10 billion Bell Canada/Philips of Holland telephone upgrade system for the Kingdom.[16] Irrespective of whatever financial transactions he may be involved in, King Fahd entrusted the most difficult governorship in the Kingdom to Muhammad, probably to assess his intrinsic capabilities. More important, and according to seasoned diplomatic observers of the ruling family, the King has confided that Muhammad had to prove himself to other senior Al Saud family members, arguing that his son's leadership potential could be demonstrated only in the critical Eastern Province. Having managed the province's various religious and ethnic problems rather well, Muhammad has enhanced his succession chances immeasurably.

Abdul Aziz bin Fahd, Minister of State. The young Abdul Aziz is being groomed for office, but chances are that his older brothers, several of his uncles, and certainly a few cousins will outrank him for the foreseeable future. It is interesting to note that the young prince is almost always part of his father's official delegation and usually sits right behind the monarch at all public ceremonies. Little is known of the many business contacts the young prince is involved in, but there is no doubt that he is well positioned.[17] In 1999, Heir Apparent Abdallah supported Abdul Aziz's appointment to cabinet minister, which, without a doubt, greatly facilitated the regent's governing capabilities. The two men apparently get along well, and the young minister secures his father's signature on all decrees that "cannot wait." In the event, and while Abdallah's brilliant move confirmed his flexibility, the Heir Apparent demonstrated that he could and would work well with his younger nephew. That was a positive sign for other rising members of the family.

Mit'ab bin Abdallah, Deputy Commander, National Guard. The oldest son of Heir Apparent Abdallah bin Abdul Aziz, Mit'ab occupies a vital position in the Kingdom. Although the official mission of the National Guard is limited—protection of the family—in reality, it is the Guard that maintains the tribal balance of Saudi Arabia. It recruits soldiers from trusted tribes throughout the country, thus strengthening the overall position of the Al Saud to rule with zeal.

Mit'ab is well liked by tribal leaders and, more importantly, by recruits who benefit from his largesse. In less than 50 years, the Guard transformed a segment of the Saudi population from destitute tribal elements into well-off, well-armed, and well-trained recruits. Unlike the regular armed forces—where a number of coup attempts were hatched (1955, 1957–59, 1969, and 1977)—the Guard never experienced an uprising. The last recorded revolt occurred in 1929, when Abd al Aziz crushed the Ikhwan, the force that preceded the Guard.[18]

Khaled bin Sultan, RSA, Commander of Coalition Forces.   The oldest son of Sultan bin Abdul Aziz, Khaled was born in 1949, entered the military, and eventually graduated from the Royal Military Academy at Sandhurst (United Kingdom). He also holds a master's degree from Auburn University in the United States. As a major general and the most senior uniformed member of the Al Saud, he was appointed commander of the Air Defense Forces (a separate service in Saudi Arabia) in May 1986, and later promoted to lieutenant general. After the Iraqi invasion of Kuwait in August 1990, he was named commander of all Arab and Muslim forces in Saudi Arabia, which gave him enormous public exposure and power. It was speculated that this, along with his concentration on extensive business interests—as well as a supposed demand to the King to be appointed chief of the General Staff—led to his dismissal in September 1991.[19] Understanding the need to protect his position, Khaled bought *Al-Hayat* newspaper—a tested platform—from the Mroueh family in Lebanon, to solidify his, as well as his father's, prospects.[20] In 1995, Prince Khaled authored a major thesis on his background and role in the War for Kuwait that, without a doubt, revealed a determination to seek power.[21] Given his military background and impeccable credentials as a nationalist, his views on a slew of issues unveiled that this rising star—despite his premature resignation from the service—retained credible chances for future service.

Indeed, on January 17, 2001—ironically, the tenth anniversary of the War for Kuwait—the royal decree appointing Prince Khaled assistant to the minister of defense and aviation for military affairs, with the rank of minister, indicates that senior family members have concluded that he would add value to the Al Saud. His return to a sensitive post further solidifies Prince Sultan bin Abdul Aziz's position within the family by strengthening the father's alliance. In turn, Khaled enhances his own credentials by assuming this new responsibility and, by inching a notch closer to the throne, he achieves yet another chance to solidify his political reputation.

Bandar bin Sultan, Ambassador to the United States.   The fourth son of Defense Minister Sultan, Bandar was trained in Britain as an air force pilot. Early on, he caught the eye of then King Faysal, who married him to one of his daughters. A capable and charismatic spokesman, Bandar has been ambassador to the United States since 1983. King Fahd has entrusted him with several important duties and missions that ranged well beyond his official position. According to knowledgeable Saudis, some of his "special" missions were problematic, including activities that were denied by Riyadh.

King Faysal recommended that Defense Minister Sultan extend public recognition to Bandar, given that birth records do not indicate his father's identity. While studying in California, Bandar remained close to the Saud princes in the universities there and, in doing so, gained entry into the inner circle of the Saudi power elite. As a result of these contacts, he was introduced to King Fahd, who needed someone to connect him directly with American government and businesses. The King trusted Bandar with that task, first as ambassador, then as security adviser. Bandar started dealing with political personalities from around the world on strategic and security issues on assignment by King Fahd.

Abdul Aziz bin Salman, Deputy Minister of Petroleum.   The fourth son of the charismatic governor of Riyadh, Abdul Aziz is deputy minister of petroleum and, in that capacity, a critical leader with his hands on the Kingdom's primary source of income. He is popular and surrounds himself with a retinue of supporters who benefit from his largesse and, naturally, support him—and his father—in other fora. He was appointed to the newly created post of undersecretary for petroleum affairs in July 1996. Previously, the prince had served as an adviser in the ministry, where he often was at loggerheads with the previous oil minister, Hisham Nazer.

Sultan bin Salman, Former Air Force Pilot and Astronaut.   Prince Sultan is a career air force pilot who flew on the space shuttle *Discovery* in 1985. He is now retired but very active in educational organizations and in a major project to rebuild the old Al Saud stronghold at Dir'iyah, outside of Riyadh. Sultan's farm near Dir'iyah is a model of modern facilities in a historical setting. Clearly, an attempt is being made to retrace the origins of the Al Saud and, equally important, to document Al Saud claims to the Najd. He is fond of the founder, to whom he refers as a "kind hearted, generous, and visionary grandfather" whom he obviously did not know. Yet, for Prince Sultan, the founder is very real. Interestingly, he often compares his father, Prince Salman, to his grandfather, drawing similarities in their character and capabilities. Prince Sultan is also active in the press, writing influential articles in local newspapers, or commenting on internal developments. In one recent essay, he admonished the minister of housing (without naming him) for lavishly spending on gargantuan facilities. He strikes his interlocutors as an influential behind-the-scenes leader with solid contacts, who may be called upon to act as a balancer.

Saud bin Faysal, Minister of Foreign Affairs. A son of King Faysal bin Abdul Aziz, Saud was educated in the United States (Princeton) and, upon his return to the Kingdom, was appointed to various posts within the Ministry of Petroleum and Mineral Resources. He was appointed minister of state for foreign affairs in 1975 after his father was assassinated, "to co-opt the best-known member of the next generation as a reinforcement against any attempt to change the order of succession."[22] Over the years, Prince Saud articulated the Kingdom's foreign policies with savvy—especially in the volatile Arab rejectionist-front arena—without abdicating its independent direction. He is close to Heir Apparent Abdallah, and with impeccable credentials, Saud bin Faysal remains one of the critical members of the Al Saud family.

Turki bin Faysal, Director-General of Intelligence. Prince Turki oversees all intelligence matters affecting Saudi Arabia and, in that capacity, protects the Al Saud from its foes—both internal and external. Appointed to his post by King Khalid bin Abdul Aziz in 1977, Turki is entrusted with several critical portfolios, including the problematic Yemen and Afghanistan questions, which naturally, remain priorities for Riyadh. His deputy, Saud bin Fahd, is an equally hardworking individual. This presence further ensures that King Fahd has a unique overview of all intelligence matters affecting Saudi Arabia. Inasmuch as intelligence duties tend to be sensitive, Prince Turki's time-tested capabilities, and unique role within the ruling family, guarantee him a privileged position.

Fahad bin Abdallah bin Mohammed, Assistant, Ministry of Defense. A career officer in the Royal Saudi Air Force, Fahad descends from the Saud Al-Kabir collateral branch of the ruling family. A highly respected director of operations for the air force, Fahad was appointed assistant minister (*wakil*) of national defense and aviation in 1984, allegedly to put Saudi Airlines back on its feet and to manage the huge Peace Shield and Al-Yamamah arms offset programs.

Secularism, Religiosity, and Political Participation

Understandably, the princes identified above insisted that their visions of life were reflected through the prism of Islam, arguing, nevertheless, that their interpretations were tolerant. Most were trenchant in their scrutiny of the Kingdom's conservative ulama, several of whom admonished the Al Saud for tolerating corruption and for doing America's bidding in the Gulf region. Prince Sultan bin Salman, for example, insisted that Shaykh al-Hawali had criticized the regime, interpreting the ills being visited upon Saudi Arabia as the result of "misunderstandings" by the Al Saud of their religion. Sultan bin Salman quoted an al-Hawali interview with *The New York Times,* identifying the secular West as the main culprit in the region, as proof of "how far out the preacher was."[23] Prince Faysal bin Salman was equally sharp when discussing Islam and the role that religion will almost always play in the Kingdom's political life. For him, the issue was a nonstarter, given the role of Islam in the history of Saudi Arabia.[24] When asked about the schisms within the Sunni world—and, of course, the difficulties associated with Shia Muslims and other offshoot sects— several princes focused on Islam's legitimizing aspects. For many, secularism carried a slew of ills that damaged Muslim societies experimenting with it. "If by secularism," one member of the family confided, "you mean nonreligious political authority, then we reject it. If you mean modernization and development, then we welcome it as long as it conforms with Islam."

A vast majority of Al Saud principals were extremely critical of Dr. Muhammad Al Masaari and the Committee for the Defense of Legitimate Rights (CDLR). One interviewee derided Dr. Al Masaari: "He is a deranged man who is dreaming of the impossible." Others were equally harsh in their assessments, indicating a uniformity of view within the younger generation on this most sensitive question. Few were ready to entertain the possibility that the CDLR could gain in popularity or that their legitimizing credentials—based on religion—could be challenged.

∼   ∼   ∼

It is not easy for the external observer to allocate portfolios amongst the various members of the ruling family in Saudi Arabia when it comes to either domestic, regional, or international affairs. This fact notwithstanding, an attempt is made here on a provisional basis. The purpose of this effort is to distinguish among the internal affairs of the Kingdom, Riyadh's relationships with its regional neighbors, and the Al Saud's foreign policy. How young princes formulate the ideological basis of their vision, shape and uphold the emerging institutions, and develop and execute the strategies that ensure their hold upon the Kingdom deserves careful attention. The following three specific issue areas will be used as guidelines in answering the above question:

1. Regional rivalries
2. Western encroachment
3. Oil policy

Regional Rivalries

The Red Sea littoral province of Hijaz, one of the most fertile and rich in the Kingdom, was incorporated into the Kingdom only some 80 years ago. Formerly under the control of the Hashemite dynasty, the Hijaz was conquered by the Al Saud not only because of the tremendous revenues generated by the pilgrimage to Makkah and Madinah, but also because control—and presumably protection—of the city provided Najdis the legitimacy they sought. The Hashemites, who entrusted their fate to British hands against the Ottoman Empire in World War I, suffered the disappointment of the Sykes-Picot agreement and the horrendous treatment of the Arabs at Versailles. Unlike the Al Saud, the Hashemites used their direct descent from the Prophet Muhammad as the legitimizing claim by which to assert their power over the two holiest sites of Islam. In other words, the Hashemite monarchy used its descent from the Prophet as an ideological vehicle by which to claim suzerainty over Makkah and Madinah, and by extension, governorship over the province. The doctrinal basis into which this ideological claim was transformed was the sharifate of Makkah, a title that the dynasty gave itself.[25]

The strategy by which the Hashemites sought to maintain their control over the province was twofold. First, accommodation with encroaching imperial powers, that is a *modus vivendi* with the Sublime Porte when it was still powerful enough to matter, and a defection to the British when the time was right. The second aspect of the strategy was one of strict religious observance and careful custodianship over the two holy places to ensure that they were not defiled. Were the two holy places defiled, Hashemite claims to rule would have been seriously impaired. As hundreds of thousands of Muslim pilgrims take part in the annual Hajj to

Makkah and Madinah, there would be no escaping a serious infringement of responsibility. Consequently, this great influx of annual visitors turned the Hijaz in general, and Makkah and Madinah in particular, into vital entities for the Muslim world.[26]

How have the Al Saud asserted control over this key wealthy province that is so important to the world's Islamic community? The Al Saud cannot and never claimed direct descent from the Prophet. It is, therefore, eminently pertinent to ask, where does their ideological claim to power over this area lie? This question becomes that much more important given the fact that the wealthy trading families of the Hijaz have traditionally regarded the inhabitants of the country's interior with some contempt. This applies particularly to conservative tribesmen from the Sudayri clan around Riyadh. Thus, a regional rivalry between the Najd and the Hijaz developed, which is latent in day-to-day Saudi politics; and the key question is, how do Al Saud princes accommodate this rivalry?

King Abdul Aziz accommodated Hijazis' view of themselves as a family apart by initially running the province as a separate Kingdom with its own viceroy. He did this by appointing Faysal, his son, as viceroy of the Hijaz, who allowed prominent families there great latitude to live their lives without undue interference. A decade later, the province was formally absorbed into the Kingdom, but it continued to have a special place by virtue of the fact that two of the most senior princes, sons of King Abdul Aziz, ruled the province in 2000. Prince Miqrin bin Abdul Aziz governed Madinah, and Prince Abdul Majid bin Abdul Aziz governed Makkah.[27] The province's importance was further reflected in the ruling family's extensive presence in Taif and Jeddah where dozens of palaces, including summer retreats, are located. Thus, two of the senior members of the ruling family have the portfolio for ensuring the tranquillity and proper integration of the Hijaz into the Kingdom.

The Al Saud's ideological claim to rule Makkah, Madinah, and by extension the Hijaz stemmed from the alliance that they formed in 1744 with the Al Shaykh family. In the Saudi view, the monarchy was the doctrinal institution into which the ideological claim was transformed. In turn, the monarchy ensured, through intermarriage between the country's secular and religious elites, that the Al Saud's claim to power was unhindered. To be sure, there may have been some justification for the caliphate, because of the direct family linkage that existed between the Hashemites and the family of the Prophet, but no such justification existed for the Al Saud. In their attempts to claim that they are the rightful guardians of the two holy sites in the Hijaz and to remedy this major lacuna, the family has had to undertake a series of strategies to boost its emerging ideological claim to rule.

The first strategy is to entrust governorship responsibilities to some of the most senior members of the ruling family.

The second strategy is, as has been stated earlier, to spare no effort to ensure that the annual Hajj is celebrated without political or social disturbances. Were there to be a serious disturbance or defiling of the holy sites during the annual pilgrimage, the Saudi regime could open itself to serious ideological and doctrinal attacks.[28]

Great efforts are made in the execution of this second strategy. Saudi princes supervise the pilgrimage committee at the Ministry of Awqaf and Religious Affairs, which organizes the annual program. Large sums of money are spent to provide for the housing and feeding of visiting pilgrims, with the intention of ingratiating and legitimizing the Saudi regime in the eyes of the Islamic community. And finally, the country's intelligence service, headed by Prince Turki, screens every visitor to the Hajj to ensure that disturbances do not occur.

A third strategy, namely that of religious good works, is also pursued to further establish the legitimacy of the Al Saud's ideological claim to rule both in the eyes of the Islamic community worldwide, the *umma,* and in the eyes of the domestic Saudi audience. Of course, members of the ruling family individually are well known for their contributions to numerous Islamic causes. Moreover, additional funds are channeled through the prestigious King Faysal Foundation based in Egypt and the Ministry of Awqaf and Religious Affairs in Riyadh, which engage in religious good works by means of charitable donations worldwide. It is worth noting that religious good works form one of the pillars of Islam that Muslims are expected to fulfill. Therefore, the Al Saud legitimize themselves by putting their oil wealth to work in promoting the faith throughout the world. This strategy of good works has the additional benefit of protecting the ruling family from attacks from right-wing fundamentalist elements, who claim that the family is not Islamic enough. Clandestine aid by the ruling family to the Mujahidun in Afghanistan, to Sunni constitutionalists in Egypt, to the FIS in Algeria, among others, further illustrates the ramifications of this strategy. Prince Muhammad bin Faysal is worth noting in this regard. Muhammad used the wealthy bin Laden family as a front through which to funnel aid to the Afghan Mujahidun in the late 1980s as well as to the FIS in Algeria in the early 1990s.[29] Individual actions of this kind by Muhammad bin Faysal and collective actions by the Ministry of Awqaf and Religious Affairs identify both the monarchy and the government with the defense and promotion of Islam.

As the family's ideological claim to rule was delicate and the institution of the monarchy rested on the claim that the Al Saud were best suited to rule Islamic holy places because of their orthodoxy, the family was very vulnerable to any allegations that they regularly engaged in behavior unsuitable for true Muslims. Such allegations undermined the very basis of the family's claim to rule. The Saudi regime's religious opponents challenged the monarchy's right to rule by raising issues of this kind. Underground Saudi opposition groups collected photographs in which Saudi princes allegedly may have been drinking, reported on mischievous behavior that had allegedly taken place either within or outside of the Kingdom at the houses of prominent Saudi princes, and made the argument that members of the ruling family were not true believers and, therefore, not suited to apply unitarian Islam in the Saudi state. It is for this reason that the ruling family is so sensitive to press reports on the behavior of its members. It is worth noting that rumors of licentious behavior by members of the ruling family—and such rumors abound among Arabs in the Middle East and Europe—are by definition extremist attacks on the monarchy and help the cause of extremist forces in the Kingdom. Fortunately for the ruling family, there are a number of princes who are strict in their religious devotions, not least amongst whom is Heir Apparent Abdallah himself. As a devout Muslim, Abdallah does much to dispel the fears that the Al Saud are not suited to govern the Kingdom because of their behavior and the equivocal adherence to unitarian Islam. By setting an example, the Heir Apparent offers the promise of continuing strict adherence to the letter of Hanbali doctrine.

Furthermore, there are a number of other devout members of the ruling family to whom one can point in countering arguments by Sunni constitutionalists to the effect that the Al Saud are unsuited to rule because of allegations of apostasy of some of its members.

The Al Saud have traditionally countered extremist diatribes by maintaining that their association with the Al Shaykh family provides them the necessary immunity. The Al Shaykh, who have typically formed the major part of the country's ulama in the past, have a vested interest in seeing the ruling family remain in power because of immense benefits to them. Thus, this key set of actors has been inclined to support continued Saudi rule. Given that the ulama do not dispose of independent means of finance and therefore can be kept on a tight string financially, they are nevertheless vulnerable to public pressures. In fact, the entire institution continues to erode and has, in recent years, come under strong attack. There are both senior and junior ulama who no longer feel compelled to support the regime, because they are disenfranchised and do not have a

stake in the system. The ruling family has to date approached these players in an autocratic manner, threatening and cajoling them to stay in line
and not question the status quo. However, this strategy cannot hold in
the long run. Secret meetings by militant Sunni constitutionalists within
the Kingdom are occurring with increasing frequency and sometimes take
place under the leadership of Al Saud family members.

One final line of defense manifests itself in yet another deployment of
Saudi oil wealth. The ruling family's attempts to deny foes an opportunity to attack it on ideological grounds, whether on the premise of the behavior of individual family members or on the grounds that the
monarchy has no Quranic base, is noteworthy. In this case, petrodollars
have been put to work gradually buying up every major newspaper and
every major radio and television station capable of broadcasting throughout the region. An example is *Al-Hayat*—owned by Khaled bin Sultan.
Another example is the *Middle East Broadcasting Company* (MBC), which
is owned by Waleed al-Ibrahim, the father-in-law of King Fahd. By buying up sources of information, the Al Saud deny their enemies platforms
from which to mount ideological attacks upon them.

Western Encroachment

The Saudi monarchy is under attack not only by traditionalists but on
the progressive front as well. The major figures in this area are the more
liberally inclined members of the haute bourgeoisie and those Saudi
citizens (whose number surely runs in the thousands) who are sent overseas for education in technical and other specialized areas. The pressure
from these sources is in the opposite direction: pressure to show more
laxity, more tolerance, more acceptance of Western ideas, less strict adherence to the tenets of Islam, greater freedom for women, availability
of alcohol, and less single-minded adherence to the strict tenets of the
unitarian school of Hanbali Islam. The attitudes and approaches encouraged by this progressive school within the Kingdom constitute a
very corrosive ideological threat to the Al Saud. If the monarchy's claim
to power rests upon its judgment that as a family it, alone, is best suited
to apply a traditionalist conservative interpretation of Islam, then any
forces that argue for a liberalization and a less strict application of that
very same doctrine are in direct contradiction to the family's claim to
rule. When taken to its ultimate extreme, if the Kingdom were to adopt
a very liberal, tolerant attitude toward such forbidden subjects as alcohol, the veiling of women, or for that matter women's rights, the Al
Saud could no longer claim that the reason they ought to rule is because

they are applying in practice the dictates of Muhammad Abdul Wahhab. If this claim to power is gone, then what is the value in having a ruling family governing the Kingdom? The administration of a state along the lines described above could also be easily undertaken by a constitutional monarchy, a democracy, or any other form of political organization. It is for this reason that the more progressive ideology (imported by technocrats and students) is so threatening to the Al Saud. The regime must, however, temper its reaction to this corrosive ideology because it must also seek to please key Western allies. The latter's view of Saudi Arabia will be impacted by the degree to which the Al Saud attempt to take into account the feeling both within their own country and in the West that they should go some way to adopting a more emancipated approach on the topics outlined above.

While King Faysal demonstrated that there was plenty of room for ingenious interpretation of Hanbali Islam—to accommodate the developments of modernization—the unitarian doctrine does act as a somewhat constraining element in the ruling family's attempts to please both its internal progressive constituency and its external Western constituencies, mollify internal conservative forces, and attempt to accommodate to modernity. The doctrinal institution used to apply these tenets is the Supreme Council of Ulama, which is asked to rule upon the Islamic nature of such controversial innovations as radio and computers. The introduction of television, after all, launched a riot in Saudi Arabia, which was quelled only by having both the radio and television repeatedly read out the Quran to assuage the feelings of conservative forces. Similarly, computers, when first introduced into the Kingdom, printed "God is Great" (*Allahu Akbar*) at the top of each page in a tip to the feelings of conservative forces within the Kingdom.

The ruling family has been careful to channel the forces of progressive thought by keeping them under its own control. The institution in question here is that of higher education and training, whether it be at the university level or for training in such areas as oil refining, exploration, etc. A majority of Saudi citizens going overseas for higher education are sponsored by the Saudi state, and by extension, the ruling family. This financial control over individuals who are going to be exposed to progressive Western ideas is in itself a means designed to help head off possible ideological threats to the monarchy's continued rule. Once in the West, Saudi citizens benefiting from education at the expense of the Saudi government are closely supervised. Offices at embassies throughout the world bear responsibility for tracking the activities of Saudi students. Within the Kingdom itself, another strategy is applied, as so-called liberal elements who returned with Western ideas are restrained by virtue of the monarchy's monopoly over sources of mass information.

The Al Saud have thus built institutions to channel and control progressive forces that might threaten their ideological claim to power, and have adopted a deliberate strategy of keeping these individuals under tight reign. Thus, it is no coincidence that members of the ruling family are in charge of youth welfare, and that intelligence organizations remain vigilant on high school and university grounds.

These facts notwithstanding, it still remains true that a large number of Saudi citizens return annually to the country having been exposed to a more liberal lifestyle in the West and expecting positions of responsibility within the government that may not necessarily be available to them. Yet, despite the Al Saud's attempts to channel and control, and despite the attempts to accommodate Western liberal thinking as well as harness whatever indifference may exist toward the monarchy's Western protectors, the regime's long-term challenges are to maintain a delicate balance between opposing forces and to accommodate an increasingly restive technocratic class whose opportunities do not match up with their expectations.

Oil Policy

One area in which the Kingdom has and indeed must accommodate the technocrats is that of oil policy and oil production. There simply are not enough members of the ruling family, with either the education or the desire, to run the huge apparatus that is needed to maintain the Kingdom's oil production and refining capabilities. Obviously, oil is one of the fundamental reasons for the Kingdom's international importance, and in a measure of that responsibility, as mentioned above, the King has placed his own son in control of the country's major oil producing province.

Interestingly, the ruling family has chosen to pursue a deliberate policy of not installing any one prince in charge of overall oil production. Instead, this job has gone to technocrats such as Shaykh Ahmad Zaki Yamani, or the former minister of planning Hisham Nazer. Although petroleum ministers report directly to the King, other princes have an influence on oil production by means of the Supreme Petroleum Council. However, it is worth repeating that no one individual other than the King has any ultimate say in this area, and the most likely reason for this is the family's desire not to concentrate the immensely important oil production function in the hands of any one prince or any one branch of the family, as this would upset the balance between the various factions within it. An institution has thus been created that deliberately keeps control of oil production decisions out of the hands of any one family faction or member, other than the King himself.

Potential Alliances

The most difficult conclusion to draw from the new leadership maze in Saudi Arabia is that of emerging alliances. To be sure, and despite many shortcomings, current alliances are functioning well. King Fahd has a first-line alliance that includes his full brothers (the Sudayris), as well as several cadet-branch supporters, including the Al Thunayan and Al Saud Al-Kabir. Fahd's second-line alliance is composed of his sons, several of whom occupy key posts throughout the government. A third alliance line for the monarch rests with the retinue of younger princes, mostly distant nephews, who benefit from Fahd's generosity.[30] Similarly, Prince Abdallah and Prince Sultan have their own separate alliances that may overlap, given the characters and issues at heart. Interestingly, few surprises exist in the cast of supporters in each alliance, as the offspring tend to stand behind their father. What is noticeably different are the many cleavages that are developing in the third line (see chart 2.2), with the sons of King Faysal supporting the Heir Apparent, for example, and, more important, with a cast of younger princes helping Governor Salman bin Abdul Aziz.[31]

Cadet Branches of the Al Saud

To rule effectively, the House of Saud maintains order within its own ranks by co-opting branches of the family that might otherwise mount a rival bid for the throne, and challenge the succession process from within. The genealogically senior branch of the family, the Saud Al-Kabir (also known as the Araif) are a case in point. As discussed earlier, in the early 1900s this branch of the family mounted a challenge to the tribal succession system, basing their claim to rule on their seniority within the family. King Abdul Aziz thwarted this threat by marrying one of his sisters, Nura, to the leading contender from the senior family line, Saud bin Abdul Aziz bin Saud Al-Kabir.[32] By acting in this manner, Abdul Aziz co-opted Saud Al-Kabir—as well as his successors—and gave them a continuing stake in the rule of his branch of the family.[33]

Over the years, the Al Saud enlarged their hold by co-opting other branches of the family that could have mounted a rival bid for power. Since the inception of the Kingdom, for example, and as discussed above, the Jiluwi have been given the responsibility of holding governorships in key provinces. Many other examples illustrate the complexity of the rul-

Chart 2.2 Possible Al Saud Family Alliances

	First Line*	Second Line**	Third Line***
Fahd Alliance	Sultan	Khaled	Muhammad b Saud
	Abdul Rahman	Saud	Mish'al b Saud
	Nayif	Sultan	Faysal b Bandar
	Turki	Muhammad	Naef b Ahmad
	Salman	Abdul Rahman	Bandar b Sultan
	Ahmad	Abdul Aziz	Saud b Faysal
Abdallah Alliance	Bandar	Khaled	Khaled b Faysal
	Talal	Mit'ab	Saud b Faysal
	Nawwaf	Turki	Turki b Faysal
	Majid	Faysal	Salman b Abdul Aziz
	Sattam	Abdul Aziz	
		Mish'al	
Sultan Alliance	Abdul Rahman	Khaled	Saud b Nayif
	Nayif	Fahd	Muhammad b Nayif
	Turki	Faysal	Faysal b Turki
	Salman	Bandar	Fahd b Turki
	Ahmad	Nayif	Nayef b Ahmad
	Badr	Muhammad	
	Abdul Illah	Turki	
	Abdul Majid		
	Majid		
	Sattam		
Salman Alliance	Sultan	Fahd	Khaled b Faysal
	Abdul Rahman	Sultan	Saud b Faysel
	Nayif	Ahmad	Turki b Faysal
	Turki	Abdul Rahman	Khaled b Sultan
	Ahmad	Abdul Aziz	Bandar b Sultan
	Bandar	Faysal	Muhammad b Fahd
	Badr		Mit'ab b Abdallah
	Abdul Illah		Fahad Al-Kabir
	Abdul Majid		Naef b Ahmad
	Majid		
	Sattam		

*Sons of King Abdul Aziz, the Kingdom's founder
**Sons of alliance leader
***Other supporters

ing family's well-crafted system of rule through intermarriages with "rival" cadet branches. Thus, the capabilities of the Al Saud to foster the development of working and effective alliances, as well as building the consensus required within the family, are the best evidence of their overall competence to rule.

Chapter 3 ∽

Perceptions of Security Concerns

The Al Saud family articulated two major security goals throughout its 65-year rule: to maintain custodianship over the holy sites of Makkah and Madinah and to preserve the commanding role of the ruling family. Both, it was posited by every ruler, ensured their legitimacy and, as a consequence, their power. Both provided stability and preserved the Kingdom from internal challenges.

Historically, nearly all family members united whenever faced with challenges. Differences were quickly resolved through negotiations, brokered agreements, and concessions, as appropriate. Above all, succession crises, which intruded on internal stability, were settled without jeopardizing existing accords. During each succession, the Al Saud chose the designated Heir Apparent as ruler, and because succession was subject to a consensus decision, disagreements within the family over a successor were never allowed to endanger existing alliances. In fact, the Al Saud diligently strove to ensure that the succession issue never escalated into an open "struggle for power" that would weaken their authority and, after 1932, the monarchy.

Similarly, custodianship of the holy cities of Makkah and Madinah bestowed upon the ruling family tremendous political responsibilities. When Abdul Aziz bin Abdul Rahman, the father of modern Saudi Arabia, consolidated his power in the 1920s, he found it necessary to promote strong ties with key tribes and influential religious figures. Abdul Aziz relied on senior family members to enhance internal stability by appointing several princes to critical defense and security posts. In response to popular demands, Riyadh adopted consensus-driven measures, which placed the country on the path to unity. Thus, the ruling family buttressed its authority by articulating a clearly defined vision of security, and by sharing power with the Al Shaykh family. In doing so, they equipped the nascent country with a decision-making establishment that, over time, developed specific institutions to protect the Al Saud from all opposition forces.

The Alliance with the Religious Establishment

To end the chaotic tribal environment on the Arabian Peninsula, Abdul Aziz bin Abdul Rahman forged a new order, adopted a unique political system, and bequeathed power to his progenitors. His transformation of the peninsula's many tribal units into a unified force ensured the formation of a modern state. By acting decisively early on, he denied leadership contenders any influence and stripped contentious tribal chiefs of their ability to rule in remote areas. The ruler deliberately placed his sons—and other family members—into sensitive regional administrative posts, without exposing the Al Saud to undue criticism.[1] To achieve his objective, he sought assistance from the religious establishment by fostering alliances with senior ulama, as well as key tribal families. Despite these efforts, rivalries developed among his successors over conflicting security perceptions, which in turn led to several costly crises.

King Abdul Aziz and the Ikhwan

Abdul Aziz bin Abdul Rahman's ability to co-opt the Ikhwan cemented the various Arabian tribes that formed Saudi Arabia. As early as 1913, Abdul Aziz led Ikhwan armies to conquer the Jabal Shammar, the Hijaz, and Asir Provinces, by convincing local leaders that the security of the country required control of these regions. However, his deliberate policies angered the Ikhwan. Between 1927 and 1930, Ikhwan troops rebelled against the ruler because they wanted to preserve their independent power base and the Peninsula's traditional socioethnic frameworks. While they did not disagree with his security goals, the Ikhwan objected to Abdul Aziz's methods, going so far as to label them as a betrayal of unitarian doctrine.

In October 1928, when the Ikhwan withdrew their support from him, Abdul Aziz called for a conference of Najdi tribal leaders. In a classic move, he challenged them to choose another member of the family to replace him if they objected to his methods. Since there were no alternative leaders, the stratagem succeeded, as Ikhwan leaders pledged themselves anew to *support and obey* Abdul Aziz. This was a clear demonstration of trust in his leadership. Not satisfied with this considerable achievement, Abdul Aziz further split the ranks of the remaining rebels with gifts and, whenever appropriate, intermarriage. These maneuvers, however, did not end the crisis. A showdown led the Saudi leader to a decisive battle at Sabila in 1929, when the powerful Najdi crushed all of his remaining Ikhwan opponents.[2]

This victory over the Ikhwan consolidated the power of the embryonic Saudi state. Al Saud forces razed Artawiya and Ghatghat, two Ikhwan colonies that caused the most trouble, and amalgamated tribal shaykhs and ulama leaders into the decision-making process.[3] Finally, the monarch established an army as well as a centralized government administration to "tame" Ikhwan forces, allowing him to govern unchallenged.

What emerged from this drawn-out ordeal was a united state under the authority of the Al Saud who, nevertheless, had to contend with a variety of internal threats to their security.

Crises Under Saud bin Abdul Aziz (1958–1964)

The most severe internal crisis faced by the ruling family started in 1958. Multifaceted in scope and substance, the crisis had root causes in the elite's perceptions of security. Under Saud bin Abdul Aziz, and despite an increase in oil revenues, mismanagement and an extravagant spending style brought the country to the verge of bankruptcy. Soaring public debt, inflation, and the fall of the riyal to half its official value affected the ruler's capabilities. The ruling family concluded that King Saud could no longer "rule." In March 1958, senior members of the family agreed to transfer executive authority to the prime minister, Heir Apparent Faysal, while allowing Saud to retain his title.

In addition to key internal requirements, Saud "neglected" primary policies at least toward Iraq, Jordan, Syria, Egypt, and the United States. A series of foreign policy blunders further separated the ruler from his archconservative Heir Apparent. Through 1957, Saud bin Abdul Aziz pursued benign policies toward Washington, and favored a rapprochement with the Hashemite monarchy in Jordan. In a dramatic volte-face, the monarch aligned himself with Egypt, as the charismatic Nasser energized Arab masses and called for the adoption of unified anticolonial policies and nonalignment in the East-West struggle. This was an untenable situation, as conservative members of the family were not about to sacrifice their security to support chimerical Arab ideals.

In March 1958, Faysal received executive authority to launch a new defense concept and strategy for the country.[4] Much of the reasons for this *transfer of power* stemmed from the linkages of internal Saudi requirements to the Kingdom's articulated foreign policies toward Egypt. To be sure, Prince Faysal, like Saud bin Abdul Aziz, recognized that Nasser's

Arab nationalist drive represented a threat to the Kingdom. Still, the Heir Apparent believed that mere resistance would be hopeless and, instead, attempted to appease Nasser while reinforcing the Kingdom's internal capabilities. Faysal proclaimed that Saudi Arabia sympathized with Arab nationalist intentions without suppressing Saudi ties with the West even as Nasser called for precisely such steps.[5] In the context of internal Saudi affairs, this policy proved divisive.

King Saud's indecision in the face of such serious challenges from other ruling family members, coupled with the Egyptian role in ousting the Yemeni monarch, forced the Al Saud to be more pragmatic. After harrowing debates, about which little is known even after all these years, senior family members and the ulama stripped power from Saud and entrusted the prime ministership to Prince Faysal on October 17, 1962. Shortly thereafter, Faysal formed a new government that excluded the sons of King Saud, as well as several commoner civil servants who had urged recognition of the Yemen Arab Republic. Khalid bin Abdul Aziz became deputy prime minister and, later, Heir Apparent. Faysal entrusted the key posts of the defense and interior ministries, as well as the all too critical post of commander of the National Guard, to his loyal brothers— Sultan bin Abdul Aziz, Fahd bin Abdul Aziz, and Abdallah bin Abdul Aziz, respectively.

These were bold moves that altered the basic makeup of the ruling family. Faysal redrew the entire decision-making process to secure the Kingdom against internal (and external) challenges, for he was convinced that all of the Kingdom's difficulties originated in festering regional crises. To highlight his new policies, King Faysal:

- dismissed Egyptian advisers within the Saudi administration;
- created a special department in the Ministry of the Interior to supervise expatriate workers;
- reorganized the Kingdom's security services; and
- obtained the ulama's consent to introduce television broadcasts for propaganda purposes.[6]

Confronted with an ideological threat from Egypt, senior Al Saud princes rallied around the Heir Apparent. Rather than reunite the monarch and his putative successor, however, the Egyptian meddling and its more problematic Yemeni corollary drove the two men further apart. Saud bin Abdul Aziz, who was still the titular head of state, insisted on representing the Kingdom at League of Arab States (LAS) summits. This order created a new turning point, at which Saud and Faysal mobilized Royal and

National Guard units to settle their dispute once and for all. In the end, Prince Faysal bowed to a decision of the ulama that, while he should retain control of the government, the monarch should represent the Kingdom at LAS summits.[7] By early 1964, tensions had grown so that King Saud's sons were openly encouraging their father to consolidate his power and oust Prince Faysal from his post. To his credit, Prince Faysal moved first to quell potential dissent. In March 1964, he authorized internal security forces to arrest the commander of the Royal Guards, a loyal supporter of Saud, which led to the dispersion of the 800-member unit. The last element of Saud's military support vanished.[8] The Saud-Faysal struggle climaxed when a formal transfer of power from Saud to Faysal was ratified by the ulama and the ruling family. In November 1964, Saud was formally deposed, and Faysal became King.

For all his mercurial policies, Faysal strengthened the hold of the ruling family, equipped the country with a sense of fiscal responsibility, and protected his brethren from internal uprisings. He aligned Saudi Arabia with Egypt when Anwar Sadat launched his October 1973 surprise attack on Israel, and helped to impose a selective oil embargo on the United States and the Netherlands (for providing military transfers to Israel), without nevertheless reneging on his fundamental objectives. For Faysal, an avowed anticommunist, the problems of the Middle East were a byproduct of the East-West conflict. There was never any doubt about which side he and Saudi Arabia were on.

The stability of the Saudi monarchy was severely tested in March 1975 when an assassin gunned down King Faysal. The monarch was shot by his twenty-seven-year-old nephew, Prince Faysal bin Musaid, who sought an audience to plead a family case. Five senior princes present in the Kingdom decided on the successor and, joined by other ruling family members, announced that the murderer was deranged and had acted alone. Such a statement was necessary to assure the country that there was no plot to incite a general insurrection. Continuity was the order of the day, as Heir Apparent Khalid succeeded King Faysal. The new ruler, in turn, elevated Fahd to fill the post he vacated.

Importantly, King Khalid delegated much of his security authority to Prince Fahd largely because of his health problems. In some ways, the relationship between Khalid and Fahd resembled that which had existed between Saud and Faysal in the 1950s, save for the level of confidence that Khalid had in his brother. As minister of the interior responsible for security under Faysal, Prince Fahd was considered far more lenient than the King in dealing with security threats. More importantly, Prince Fahd was more openly "understanding" toward the United States, acknowledging that the special relationship between the two countries was benefiting the Kingdom too. The Heir Apparent distanced himself from controversial policies, demonstrated leniency toward dissidents, including those operating within the armed forces, and pardoned a number of prisoners. Moreover, Heir Apparent Fahd ordered that political detainees be rehabilitated, while Interior Minister Nayif bin Abdul Aziz reorganized and expanded the internal security services, which enabled it to monitor expatriate workers and suspected radical elements more closely.[9]

Still, despite these steps, family disagreements erupted, as sympathy among younger princes toward opposition religious groups increased. For example, strains between the Sudayri and Jiluwi branches of the Al Saud reached a crescendo in 1975 when the former pressed on with their demand that Prince Abdallah relinquish the command of the National Guard. Conservative Jiluwis, on the other hand, encouraged Prince Abdallah to resist this demand. This confrontation occurred as the regular armed forces, under Defense Minister Sultan, and security services, under Interior Minister Nayif, were being rapidly upgraded.[10]

The 1970s Challenge to Prince Abdallah

For a variety of reasons, dormant rivalries in the ruling family were rekindled in the late 1970s. When King Khalid was rushed to London for urgent medical treatment in February 1977, Heir Apparent Fahd, and other senior officials, demanded once again that Prince Abdallah surrender control of the National Guard. It was widely believed that Fahd bin Abdul Aziz and several of his brothers wished to replace Abdallah as second deputy prime minister and second in line of succession with Sultan and thus consolidate the so-called Sudayri hold on the government. The effort failed because Prince Muhammad, and other senior leaders, rejected it. They perceived the move as a destabilizing step that did not serve the Kingdom's best interests. Muhammad was also concerned with the pro-Western stance adopted by Riyadh. He reiterated that consensus must be reached on vital matters, especially over the Kingdom's Arab identity and, more important, on its vital foreign policy initiatives. When Prince Fahd met Egyptian President Anwar Sadat and Syrian President Hafiz Assad a few months later, the Heir Apparent ostensibly coordinated the Saudi stance with those of Egypt and Syria. In reality, Fahd's pro-American penchants caused discord among conservative Saudis, as Egyptian and Syrian policies shifted markedly from agreed measures.[11]

Such displays placed the "Sudayris" under pressure from the more conservative forces in the ruling house. The nearly simultaneous collapse of the Iranian regime, the signing of the Egyptian-Israeli peace accords, and the outbreak of the war between the two Yemens—as well as internal uprisings influenced by events in Teheran—triggered a critical policy debate among Saudi leaders that resulted in a political defeat for Fahd. Indeed, his hasty departure from the Kingdom for a long self-imposed vacation was telling.[12] Prince Fahd's temporary political decline meant that his ability to maintain a consensus was weakened. The Heir Apparent was unable to pursue a coherent security policy that could insulate the Al Saud from regional upheavals that, in turn, transformed the area throughout the 1970s. Prince Abdallah bin Abdul Aziz, known for his attempts to moderate the Kingdom's security policies with Syria, Iraq, and Iran, favored a disengagement from the U.S.-Saudi special relationship and, at least in the pre-1990 period, succeeded in guiding the country's foreign policy direction.

Uprisings in the Eastern Province (1950–1990)

An equally important internal fissure was the sensitive Sunni-Shia divide that was most prominent in the critical oil-producing Eastern Province. Over 500,000 Saudi Shias lived in the oil-producing Eastern Province in the early 1990s. A religious minority, Shias faced intimidation from strict unitarian teachings. At the time, the unitarian majority confined the Shia by banning their literature and denying them key professions, including sensitive military responsibilities. As the Shia community comprised a large percentage of workers in the oil industry, their presence was perceived as a major peril as well.

In response to perceived unitarian indifference, Shias went on strike in 1953 and again in 1956, 1970, and 1979. Aramco workers (both Saudi and expatriate) sought to rectify their perceived economic grievances and, taking advantage of the situation, made specific political demands to improve their social standing. For the ruling family, Aramco's early years were troublesome, primarily because the corporation provided radical Arab governments an object of the colonial paradigm. In the event, Aramco became the focal point for all of the Kingdom's socioeconomic problems, as Saudi Arabia was the only Arab Gulf state where both local and expatriate workers participated in protests against the Al Saud. For Riyadh, this was a security dilemma that threatened its ability to export oil and continue modernization programs on its own terms. At times, the confrontation was mild, whereas on other occasions it was downright dangerous.[13]

An official visit to the Eastern Province by King Saud bin Abdul Aziz in 1953 prompted an estimated 13,000 Shia oil field workers to protest against their poor treatment. The demonstration led to a strike, and for three weeks, oil production was brought to a complete halt. To be sure, Arab nationalist ideologies played a role in influencing these workers to manifest xenophobic and anti-Western sentiments.[14] Nevertheless, Riyadh was concerned that the strikers attracted sympathy among the armed forces. At the time, Saudi soldiers in the Eastern Province participated in the strike, coordinated the assault on the U.S. consulate, and joined Aramco employees in strengthening the antimonarchical National Reform Front.[15] Although the strike prompted Aramco to introduce fiscal reforms and improve working conditions, the ruling family opposed the vast majority of the demands—on security grounds—arguing that the petroleum industry could not be jeopardized by any concessions. Instead, the Al Saud quelled the uprising by dispatching army troops.[16] In addition, the ruler issued a decree recalling all Saudi students abroad, divesting those who failed to return of their citizenship, with the exception of those who were studying engineering, law, and medicine.[17]

The next Shia uprising occurred in May 1956, when King Saud bin Abdul Aziz visited Aramco facilities at about the same time the U.S. lease on Dhahran Air Base (DAB) was about to expire. Once again, Shia workers demonstrated by carrying banners condemning "imperialism" and demanding elected trade unions. Strikes continued throughout the summer, culminating in riots after Egyptian President Nasser visited Dhahran in September 1956. Nasser was met by tumultuous support that deeply troubled the Al Saud family.[18] At the time, Riyadh was concerned that these Shia strikes were an extension of Nasser's Arab nationalist struggle against perceptions of Western "colonialism" in the Middle East and, not insignificantly, that the Al Saud were associated with it. Coincidentally or not, the Kingdom decided not to renew the Dhahran Air Base agreement, even if the facility cemented the nascent Saudi-American security relationship.

King Faysal paid attention to the Shia throughout the 1960s, which, to a certain degree, reduced tensions. Although no core problems were resolved, Faysal used his immense persuasive skills to eliminate inherent mistrusts. With the sharp rise in oil prices starting in the early 1970s, however, Shia unrest in the Eastern Province rekindled the anxiety among members of the ruling family. The Al Saud responded once again with duress. In the late 1960s and early 1970s, for example, the National Guard arrested thousands of Shias after the latter demonstrated against the regime.[19] Little was different in their fundamental demands: human and economic rights.

To further ensure Al Saud security interests, in 1975 King Khalid and Heir Apparent Fahd moved to placate the Shia by allocating considerable financial support to build communications and industrial infrastructures in the Eastern Province. Without a doubt, these measures improved the educational system in the area, and, in a remarkable development, a number of Shias were provided with secure government posts. The majority Shia population, nevertheless, remained confined. By the late 1970s, developments in Iran had spilled over among Saudi Shias. In 1978 and 1979, riots broke out, setting off confrontations in several Eastern Province cities and villages.[20]

In November 1979, in commemoration of the death of Imam Hussein, Shias in Qatif demonstrated throughout the city, carrying anti-Western banners and pictures of Ayatollah Khumayni. National Guard units opened fire, killing 17 people and wounding hundreds. Prince Ahmad bin Abdul Aziz flew to the Eastern Province, where he promised massive investments in the development of Al-Hasa's economic infrastructure, education system, and other services. Despite attempts to pacify the Shia with increased subsidies, tensions rose, persuading the Al Saud that they could not discriminate against their own citizens without great sacrifice. This was a lesson learned, as aid began to flow to Shia businessmen and vocational centers, as well as to higher education institutions that were established to cater to special regional needs.[21]

In the 1980s, Saudi Arabia became more sensitive to the Shia plight, as the ruling family reversed its internal policies. To be sure, the perceived Iranian threat to the Saudi "state," as well as the outbreak of the Iran-Iraq war, highlighted the scope of the danger. The Al Saud could not insulate themselves from Shia attacks by merely pumping more funds into the Eastern Province. Political reforms were necessary and a consensus soon emerged on their utility. In September 1980, after the start of the Iran-Iraq war, Riyadh bolstered its armed forces in the Eastern Province, tightened existing security measures around oil installations, and adopted new safety steps to protect essential installations. Surveillance of the Shia population increased substantially. Although Iran whipped up tensions between Riyadh and the Saudi Shia population, no new riots occurred, despite minor acts of violence. The few terrorist activities were rapidly defused.[22]

These significant developments notwithstanding, the Eastern Province has remained relatively calm since 1990, due to increased contacts between the Sunni majority and the Shia minority. Saudi security interests dictated that renewed contacts succeed. In the wake of the War for Kuwait, the ruling family mitigated both Iranian and Iraqi abilities to influence its Shia population, an effort that culminated in a meeting between King Fahd and exiled Shia leaders in 1993 to reconcile and improve relations. The monarch released 40 detainees, and Interior Minister Nayif bin Abdul Aziz allowed Shia dissidents to return home safely. In return, Shia dissidents abroad halted publication of their monthly anti-Saud newsletters and agreed to stop attacking the government from their foreign bases.[23]

The 1979 Makkah Mosque Takeover and the Neo-Ikhwan

The ruling family was literally rocked to the core by the Makkah Mosque takeover that was carried out by hundreds of neo-Ikhwan supporters who stormed the Masjid Al-Haram, holding it hostage for three long weeks in late 1979. Led by Juhayman Al Utaybi, they demanded that worshippers recognize Muhammad bin Abdallah Al Qahtani as the long-awaited Messiah, distributed a prepared statement that condemned the Al Saud, and accused them of corruption and the befriending of Western infidels. They also called for the eradication of all signs of Western influence in the Kingdom, including television.[24] The group held out for three weeks before its harried members were "flushed out" by Saudi troops, aided by Jordanian volunteers and French counterterrorism advisers. Sixty-three individuals survived the assault and all were executed in public. The message to the populace was clear: the Al Saud would not tolerate uprisings against the regime.

This major incident clearly illustrated, however, that Riyadh had underestimated dissent within the Kingdom. Those who participated in the mosque takeover hailed from a broad spectrum within the population, belonging to various groups, including:

- the Al-Mushtarin sect;[25]
- the Shammar, Harb, and Utaybah tribes;
- National Guardsmen; and
- Muslim Brotherhood supporters from the Hijaz.[26]

The wide-ranging composition of the group suggested that this was not the work of fanatical fringe elements. At the time, many argued that the rebels had planned their operation in an urban area, despite efficient Saudi intelligence services, to drive a point home. Still, few dissenters were deterred by internal security forces, and what was even more telling was that their armaments originated from Saudi military stocks. The fact that National Guardsmen, and regular armed forces personnel, may have been involved in the uprising led the ruling family to launch a purge within suspected air force, tank, and infantry services.[27] Consequently, the incident exposed rivalries within the military because of the latter's poor performance in regaining control over the mosque complex without outside assistance. A more fundamental question was raised as well: Given its performance in 1979, could the National Guard fulfill its mandate to protect the Al Saud?[28]

The Makkah incident forced King Khalid to address deep-rooted issues that would prevent future uprisings. Prince Turki bin Abdul Aziz articulated King Khalid's position when he stated that "Makkah showed us we could be caught off guard. As a result, we expect others to try something."[29] First, the Saudi monarch embarked on an unprecedented campaign to accommodate dissent and control the political damage created by the uprising.[30] For example, the Al Saud provided generous grants for land purchases as well as outright loans to select individuals.[31] Second, King Khalid and the ulama agreed to cooperate even more closely on issues affecting the country's security. Religious authorities viewed the Makkah uprising as a clear threat to the unitarian alliance as well as a challenge to their credibility. It was for such reasons that they sanctioned the storming of the Holy Mosque and denounced the rebels for their actions. Saudi rulers reinforced the ulama call to carry out strict controls on everyday life to reemphasize the importance of their 1744 alliance.[32]

Sunni Extremism

Even before the epoch-making 1979 Makkah Mosque takeover, Sunni extremism had gained prominence in Saudi Arabia, starting in the early 1960s after its failures in Egypt. Known as the Salafi movement, its adherents accused the Al Saud of encouraging the erosion of basic Muslim values and giving tacit approval to the corruption that accompanied modernization. In addition, Salafis argued that the ruling family betrayed its sacred duty by allowing Westernization and permissiveness.[33] Following strict Sunni teachings, extremist believers further opposed giving greater rights to the Shia. As Riyadh embarked on improved ties with Shias in the late 1980s and early 1990s, Sunni extremists feared that accommodation between the ruling family and members of the Shia minority sect would single out the Salafi movement for retribution.[34]

In the wake of the War for Kuwait, Sunni extremism against the ruling family grew once again, as Salafis entrenched in Qasim demanded reforms in domestic politics and criticized Riyadh's reliance on Western forces.[35] In May 1993, Salafis announced the creation of a human rights group—the Committee for the Defense of Legitimate Rights (CDLR)—to eliminate injustice, support the oppressed, and defend the rights prescribed by the

Shariah in the Kingdom.[36] The official response to the CDLR was swift. Neither the ruling family nor the ulama wanted to contend with a second extremist threat within the Kingdom. Ulama leaders denounced the committee as an illegal organization. The strong reaction was consistent with King Fahd's warning—which stressed his opposition to such movements—despite repeated calls for greater tolerance and respect for individual human rights.[37] Subsequently, a crackdown on Salafis was initiated, especially after authorities confiscated weapons and ammunition at an Asir-area training camp in October 1993.[38]

Stability and Factionalism in the Armed Forces

The discontent that the ruling family faced, and that divided the Al Saud, was not relegated to the religious and political realms. Factionalism within the armed forces, linked to both internal as well as external causes, was also present. Although soldiers sought increased benefits as the armed forces developed, many officers were exposed to Arab nationalist ideologies that clashed with the Kingdom's unitarian character. Over the years, young, discontented nationalist military personnel—including members of the ruling Al Saud family—represented the most serious opposition in the Kingdom, seeking to emulate military uprisings in neighboring countries. Riyadh managed the military and, in doing so, further entrenched Al Saud rule. Over the years, the family withstood several potential coup attempts, but senior members handled each with determination.

Uprisings in the 1950s

All regular Saudi military services were at their embryonic stages in the early 1950s, as they lacked prestige and were easily counterbalanced by the National Guard. Still, the institutions were well on their way and, irrespective of performance, provided the regime with a skeletal military framework. The event that exacerbated internal military threats, however, was King Saud's 1954 decision to invite an Egyptian military mission to replace American advisers.[39] So-called Saudi Free Officers mounted a failed coup a few months later as an anti-American movement emerged amongst the military. By the spring of 1955, a slew of officers had been arrested, tried, and executed. During the trials, it became apparent that leaders had planned to oust the King and replace the monarchy with a republican government.

This was not the only such attempt. In 1955, the Al Rith tribe in northwestern Jizan—entrenched in the Jabal Qaha—demanded greater religious rights. Riyadh responded by dispatching air force planes but failed to subdue the rebellion. This uprising was supported by at least 12 officers from within the ranks.[40] A clear pattern emerged, as rivalries within the ruling family influenced developments in the armed forces.

Importantly, when King Abdul Aziz bin Abdul Rahman sought to build up the armed forces—ostensibly to respond to increasing threats from regional foes—he was, simultaneously, taking the necessary steps to protect his personal power from rival princes.[41] Unfortunately, the 1954 coup attempt alerted the Al Saud to serious problems within the military. Consequently, King Saud suspected the regular armed forces, even if Saudi nationalists in the military survived repeated purges. Antimonarchical activities continued. Between 1957 and 1959, thousands were periodically arrested—some executed—for subversion and mutiny. Many arrests were linked to the struggle among senior princes over control of the armed forces.

Royal Saudi Air Force Defections (1962)

Between 1958 and 1962, the establishment of the United Arab Republic persuaded many more Saudi officers to join the Free Officers movement. In 1958, for example, cadets and officers demonstrated against termination of the services of the Egyptian military mission in Saudi Arabia.[42] Not surprisingly, sympathy for Nasser continued among the military up until the 1962 revolution in Yemen, and, amazingly, the Saudi military appeared to be far more loyal to Nasser than to the Al Saud. Between October 2 and 8, 1962, four Saudi aircraft crews defected to Egypt, carrying arms destined for rebel forces.[43] In response, the ruling family grounded the entire air force, while Riyadh asked Washington to patrol Saudi airspace.[44] A repeat of these events occurred a month later, although on a more serious note. In November 1962, palace guards discovered a conspiracy against the Saudi monarchy when Saudi air force pilots—all members of the ruling family—planned a coup in Riyadh. Before the conspirators could be arrested, however, the pilots defected to Egypt. Once again, King Saud grounded the entire air force fleet, and ordered storage batteries from royal guard tanks removed.[45] Embarrassed by the scope and substance of these events, senior members of the family scrambled to address emerging schisms within their ranks, and this too contributed to the differences between King Saud and Heir Apparent Faysal.

Coup Plots (1969–1977)

Unfortunately, Saudi Arabia was not immune to upheavals elsewhere in the Arab world, as these episodes clearly illustrated. As tensions grew throughout the region, conservative regimes in Libya, Sudan, and Somalia were overthrown by military officers. In June and July 1969, military supporters of the Popular Democratic Front, the National Front for the Liberation of Saudi Arabia, and the Federation of Democratic Forces in the Kingdom were all implicated in a new coup attempt. This time, the plotters included 60 air force officers and the director of the air force academy in Dhahran. Their plan called for an attack on the monarch and senior princes by bombing the royal palace from the air and then proclaiming the Republic of the Arabian Peninsula. Also involved were various former and active garrison leaders. In the event, hundreds of officers were arrested in the wake of this latest coup plot, which yet again resulted in a full grounding of the air force for several more weeks. When flying resumed, it was without munitions for some time.[46]

To be sure, Saudi authorities learned the lessons of these coup attempts, and to address them, Riyadh initiated an intensive program to refurbish its intelligence services. The program devoted special attention to the National Guard.[47] It also started to screen foreigners wishing to enter Saudi Arabia and encouraged the replacement of Arab expatriate workers with non-Arab Asians wherever possible. Significantly, senior ulama supported these Al Saud decisions.[48]

Not surprisingly, the 1969 coup attempt ignited a serious debate within the ruling family over the future of the armed forces. A vocal faction led by conservative elements opposed further modernization programs, with Prince Abdallah arguing that the National Guard, rather than the regular armed forces, should be relied on to perform specific duties. A second faction, led by King Faysal, Prince Sultan, and Prince Fahd, concluded that the coup attempt did not justify a total halt to the modernization and expansion of the armed forces. Their argument gained momentum after London announced its decision to withdraw from the Persian Gulf by 1971, which, in turn, would create a military vacuum in the region.[49] As the 1973 October War galvanized Arab forces, the ensuing stalemate rekindled military modernization efforts throughout the region, and Saudi forces have committed to a steady buildup ever since.

In the summer of 1977, reports circulated that Saudi officials had uncovered another coup attempt launched by air force personnel at Tabuk. In this instance, authorities relied on Egyptian and Jordanian military intelligence services to suppress the potential rebellion.[50] With the exception of three pilots who escaped to Iraq, all plotters were arrested, and for a time all aircraft flew for only 30 minutes, without ammunition. To avoid any further uprisings, the ruling family doubled salaries for all civil servants, soldiers, and NCOs, as it attempted to restore order among disenfranchised members.[51]

The Armed Forces in the War for Kuwait

If internal tensions continued throughout the 1970s and 1980s, the 1990 Iraqi invasion of Kuwait permanently altered the ruling family's perceptions of the armed forces. Facing imminent danger, Saudi officials prepared their soldiers to expect the worst and succeeded in rallying support for their assertive policy—to oust Iraq from Kuwait and to stay in power. Thousands of Saudis volunteered to join the army and civil defense forces before the outbreak of hostilities in January 1991. In addition, and for the first time since the 1979 Iranian Revolution, Saudis welcomed Shia volunteers into the ranks.[52]

In yet another dramatic change, Riyadh allowed foreign supervision of its troops in 1990, and took an even larger step by granting American commanders full control of Saudi forces during any offensive. In January 1991, King Fahd reviewed more than 5,000 troops from the international coalition assembled near the Kuwaiti border. The monarch was joined by Defense Minister Sultan and U.S. general Norman Schwarzkopf, commander of all coalition forces.[53] Despite assertions to the contrary, the Saudi armed forces played an active role in the fighting, as Royal Saudi Air Force (RSAF) units flew an estimated 6 percent of the total number of sorties flown by the coalition.[54] Even though limited in efficiency, the RSAF flew regularly and performed well. Captain Ayed Shamrani was credited with the first reported air kills by the RSAF in January 1991 when he downed two Iraqi jets over Saudi territorial waters. Although the Saudis benefited from the allied victory against Iraq, the 1991 war alerted the ruling family to serious deficiencies in their fighting capabilities. Consequently, the Kingdom began a major expansion of its armed forces. In an April 15, 1991, address to the nation, King Fahd stated:

> Regarding the building of the Armed Forces, the main lesson to be learned from the Gulf crisis and the experience of our forces, which did extremely well, and out of the reality in which we live today, we in the Kingdom of Saudi Arabia have made a decisive decision to immediately embark on expanding and strengthening our Armed Forces, providing them with the most effective and most advanced land, sea, and air weapons the world has produced as well as advanced military and technical equipment.[55]

These comments marked a major departure for Saudi Arabia, since it appeared that the Kingdom accepted responsibility for its own security instead of relying on extraregional powers. Saudi military planners sought to double the number of men under arms, purchase the necessary hardware to arm recruits, and initiate rigorous training programs to prepare them for any eventuality. Despite this newfound realism, Defense Minister Sultan ruled out the introduction of conscription.

In June 1991, during a visit to the King Faysal Air Base, Prince Sultan revealed that the Kingdom was unable to absorb a large number of recruits because of limited capacity at its training centers. His comments illustrated lingering apprehensions about a conscript army that could become a fertile breeding ground for opposition forces.[56] Significantly, these plans neglected to emphasize the status of the National Guard. Whether Heir Apparent Abdallah was sidelined—for arguing with the King over how Saudi Arabia should have conducted itself during the war—is difficult to determine. Still, the lack of attention on this pivotal service was all the more remarkable at a time when challenges abounded. At the time, the combination of hostility and mistrust that Riyadh felt toward other Arab countries, even those that had supported it during the war, appeared to be a factor affecting Prince Abdallah's status.[57]

Security Perceptions

King Abdul Aziz's objective to establish a "nation" that ensured the continued rule of the Al Saud was shared by his progeny. Since 1932, the Al Saud had maintained their hold on power and kept the country intact, despite numerous challenges to their rule. Nevertheless, a mood of discontent lingered amongst the Saudi population, which defied Riyadh directly. For example, in September 1993, a gunman tried to storm a court in Riyadh, firing several shots and wounding a civilian passerby. The gunman was allegedly linked to extremist groups, although his sect was unknown.[58] Similar incidents rocked the Kingdom periodically, including a major bombing at a National Guard facility in Riyadh (1995) that killed several, and the 1996 Khobar Towers bombing near Dhahran that killed both Saudis and Americans.[59] As the ruling family could not contemplate, or accept, a weakening of its authority, Riyadh responded to these challenges by:

- accommodating religious leaders further,
- tolerating the Shia in the Eastern Province, and
- providing the armed forces with additional benefits.

Simultaneously, and as the Al Saud faced several external security threats—which, in the wake of the War for Kuwait, altered their defense behavior—Riyadh's reliance on Washington and other Western powers lost its luster. Still, Iraq and Iran retained their respective menacing postures toward the Kingdom. Yemen pressured Saudi leaders to accept greater democratic norms, especially its limited democratization process, or face the risk of a spillover effect that would cause internal upheavals.[60] Against a plethora of regional developments, the ruling family:

- continued its defense purchases from Western sources, even if it preferred that "pre-positioning" be undertaken in neighboring countries;
- contained Iraq, pending its anticipated leadership implosion;
- placated Iran, especially its challenge to deny Riyadh custodianship of Makkah and Madinah;
- worked with the GCC to enhance regional defenses; and
- negotiated a mutual defense agreement with Egypt.

How senior Al Saud officials—including those identified above—perceived internal and external threats facing the Kingdom in the aftermath of the War for Kuwait deserves further attention. For illustrative purposes, four specific issues are examined next: religious and secularist internal opposition to the Al Saud, and the Iraqi and Iranian external threats.

The Religious Opposition

In the aftermath of the 1991 War for Kuwait, Riyadh has been confronted with a growing Islamist movement calling for sweeping changes in the Kingdom's political and social life. Although such a call seemed unnecessary in a country that based its entire legitimacy on the Shariah (Islamic law), maintaining that the Quran was its constitution and that "democracy" remained an alien concept, what was more unusual was the regime's response to such suggestions. The religious challenge in Saudi Arabia manifested itself on two levels: first, within the clergy, and second, between the clergy and the Al Saud.

Key religious leaders opposed to the Kingdom's future political and defense posture argued that the government's investments had been largely wasted. Simultaneously, younger religious leaders sought to reinterpret, and ultimately oppose, the teachings of more conservative elders viewed as being "closed," even "corrupted" by the Al Saud. How had this religious challenge been articulated in the immediate past and how could it impact on the future?

The origin of the Islamist challenge may be traced to two petitions addressed to King Fahd by groups of religious scholars and intellectuals in May 1991 and September 1992. The first called for the creation of an independent Majlis al-Shura (Consultative Council) with the power to debate and legislate domestic and foreign policy matters, for equality before the law of all Saudis irrespective of rank and stature, for a redistribution of wealth, for the accountability of all officials, and for stricter adherence to Islamic values.[61] The second petition (with 107 signatories) elaborated on these demands, drawing attention to public mismanagement and corruption. More daring than the first, this second petition made detailed recommendations for remedial action, including granting the clergy a far greater role in the decision-making process and calling for severe cutbacks in government expenditures. Other recommendations concentrated on the need to exclude foreign cultural influences (by restricting access to satellite dishes, for example), limit Western contacts (especially arms purchases), and increase the state's ties with fellow Muslim countries.[62]

Many of the signatories of these two petitions were men of religion—prayer leaders, preachers, jurists, and teachers—from the Najd, especially Riyadh, the cradle of the unitarian (Muwahiddun) movement and the traditional power base of the Al Saud. Among the more charismatic preachers stood Salman al-Awdah and Safar al-Hawali, who since 1991 had posed a direct challenge to government authorities. In 1993, they championed the CDLR, which called for profound political changes in the Kingdom.[63] Still, the essence of the two petitions was a *demand* to change Saudi Arabia's basic political structure, involving a major transfer of power from the ruling Al Saud family to a self-appointed elite of religious puritans. Most of these clerics were young and also opposed the senior ulama in the Kingdom, because, they alleged, these old men had been co-opted a long time ago. In other words, the young clerics pointed to an existing wedge between them and members of the religious establishment that, ironically, included compromised religious figures.[64]

The Al Saud Response

Not surprisingly, both of these petitions were denounced as being misguided and divisive by the members of the Supreme Council of Ulama. Only seven ulama refused to affix their names to the official response and, for their inaction, were quickly "retired," to be replaced by more liberal blood. Significantly, the regime's long-promised Consultative Council was finally inaugurated in late December 1993, as Riyadh cautiously responded to growing pressure for political participation. The majority of the 60 appointed Majlis members were Western-educated technocrats and academics, with only a handful of religious notables, selected for their loyalty. Most of the Islamist critics of the regime were excluded from membership in what has now become an advocate institution.[65]

The Al Saud responded to the Islamist challenge with a blend of indecision and appeasement. After all, it was in King Fahd's nature to avoid confrontation. The apparent expenditures of the ruling family, against the pressures of severe budget problems, made the regime vulnerable to criticism. Nevertheless, the Al Saud have sought solace in their puritanical ways, rejecting calls for reform, and have played religious forces against each other. Although they had been somewhat successful in the past, the Iranian Revolution amply illustrated that monarchies, even those of the powerful variety, could not sustain themselves in power unless they adapted to changing circumstances.[66] To their credit, the Al Saud adapted, but only as necessity compelled them to act.

The Worldly Opposition

On May 3, 1993, six high-ranking religious Saudis publicly defied the Al Saud by announcing the creation of the Committee for the Defense of Legal Rights (CDLR). Their mission was to "struggle for the elimination of injustices, the restoration of legitimate rights and guaranteeing the people's right to express their opinions freely and to live in honor and dignity in an environment of equality and justice."[67] Their action, the six further declared, was prompted by a desire "to stop societal decay."[68] They supported genuine reforms, but despite the overall moderate tone of the announcement, Riyadh immediately dismissed all six from their official positions, arrested them, and subjected them to rigorous interrogations. A few months later, the CDLR's spokesperson, Dr. Muhammad Al Masaari, clandestinely crossed into Yemen, and from Sanaa traveled to London. He asked for political asylum. King Fahd's repeated attempts to persuade then prime minister John Major to expel the doctor from Britain have been to naught.

Al Masaari, a physics professor, kept a long beard but was a most affable character. He displayed a charming personality, in the manner of a proud Saudi. Under his leadership, the CDLR's communiqués became professional. Information on repression in the Kingdom, the turpitude of the ruling family, especially its alleged submission to Western diktat, were routinely faxed to thousands around the world, including those in the Kingdom. CDLR communiqués were also posted on the Internet, which in effect meant they were accessible to just about anyone who had a minimum interest in Saudi Arabia.

To be sure, the relative success of the CDLR was one of the direct consequences of the War for Kuwait, which traumatized Saudi society. The presence of close to 500,000 non-Muslim soldiers on Islam's holiest land, coupled with the Kingdom's lack of capability to defend itself—despite billions spent on expensive Western equipment—as well as the systematic assault on Iraq, a fellow Arab and Muslim state, raised several questions among nationalist Saudis. CDLR leaders articulated that many Saudis were openly discussing the merits of all that had gone on with the War for Kuwait, acknowledging that most had rallied behind the King because they were scared of Saddam Hussein. When the war ended, however, many asked difficult questions, including whether it was necessary to rely on Westerners for their protection.

The CDLR was of interest because it had taken the lead on the world stage in opposing the ruling family.[69] It appeared to be well informed, indicating a substantial network of supporters inside Saudi Arabia, though nowhere near as extensive as claimed. CDLR leaders spoke in rather overblown terms of the coming fall of the Al Saud ruling family, which, naturally, irked royals both senior and junior. Dr. Al Masaari argued that a sudden change could occur either because of the death of King Fahd or because of a severe economic recession caused by another drop in the price of oil.[70] Al Masaari postulated four scenarios for the future of the country. It must be emphasized that these scenarios were known to the junior princes, who discussed them openly among themselves and with visitors.

His first scenario involved a confrontation between ruling family members and the Islamist opposition. Once the clash intensified, the military would intervene to stage a coup. According to Al Masaari, and under such circumstances, the army (with U.S. backing) or the National Guard (with British aid) might well intervene to save the day. Importantly, this scenario would probably produce a government that would not welcome the CDLR.

The second scenario involved Islamists coming to power. Al Masaari anticipated that Islamists would have no choice but to impose economic austerity measures, although he hoped that the new regime could keep the state together. Alternatively, the state could split and descend into civil war. He further argued that rival princes were arming themselves and building their own power bases to prepare for this eventuality, or indeed to fight over the succession when King Fahd died. A civil war, he stated, could be backed by outside powers. Not one to assume that most of what goes on in a country is exclusively domestic in nature, Al Masaari actually believed that Western powers, including the United States, aimed to separate the Najd from the Hijaz, to control the oil-rich areas without having to bother about the religious baggage of the western provinces. Obviously, such a scenario concerned Riyadh, and as the director-general of intelligence Prince Turki bin Faysal emphasized, "We must keep the Islamists under full control or they will cause much trouble."[71] Other officials were more confident, arguing that the Saudi state could gain the upper hand if a confrontation ensued.[72]

A third scenario was gradual change. This would involve a younger, reformist prince taking over in a palace coup and making substantial reforms. Al Masaari did not believe that this was very likely, because of potential infighting among rival princes, especially if the decision were made to skip to the younger generation.[73]

Finally, Al Masaari's fourth scenario was that there would be no change at all. He argued, however, that this was not possible unless the ruling family negotiated with Islamists, slowed the drive toward peace with Israel, distanced the Kingdom from the West, controlled the budget deficit, and cut military spending (all of which were demands made by the CDLR in its regular newsletters).

Despite Al Masaari's complex views, CDLR statements of objectives merely listed removing the injustices of the Saudi regime, enabling the people to limit the government's powers, bolstering the independent role of the judiciary, and ending alleged abuses perpetrated in the name of Islam. In his public pronouncements, Al Masaari called for the fall of the Al Saud, insisting that under no circumstances would he engage in a dialogue with them.[74] It was important to note in this context that little criticism was lobbed against the Heir Apparent, deputy prime minister, and commander of the National Guard, Abdallah bin Abdul Aziz, in most CDLR newsletters.[75] Speculation on sponsorship or funding support from Heir Apparent Abdallah to Al Masaari continued, although this was unlikely and, more importantly, impossible to verify. The spokesperson for the CDLR insisted that the institution of monarchy was illegitimate in Islam (echoing comments made after and since the 1979 Iranian Revolution by Ayatollah Ruhollah Khumayni and his successors) and that in modern times full democracy should be adopted in Arabia. This last call was diametrically opposed to King Fahd's pronouncements on the matter. Most senior members of the family concurred. To date, Dr. Al Masaari has not proposed a public program for a new *Arabia,* although he may have contemplated such a program in the mid-1990s.

Although it is difficult to properly assess the degree of influence that the CDLR enjoyed in Saudi Arabia, it was clear that some form of influence was present, its internal divisions notwithstanding. To date, the CDLR's greatest weakness—its lack of progress beyond opposing the status quo—has meant that no program for power has ever been formulated. Even if the CDLR was "thinking" of such issues, it did not articulate them. Lack of a full-blown agenda did not mean, however, that the CDLR was not expressing some of its ideas.

CDLR newsletters made frequent references to the capitalist economy that led to imperialism and the "looting" of "other peoples."[76] Stories on the imperialist attitude of the West, and how this could be changed only if Westerners stood up to their governments and their capitalist "rulers," appeared frequently. According to Al Masaari, "the American [or British] people d[id] not need a sick Boeing [or British Aerospace] and their like, that sell unnecessary arms to the Kingdom and maintain the imperialists in Washington or London [the masters] and the tyrants in Riyadh [the slaves] in power." Al Masaari insisted that Western oligarchs should "get off the backs" of the Arabs and that the international order, epitomized by the United Nations and the International Monetary Fund, was composed of Western, secular, and liberal institutions, in which other cultures/beliefs were not represented.[77] The CDLR wanted nothing to do with these organizations that were helping starve a million Iraqi children, he asserted, but, at least on this score, what Al Masaari articulated was not all that different from what some Arab and/or Muslim presidents and monarchs were saying too.[78] In the event, Al Masaari linked Western policies in the Gulf region with those pursued by Riyadh and, in doing so, labeled the Al Saud as lacking in independence. Such omissions, presumably, illustrated the harmful nature of Saudi policies and the urgent need for reforms.

The CDLR's Influence

In surprising contrast to most Western reporting on the Middle East, the CDLR received significant and sympathetic coverage, presumably because human rights groups, such as Amnesty International, emphasized the deteriorating human rights situation in the Kingdom. Not surprisingly, several European governments, led by Britain, reacted negatively to this coverage.[79] Still, because of their influence in London—from where they easily tapped into the large electronic web of Saudi Arabia—the CDLR called for political mobilization against the Al Saud. In 1995, it issued four calls to gather after Friday prayers in designated mosques, to demonstrate against Riyadh.[80] These CDLR calls asked citizens to assemble in the courtyards of eight mosques and make themselves heard.[81]

The calls proved successful and Riyadh took notice. It quickly clamped down on demonstrators, dispersing them on the grounds that they were illegal. Sit-in protests, even those that lasted but a single hour, proved to be too risky. Few of those present sought the necessary permit or queried about the legality of such a document. After all, gatherings in a mosque were a basic Islamic duty, and the onus was on the authorities to justify why Muslims should not engage in Islamic activities. As a different tactic, Riyadh then engaged in sending several countercommuniqués, in an attempt to confuse those who intended to gather. In the event, the effort backfired when CDLR officials in Saudi Arabia informed their London office of what had transpired.

The Al Saud Response

Al Saud responses to CDLR activities between 1993 and 1999 failed to produce what was needed to bring the opposition to its knees. Several members of the ruling family acknowledged that Saudi Arabia and the Al Saud had a "CDLR problem." Although no one thought that criticizing or not criticizing CDLR activities would advance their careers, many were deeply offended that the monarch was not taking stricter measures to clamp down on dissidents. Junior officials concluded that remaining silent or trying to influence the CDLR indirectly (by pressuring Britain to expel Dr. Al Masaari, for example) was not enough. One ranking member of the family, for example, posited that all CDLR sympathizers—not just leaders—ought to be questioned and, if found liable, "expelled to Afghanistan."[82] When Riyadh sentenced several CDLR sympathizers to death in 1995, and actually carried the sentences out, its deterrence policy also failed to make a dent. Rather than be intimidated by the dramatic rise in executions, CDLR sympathizers instead mobilized in their opposition.[83] The CDLR argued that executions at the end of the twentieth century were no longer valid state activities and, besides being barbaric, violated all norms of international human rights covenants.

What concerned Riyadh about CDLR activities was the spread of its *message* among the rather subdued Saudi population. There was also a significant swing in public opinion against the ruling family, as displayed by open criticisms that most Western visitors have been exposed to in recent years. Noticeably, past reticence to vent frustrations against the Al Saud has given way to a more relaxed approach. Strangers voice their views publicly, complaining about corruption, their own economic plight, and the exposure to outside influences (meaning the American military presence). Under certain circumstances, this defiance could easily translate into a formal civil disobedience program, something that the CDLR wished all along. In addition to its peaceful sit-ins, the CDLR called on its sympathizers to "support leading ulama," attempting to create a wedge between the government and influential clerics. In a textbook case approach, and through its *actions,* the CDLR placed the onus on Riyadh, arguing that the regime must be accountable because it was in power and was entrusted with the responsibilities of governance. This, in effect, was the equivalent of calling the Al Saud's bluff that they were the "custodians of the holy mosques." If that were the case, as the CDLR argued—and many Saudis were inclined to believe—then the Al Saud ought to behave as custodians. In other words, custodianship over Islam's holiest shrines came laden with a moral code of conduct that needed to be fully satisfied. When it allegedly was not, then it was legitimate to oppose such a regime, and such rulers.

Such defiance concerned the Al Saud. Starting in the mid-1990s, Riyadh clamped down on this raging "debate" by emphasizing the good deeds performed toward Islam, in Saudi Arabia itself and the Islamic world at large. But the need to undertake such efforts also resulted in a massive grinding down of decision making throughout the government, bringing the process to a slow halt.

In addition to CDLR calls for change, thousands of young men within the Kingdom's eight (male) universities added their voices to incite the population to mobilize against the regime. Similarly, some business leaders also opposed Riyadh's attempts to control every aspect of economic life in the Kingdom, calling for their input on the state's economic regulations. Saudi business leaders demanded greater rights and responsibilities for business decisions instead of relying on the government to monitor and dictate economic policy. At a time when Riyadh was running considerable budget deficits and depended on sorely needed funds from local financial institutions, the influence of the business community could not but grow in importance. Simply stated, the Al Saud could no longer assume the loyalty of the vibrant business community and needed, to the degree that was possible, to share power with it.

Ironically, the CDLR was substantially weakened starting in 1996, not because of any steps taken by Riyadh, but because of the legal and financial costs of operating out of an increasingly hostile British environment. Riyadh cracked down on the money trail and this too was felt by Al Masaari, who was preoccupied with his day-to-day survival.[84]

Yet because Western-educated Saudis faced the prospect of unemployment, many were inclined to believe what "opposition voices" churned out. Riyadh was at a loss as to how best to handle this crucial problem. A portion of the Saudi population was frustrated, seeking audiences with governors and senior Al Saud members to express bafflement over their prospects, even if such meetings did not produce desired outcomes. Simply stated, the regime could no longer guarantee employment to all because of severe budget deficits that necessitated spending reductions. Even more challenging than the threat of liberal opposition was the potential impact of exponential changes on the Kingdom's social cohesion. In the mid-1990s, a mushrooming phenomenon of nongovernmental organizations, led by women and human rights groups as well as other activists, gathered momentum throughout the country. Individually or in groups, many Saudis discussed their sociopolitical needs, and demanded greater rights. By doing so, they signaled to the government their inherent displeasure and, by calling for effective policies that would recognize fresh perspectives, challenged the Al Saud to take risky steps to their rule. Nevertheless, opposition forces left their marks on the Al Saud, as the debate reached the highest levels within the family. Although the monarch and his Heir Apparent were preoccupied with a variety of issues, they could not ignore internal currents that divided the family and the country. What young princes, members of the intelligentsia, and the population at large thought of the religious and secular opposition to the Al Saud was important and could not be ignored. Unaddressed, they would further muddy perceptions of a threat, both of the local and international varieties.

The Iraqi Threat

Although official Saudi perceptions of the Iraqi threat were well known, they became even clearer after Khaled bin Sultan published his memoirs, discussing, for the first time, a major regional concern from the Al Saud point of view. Far less was known about Saudi public opinion toward Baghdad and how the younger generation reacted toward it, especially a decade after the end of the War for Kuwait.

Not surprisingly, and in the aftermath of the War for Kuwait, the Islamist opposition commandeered the *Iraq question* from the Al Saud. Critics of the government constantly asked—and some continue to ask—what did $300 billion in defense investments over the past half century buy the Kingdom? More importantly, ordinary Saudis queried, was it necessary for Riyadh to call on foreign powers to defend the country?

Inasmuch as answers to these questions may be straightforward within the Al Saud, there was no uniformity on how to deal with Iraq. To be sure, and without exception, Saddam Hussein was identified as a regional nemesis that needed to be checked. Khaled bin Sultan was adamant in his assessment of the Iraqi leader, positing that Riyadh could not expect to be able to set its differences with Saddam Hussein aside. "Saddam's invasion of Kuwait in August 1990," he wrote, "posed the gravest threat to Saudi Arabia's security that I had yet encountered in my military career. Our vital, oil-producing Eastern Province—the principal source of our national wealth—lay open to his mechanized and armored divisions."[85]

This view was shared by senior Al Saud officials for most of 1990 and 1991. In August 1990, for example, King Fahd reportedly confided in President George Bush that he had tried to resolve all Iraqi-Kuwaiti differences. According to the former president, the Saudi monarch agreed with him that President Saddam Hussein attacked and occupied Kuwait because he was a conceited individual. "He doesn't realize that the implications of his actions are upsetting the world order. He seems to think only of himself. He is following Hitler in creating world problems—with a difference: one was conceited and one is both conceited and crazy. I believe nothing will work with Saddam but the use of force."[86]

In August 1990, Prince Khaled bin Sultan clarified his perceptions of the Iraqi invasion and whatever "motives" the Iraqis may have had to occupy Kuwait. He declared that Riyadh did not believe that Iraqi soldiers were willing to kill their brothers and neighbors who had supported them during the Iran-Iraq war. "The Iraqi regime," asserted the general, "pushed its soldiers into Kuwait without their knowledge. It forced them to get involved in an adventure that conflicts with their convictions and morals. And I do not think they will agree to achieve their leadership's unjustified ambitions, except under threats and terror."[87] Khaled was unequivocal when he added that the Iran-Iraq war was a conventional war, in terms of equipment, training, preparedness, and armament, and that the planned confrontation—which the Iraqi president did not understand—would be qualitatively different. The Saudi further asserted that the latest military technology would shock Iraq.[88] Finally, Khaled opined that President Saddam Hussein had pushed himself into a dark tunnel and that he, before anyone else, must consider how to extricate himself from the dilemma. "As for us," the Saudi commander concluded,

we believe that his withdrawal from Kuwait, the restoration of its legitimacy, and the elimination of the subsequent results of his invasion of it are the foundations for a solution. This is because Saddam Hussein has failed to annihilate the ruling family in Kuwait and to polarize the opposition to form a national government to back his ambitions. He has also failed to avert Arab and world reaction, which has besieged him and could destroy him, his regime, and oppressed people. He also failed to assess the Saudi position as he wanted to continue to wreak havoc in the region and attack our country. He did not, as I said previously, expect the wise Saudi leadership to take a swift decision to seek backing from brothers and friends.[89]

To be sure, these perceptions were formed at the height of the military buildup, when morale was at a premium given the many uncertainties associated with the war. Still, conservative views were not limited to the Saudi monarch and his military advisers. Even Heir Apparent Abdallah, who was far more skeptical of what coalition forces would be able to accomplish, joined the bandwagon.

Speaking to Saudi troops before they were to be dispatched to oust Iraqi forces from Kuwait, Prince Abdallah declared:

> On my way to you, I wished the purpose of my visit to you was to bid you farewell and to see you, along with your brothers and comrades in arms in the valiant Iraqi army and in all the Arab armies proceeding to restore the usurped and legitimate rights in Palestine. But regrettably, God's will cannot be averted. However, hope continues and it will not die in our souls, God willing. What I wish to tell you now is that the camps that stretch in front of me are swollen with my brothers and yours, the sons of the Kuwaiti people who have fled their country, the dearest land to their souls. I urge you to treat them charitably, to respect them, and to facilitate all their affairs.[90]

The Heir Apparent added that the Iraqi people were part of the Arab world and that Saudis shared much with Iraqis. He continued: "We are partners for better or for worse. Our fear is that a defeat will be inflicted upon them, dividing and scattering their ranks and fragmenting their unity into ethnic groups and into sects." In his most severe warning, Prince Abdallah warned that Riyadh had done its "fraternal duty," and had no apologies.[91] As if pleading with the Iraqi strongman, Prince Abdallah concluded that "the Iraqi president still ha[d] in his hand an opportunity for peace and for averting dangers from our nation and our peoples."[92]

For the better part of 1990, senior Al Saud officials returned to these same themes, while shaping and articulating their policies toward Iraq. In September 1990, for example, Foreign Minister Saud bin Faysal argued that the Iraqi invasion was an international issue that should be decided by the United Nations and not through an Arab solution.[93] Addressing his troops at King Khalid Military City a few days earlier, Defense Minister Sultan explained how it pained his soul "to see [how] the Iraqi Army, whom [the Saudis] stood by for eight difficult years, supporting it and supplying it with weapons and money, and developing its capabilities" was behaving.[94] "Despite the risks," Prince Sultan continued,

> we threw our political, material, and moral weight behind [Iraq] at international gatherings, to rescue it from destruction, disintegration, and collapse under the gravity of

blows—it pains us to see it turning from a shield defending the Arab nation into a sharp sword cutting wombs, destroying sanctity of fraternity, and shattering the ties of neighborliness and kinship. [Baghdad] destroyed the noble sentiments of souls when it became a tool of destruction and oppression in the hands of an opportunist and heedless leadership, which turned its back on all values and exhausted its people in a fierce war that destroyed everything and burdened Iraq with debts, after it had been one of the richest Arab countries, for no other objective than the satisfaction of a personal arrogance that was not satisfied with the hundreds of thousands of Iraqi martyrs who fell for no objective or justification; thus he [Saddam Hussein] returned to his adventures, and only God knows how many souls they will harvest if the Iraqi leadership persists in its offense, pomposity, aggression, and intransigence and does not withdraw its army from sister Kuwait and does not stop displaying its forces to terrorize and blackmail its sisters and neighbors.[95]

By October 1990, when the military buildup had reached a point of no return, Foreign Minister Saud bin Faysal entrenched his perceptions of the Iraqi leadership. He concluded that Saddam Hussein would not retreat one millimeter. "He has Iraqicized Kuwait," he declared, and "reject[ed] any negotiations on the topic. He is determined to stand up against international law and against the community of peoples."[96] Prince Saud bin Faysal labeled Saddam Hussein a liar and hypocrite because "he has not done anything for the Islamic and Arab causes . . . on the contrary, the Iraqi leadership led by Saddam Hussein has only brought misery to Arabs and Muslims . . . desecrat[ing] many holy sites—be they Islamic ones or others."[97]

By late 1990, Saudi leaders, both senior and junior, were clear in their opposition to Saddam Hussein's military actions against Kuwait. Prince Mit'ab bin Abdallah determined that he did "not believe Iraq's capabilities would be able to resist the huge deployment defending the Kingdom of Saudi Arabia."[98] For his part, Khaled bin Sultan prepared his constituents for the possible use of chemical weapons by Baghdad, even if Prince Bandar bin Sultan asserted that Saudi Arabia was prepared for chemical warfare.[99] Noticeably, however, no weapons of mass destruction were used during the War for Kuwait, by either side. A few months after hostilities ended, King Fahd posited that the "ruler of Iraq, who was blinded by his aggressive greed which left him unable to see the path of right, insisted that matters should proceed in the direction they did, resulting in catastrophe, defeat, and loss for him."[100]

Still, among the next generation of Saudi leaders, one detected a shift in attitude toward Iraq. Many asked whether it would not be better to remove Saddam Hussein and save the Iraqi people. Fahad bin Abdallah bin Mohammed Al Saud, the assistant to the minister of defense, for example, wished that the "Saddam Hussein nightmare would go away." He contemplated a military coup as an ideal solution that would restore stability to Baghdad and save Iraqi masses from the repercussions of the United Nations–imposed embargo. "Otherwise," he said, "our task would be far more difficult after Saddam Hussein is gone."[101] Others believed that a distinction was necessary between the Iraqi leadership and people. Younger princes, in particular, were acutely aware that the Iraqi dilemma could perpetuate a slew of problems for Riyadh, some of which would be difficult, if not impossible, to resolve.

Speaking in early October 1999 in Washington, D.C., Prince Faysal bin Salman posited that change in Iraq required policy changes. He observed that

Saudi Arabia [stood] behind the implementation of the United Nations resolutions in Iraq, yet Saudi Arabia will not unilaterally step into Iraqi internal affairs. The ideal balance of power in the region includes a united, stable Iraq, which respects its political boundaries. This is quite different from the balance of power in the 1960s to 1980s, which encouraged an arms race and the desire for hegemonic power.[102]

Prince Faysal emphasized the importance of Iraq being reintegrated into the trade system and "hoped that economic relations would enforce political cooperation." Nevertheless, "until change in the regime takes place, this is all wishful thinking," clarified the prince.[103]

Whatever misgivings Al Saud members had of the Iraqi strongman, few wanted to entertain the idea that Saudi Arabia might have to provide financial assistance to Iraq, and even fewer were willing to contemplate Baghdad's strategic value vis-à-vis Teheran. The belief that the Kingdom could buy security from Baghdad proved false after 1990, and next-generation leaders drew the correct lessons. The words of the former Saudi first secretary at the United Nations, Muhammad al-Khilewi, rang true. Al-Khilewi asserted that the Kingdom had provided Iraq with up to $5 billion to pursue its nuclear weapons program in the 1980s, on the understanding that Iraqi nuclear weapons technology would be shared with the Kingdom. Western defense analysts did not rule out Saudi discussions on the subject but never took seriously Saudi aspirations to acquire nuclear weapons by this route, on the grounds that Iraq might well have promised cooperation yet could never have been expected to deliver.[104] Even if few Al Saud leaders believed Al-Khilewi, they nevertheless took note of his declarations, hoping to draw yet other lessons.

In the end, and no matter how convoluted Riyadh's policies toward Baghdad seemed between 1932 and 1990, it was significant to note that younger Al Saud members differentiated between the Iraqi people and the hegemonic policies pursued by successive Iraqi strongmen. That was certainly a novel development in the region, where a generation of leaders had pursued conformist policies, cajoled dictators, and, fearing catastrophe, failed to trust their own populations. Arguably, the 1990 Iraqi invasion of Kuwait, as well as the Iranian Revolution, altered many such perceptions.

The Iranian Threat

With few exceptions, Al Saud family members perceived Iran as a genuine regional threat, one which needed to be handled with kid gloves. In this instance, the Al Saud considered the Islamic revolutionary regime as an ideological foe that was strong—and getting stronger—and one that remained a troubling neighbor. Although a consensus existed on the Iranian threat, views differed on how to deal with Teheran and, equally important, on whether to follow the U.S. lead in the area.

Several younger Al Saud officials believed, for example, that Saudi Arabia should not follow the American perception of Iran but distance itself from Washington. Others argued that U.S. and Saudi interests regarding Iran did not coincide. What was curious, and somewhat misplaced, was the outlook that key princes held as to how best to deal with revolutionary Iran.

Those who perceived the Islamic government as a threat to the fundamental construct of the Kingdom, namely, Riyadh's claims to the custodianship of the two holy places, were keen to match Iran missile for missile and airplane for airplane. Khaled bin Sultan, in particular, adopted a larger strategic view, positing that Saudi Arabia needed to deter both Iraq and Iran militarily, lest Baghdad and Teheran assume that Riyadh would not defend itself or call on allies to help defend it.[105] The Iranian threat was on the young generation's mind even as Riyadh embarked on a rapprochement with Teheran in the late 1990s. Some members of the ruling family articulated clear ideas as to how best to behave with Iran—bearing in mind the ideological divide that separated them from their neighbor—and considered it their "duty" to stand up to religious fervor and regional hegemony. Others were more pragmatic, given inherent Iranian capabilities. Many agreed, nevertheless, that Iran represented a concrete challenge to Saudi Arabia's own regional aspirations.

Elite Views Toward Iran

Despite Khaled bin Sultan's remarks that Saudi Arabia "had no fear of Iran as an Islamic country" but was merely concerned by "its radical political views and its attempt to export its revolution," in November 1978, Foreign Minister Prince Saud bin Faysal emphasized that Riyadh believed the Shah should remain in power because his achievements were "an example for the development of any state."[106] In January 1979, then Heir Apparent Fahd bin Abdul Aziz expressed the Kingdom's support for the Shah, ostensibly because the Pahlavi regime was legitimate. He declared that the disturbances in Iran were an internal concern, and expressed the hope that Iranians would put an end to the bloodshed among themselves without foreign intervention.[107] At the time, Riyadh assumed that Teheran's powerful allies, led by Washington, would support the Pahlavi regime and, in the aftermath of the revolution, adopted cautious policies. Without a doubt, the fall of the Shah stood as a painful example of a monarchy gone astray, especially when erstwhile Western champions of Iran's ruler did not lend a hand.

Prince Abdallah bin Abdul Aziz viewed the emergence of the new Islamic Republic of Iran as a fait accompli and, even if he harbored any misgivings, pretended that his country could do business with Ayatullah Khumayni's regime. Relations between the two regional neighbors, he declared, were based on Islam. Twice in 1979, Prince Abdallah opined that ties between Saudi Arabia and Iran were based on mutual respect and that they were improving, even if Riyadh was fearful of any spillover effects of the nascent Islamic Revolution, stating:

> You can see that the ties between Saudi Arabia and the Islamic Republic of Iran did not [depend] on material interests and political geography.... The material potentials— money and oil—possessed by the Islamic Republic of Iran and Saudi Arabia, and by the Islamic and the Arab worlds, will be utilized and directed by the Islamic spirit. The fact is that we are very relieved by the Islamic Republic of Iran's policy of making Islam, and not heavy armaments, the organizer of cooperation, a base for dialog and the introduction to a prosperous and dignified future."[108]

For his part, Defense Minister Sultan elaborated that the Kingdom's strategic situation was based on Islamic ideology—as well as its Arab ties—and that events in Iran did not introduce any decisive changes in strategic direction.[109] In reality, Saudi Arabia was embarked on one of its most crucial strategic reevaluations, which portended to develop the wherewithal to deter Ayatullah Khumayni's government from spreading its revolutionary zeal to the lower Gulf. Riyadh was on the defensive as Teheran's repeated and vitriolic attacks against the Al Saud—for being un-Islamic and, allegedly, unworthy of ruling over Islam's holiest shrines—increased in frequency and tempo. In February 1980, Heir Apparent Fahd went so far as to declare that Saudi Arabia was already an Islamic state, and that Iran finally became one.[110] Both King Khalid and Prince Fahd congratulated Iranian president Abolhassan Bani-Sadr on his election, but that was the only formal recognition of the regime's leadership, yet another illustration of the truncated dialogue between Iran and Saudi Arabia.[111]

Evolving Elite Views Toward Iran

Saudi perceptions of Iranian views evolved for the better part of the 1980s. As the Iran-Iraq war raged in intensity, Riyadh took additional measures to enhance its limited security capabilities and, not an unreasonable objective, to benefit from the opportunity provided by the conflict. Prince Khaled bin Sultan acknowledged, for example, that the acquisition of Chinese missiles was partly linked to the Iran-Iraq war. "Iran's new leaders," he opined, "attempted to belittle our standing in the Muslim world and undermine our role as guardians of the Holy Places. The danger became more acute with the outbreak of the Iraq-Iran war in 1980, which from the start carried with it the threat that other Gulf states might be sucked into the conflict, ourselves included."[112]

Other members of the Al Saud chimed in with various evolving views as well. In October 1980, for example, Prince Saud bin Faysal addressed the United Nations General Assembly, where he declared that Saudi Arabia would support international participation in resolving the conflict.[113] A year later, Heir Apparent Fahd bin Abdul Aziz stated that the Iran-Iraq war was a calamity for the Islamic world and should be stopped by agreement to avoid further splits.[114]

These calls for ending the war notwithstanding, Saudi Arabia and several conservative Arab Gulf monarchies initiated elaborate mechanisms— mainly financial—to support Baghdad. Although Defense Minister Sultan was correct in stating that Saudi Arabia was not aiding Iraq in providing training to Iraqi soldiers, the financial spigot was gushing.[115] On January 15, 1991—that is, two days before hostilities in the War for Kuwait were launched—the Saudi monarch revealed that Riyadh had given Baghdad $25.7 billion.[116] Even if the Saudis were embarrassed by these revelations, they insisted that the Kingdom's assistance at the time was to help Iraq overcome Iran. In December 1981, for example, Prince Abdallah bin Abdul Aziz asserted that Saudis were surprised by the latest Iranian constitution, which perpetuated sectarianism. The lexicon used by clerical leaders focusing on exporting the revolution was crystal clear as well.[117] A few months after acceding to the throne, King Fahd stated that the continuation of the Iran-Iraq war would surely lead to serious interference (from abroad), and asserted "that Iraq [wa]s looking for an end to the war." The Saudi ruler further declared that "the kingdom's position

[wa]s that Riyadh [would] make every effort to end the war regardless of accusations on radio."[118] Repeatedly, Saudi officials called for caution as well as an end to the conflict, although their calls fell on deaf ears. Prince Abdallah called on both sides to bargain for a peace settlement.[119] In February 1984, King Fahd welcomed Iraqi proposals to end the war with Iran.[120] Aware that such a position could be misinterpreted, Defense Minister Sultan announced that "Saudi Arabia [wa]s always on the side of right and justice," and that it did not take sides in the war even if the evidence was contrary. "Our relations with Iran," emphasized Prince Sultan, "whether political or otherwise, [will] continue."[121]

If these statements contained contradictory elements, they reflected the difficult choices available to Riyadh on the one hand, and the level of debate under way within family circles on the other. During the "War of the Cities" in 1985, for example, Saudi Arabia felt an imminent threat to its security even if few could fathom how it would manifest itself. "After a careful study of Iranian capabilities," Prince Khaled bin Sultan revealed,

> we concluded that Iran was unlikely to launch a land offensive against us. To do so would have meant coming through southern Iraq and Kuwait or mounting a major amphibious operation. Sending an army across the Gulf would require a huge logistics effort which would dangerously extend and expose Iran's supply lines. Iran lacked the capability for such an adventure. Already locked in battle with Iraq, it was unlikely to contemplate opening a second front.[122]

A year before Iran accepted a cease-fire, King Fahd wished that Teheran would move in that direction, because Riyadh wanted to cooperate with a "stable" Islamic Republic.[123] By early 1988, Saudi-Iranian relations had entered a new phase, even if the monarch was harsh in his conclusions. Senior Arab officials, the Saudi leader confided to *Al-Ahram,* "expressed their strong denunciation of the shameful acts undertaken by the ruling regime in Iran against its neighbor Arab countries and others."[124] Inasmuch as these views fluctuated, they were directly tied to the conduct of Iranian pilgrims at the annual Hajj, where disturbances continued.

King Fahd justified the Kingdom's refusal to allow Iranian participation at the 1988 Hajj on the grounds that Riyadh could not cope with the added security responsibilities for large numbers of Iranian pilgrims.[125] More specifically, the monarch identified the behavior of Iranian pilgrims, stating that the pilgrimage was "a ritual and ha[d] nothing to do with raised placards or uttered slogans or abuse, nor [wa]s it an occupation of the holy mosque or murder of innocent pilgrims."[126] These were strong words uttered in frustration following the deaths by stampede of hundreds of pilgrims. Still, King Fahd did not rule out a resumption of diplomatic ties between Iran and Saudi Arabia, even if major conditions were attached to any such steps. In the ruler's own words:

> I do not know where it will end. We say the spirit of tolerance should not make the Iranians think we are weak. We hope Iran will not act too irresponsibly. We do not want it to test our people's ability to defend themselves. The question is: What does Iran want from all that is happening? Iran has harmed relations not only with us but also with its neighbors and the whole world. We ask Iran: For how long will this war continue—a war that is destroying Muslims and depleting their money? Iran has tested Iraq's defense strength for more than eight years. This is a sufficient sign for Iran that it is difficult to penetrate Iraq's defensive strength. Moreover, Iran has attacked Kuwait and the UAE and struck at our merchant ships. Who benefits from this? Why undermine peace in the region while it is possible to attain coexistence and spare Muslims' blood and money? Iran has tried many times to undermine security in the Gulf region, the Arabian peninsula, and the world. What has Iran gained? Iran has gained nothing. When talking about Iran here, we do not presume that there are no masterminds in Iran, but we want reason and logic to triumph so that peace will prevail in the region. We want the moderate minds to play their role in Iran.[127]

Whether these words, as well as various diplomatic contacts, persuaded Teheran to finally accept a cease-fire is difficult to determine. Still, after August 1988, Saudi officials identified a greater Iranian flexibility in ending the war.[128] Foreign Minister Saud bin Faysal concentrated on the cessation of rhetoric between Riyadh and Teheran, declaring that there were no reasons to rule out the restoration of diplomatic relations between the two countries.[129] King Fahd elaborated:

> At our end, we stopped media campaigns against Iran. However, no contact has been held so far. We believe that Iran is an Islamic country in this region. However, at the same time, we do not believe in interfering in internal affairs. Iran is in a good position and possesses all the components of a good state. It has large lands, rivers, plains, valleys, and mountains. It has a population density. It has all that can enable it to live in peace without interfering in others' internal affairs. We want good relations with everyone. We want Iran to become a strength for Islam.[130]

By late November 1988, a schism had emerged within the family, as Prince Sultan bin Abdul Aziz redefined the Iranian security threat. He emphasized that even if Saudi Arabia were to restore full diplomatic relations with Iran, Riyadh could not tolerate business as usual at the annual Hajj. For Prince Sultan, Iran had to abide by its quota—hovering around 40,000 per year even if more than 150,000 made the trip on a regular basis—and must not transform the pilgrimage into a political event. The defense minister added a new twist, underscoring the importance of restoring relations between Iran and Iraq and between Iran and several other states.[131]

As if by coincidence, Saudi Arabia signed a nonaggression pact with Iraq in March 1989, which reaffirmed their mutual interests in the wake of the Iran-Iraq war. The accord called for a pledge not to use force, to resolve disputes through Arab League regulations, and to reject interference in internal affairs.[132] Even if Riyadh presented its latest accord with Baghdad as part of a regional balance-of-power reorganization, in reality it was alarmed by the large and idle Iraqi military presence on its northern border. King Fahd clarified that the Saudi-Iraqi accord was a "nonaggression pact" and, since both countries abided by the League of Arab States Defense Pact, it was not surprising to see it couched in such rhetoric. To be sure, the treaty included articles that were part of earlier LAS accords between Arab states, but the urgency of adding a bilateral feature reflected the growing Saudi concern with Iraq, following the August 1988 Iran-Iraq cease-fire. Within a year, the Saudi apprehension crystallized, when Iraq invaded Kuwait and threatened Saudi Arabia.

An Assessment of the
Iraqi and Iranian Threats

"Where is the interest of Iraq and its people in what Saddam Hussein is doing to his country and the Arab nation?" asked King Fahd in October 1994.[133] Inasmuch as the Saudis drew specific lessons from the Iraqi invasion of Kuwait and its aftermath, it was clear that a Rubicon was crossed and that relations between Riyadh and Baghdad—despite their 1989 nonaggression pact—would not improve dramatically. Defense Minister Sultan denounced various Iraqi troop movements to the Kuwaiti border but stressed that the Kingdom attached extreme importance to the safety and unity of Iraq. "Saudi Arabia holds the Iraqi regime responsible for the suffering faced by the brotherly Iraqi people," he declared, and called on "the Iraqi regime [to] implement all the Security Council resolutions including the release of prisoners of war."[134] A few years after the end of the War for Kuwait, relations between the Gulf region's two largest Arab states remained moribund, even if Foreign Minister Saud bin Faysal separated Iraq from President Saddam Hussein. Speaking at the United Nations in October 1995, Prince Faysal declared:

> We look forward to the return of fraternal Iraq to the fold of the international community as a responsible member carrying out a constructive role in the international arena because its noble people are known for their capabilities and energies. The suffering of the Iraqi people will remain a source for our anxieties and preoccupation. We will continue to work to maintain the unity of Iraq, its sovereignty, and territorial integrity.[135]

In late 1995, that is, before the dramatic improvement of Saudi-Iranian ties, Prince Saud bin Faysal did not mince his words toward Iran and its putative designs on the UAE's Abu Musa and Tunbs islands. At the time, Riyadh supported Abu Dhabi's efforts to find a peaceful solution to the continued Iranian occupation.[136] Nevertheless, the election of a pragmatic Iranian leader to the highest office provided Saudi Arabia a golden opportunity to enhance its regional policies.

When President Mohamed Khatami galvanized a large portion of the Iranian electorate, Riyadh took note and, not surprisingly, sought new ways to improve bilateral relations.[137] Shaykh Abdulaziz Al-Tuwayjiri, the deputy assistant commander of the National Guard, and a close confidant of Heir Apparent Abdallah bin Abdul Aziz, predicted that Iran and the Arabs were

> heading for more cooperation and coordination which will enable them to take their natural place in the world and to serve the Islamic nation. Yes, Riyadh and Teheran had to make the initial move. I believe that the caravan will go ahead and no one will miss it because this is not possible. Nations will die if they miss the caravan of dialogue, cooperation, and partnership.[138]

Since the end of 1997, Heir Apparent Abdallah bin Abdul Aziz has steered the Kingdom's ties with the Islamic Republic of Iran from an attitude of benign neglect to one of active engagement. In fact, improved relations with Iran have emerged as the cornerstone of Saudi Arabia's objective for regional supremacy.[139] While relations have been warming for nearly two years, the first results of this rapprochement appeared at the March 1999 OPEC meeting, when the Saudis stunned observers by agreeing to a new set of oil production quotas that were highly favorable to Iran. In response, petroleum prices rose, as did hopes for more breakthroughs between the two traditional competitors. While these moves may seem to indicate a clear gain for Iranian foreign policy in general, and for President Mohamed Khatami in particular—as the latter successfully ends his country's political isolation—in reality, Riyadh gained most. Indeed, Saudi Arabia extended its welcome mat to visiting Iranian president Khatami in May 1999 and further drew concessions from the latter on key regional issues, including a pledge to help reduce tensions throughout the area. That the Saudis have effectively mollified and won the support of Iranians on various other concerns, ranging from a commitment to coordinate policy toward Afghanistan to joint investment policies, were further indications of the progress under way.[140] Even sensitive defense questions were discussed, following Saudi Defense Minister Prince Sultan's visit to Teheran in early May 1999. At that time, Ali Shamkani, the Iranian defense minister, told his Saudi counterpart that he saw "no limit" to ties with the Kingdom and went so far as to proclaim that Iran's entire defense capability will be put at the disposal of its Saudi "brothers."[141] The hyperbole aside, and although no formal defense accord was initialed during Khatami's visit to Saudi Arabia, these high-level discussions reduced the overall military tension in the Gulf region.

These latest developments were the result of a carefully designed policy to redress the balance of power in the Gulf region. In February 1998, or barely a few months after Prince Abdallah bin Abdul Aziz's participation at the December 1997 Teheran Islamic Conference Organization Summit, National Guard Deputy Commander Mit'ab bin Abdallah received former president Ali Akbar Hashemi Rafsanjani. The symbolic visit, at the National Guard Riyadh headquarters no less, elicited the following remarks from Prince Mit'ab: "We deeply believe that the capabilities and the military forces of Iran and Saudi Arabia can serve as a unified force in pursuit of the aims and interests of the Islamic nations."[142] Even if the statement was diplomatic verbiage, it carried a good deal of symbolism and, naturally, became the harbinger of improved ties. Prince Sultan bin Abdul Aziz assured his interlocutors—in Teheran—that there were no disputes between the two countries and that priority would be given to security issues before all other bilateral concerns—ranging from economic to cultural and social topics—are addressed. There was no mention of the Hajj or of any Iranian participation and at what quotas.[143] In fact, Riyadh was so enthusiastic that it sacrificed its long-established ties with the United Arab Emirates to cement its nascent diplomatic overtures with Iran.[144]

In the end, Riyadh embarked on these initiatives both to check the growing Iranian and Iraqi influences in the Gulf area and, equally important, to strengthen the position of the Kingdom on the regional checkerboard. From the perspective of Saudi leaders, the Iran-Iraq war as well as the War for Kuwait had engulfed the Kingdom in a two-decade-long military and political turmoil, when much of what occurred in the region had spilled over with significant internal consequences. Heir Apparent Abdallah bin Abdul Aziz, supported by a slew of younger-generation princes, vowed to guide Saudi policies and strengthen Riyadh's regional standing.

Chapter 4 ⌇

Direction of Family

If policymakers had any doubts about Saudi Arabia's commitments to the security of the Persian Gulf region, they were completely erased in the aftermath of the 1990 Iraqi invasion of Kuwait, when Riyadh joined with its regional and international allies to defeat Saddam Hussein. Saudi Arabia has, time and again, amply demonstrated that its own global interests coincided with those espoused by the Western industrialized states, that it needed strong allies to protect conservative Arab Gulf regimes from powerful regional hegemons, and that the relationship was of mutual economic benefit. To be sure, Riyadh disagreed with several of its Western allies on how best to solve the long-festering Arab-Israeli conflict, for example, although it never allowed that crisis to damage long-term Saudi-Western relations. At stake were global economic issues hovering around petroleum. At stake was the future of the Al Saud ruling family.

To better ascertain what views many of the individuals cited above may have of security concerns, three specific possible scenarios are used below that will, in turn, be analyzed against the background discussed above. These are responses to internal opposition cases, and they are used solely for illustrative purposes.

A Family Corrective Move

Momentous events rocked Saudi Arabia between 1958 and 1964 when then Heir Apparent Faysal bin Abdul Aziz organized King Saud's removal from power. It is quite possible to see this historical scenario being duplicated when Heir Apparent Abdallah bin Abdul Aziz accedes to the throne.[1]

The Challenge

Following Al Saud traditions, a future King Abdallah bin Abdul Aziz could well appoint Defense Minister Sultan his Heir Apparent. As both men are already well advanced in age and, more important, increasingly influenced by their offspring, policy disagreements could polarize the government into at least two camps. A rebellion within the family could ensue, pitting younger, more dynamic princes against family elders who, presumably, would insist on maintaining the family's internal cohesion intact. The result could be a full-fledged internal family uprising that jeopardizes the King's rule. Under such a scenario, King Abdallah bin Abdul Aziz would be cornered, charged with mismanagement, and, worse, accused of threatening Al Saud legitimacy. A series of subclans would emerge around mid-level princes from cadet branches to force an outcome. As in the past, cadet branches would be used to realign the family's internal structure, orchestrated by powerful senior officials. The result of such dramatic political associations would be a forcible removal of the monarch. It would also neutralize his sons in the National Guard. As Heir Apparent, Sultan would have been compromised; another son of King Abdul Aziz, perhaps Prince Nayif or Prince Salman, would be chosen to maintain family priorities intact. The scenario would unfold as the Kingdom returned to a modicum of stability, although at a high political and social cost. A son of Abdul Aziz would emerge as ruler even if internal family and religious disputes abounded.

The Response

Throughout Saudi Arabia's history, the Kingdom has faced numerous external and internal threats from tribal uprisings, Shia and Sunni fanaticism, and Arab nationalism. The Al Saud's enemies sought to oust the ruling family from power but were unable to unite under a common banner. Interestingly, attempts to disrupt the political and social fabric in the Kingdom occurred within a four-year period after each succession. Revolts within the military in 1954 and 1955 as well as uprisings between 1958 and 1960 occurred under the troubled rule of King Saud bin Abdul Aziz.

The Al Saud family best resembles a papal conclave in selecting one of its own to succeed as ruler. Still, there are tensions in the 1744 Al Saud/Al Shaykh alliance, with young ulama rejecting traditional consensus (ideological tensions), disenfranchised ulama operating independently (doctrinal tensions), and business elites seeking expanded political voices. Further impediments to orderly change come from Western-educated technocrats searching for guaranteed employment, and women's associations and human rights activists organizing and demanding additional privileges. All of these indicate that a heightened awareness among the Saudi elite and population is under way. Although it is difficult, these trends are not impossible to identify.

Among the more interesting challenges facing the Al Saud is the level of policy discussions in open fora. Because the Kingdom's media outlets remain under the strict control of the government, Riyadh has had to respond to the proliferation of alternative means of communication. In the aftermath of the War for Kuwait and the prolific introduction of satellite dishes, for example, Saudi authorities have increased their own levels of public discourse, simply to compete with foreign sources. Moreover, the increased reliance on facsimile messages essentially meant that any document could be easily and exponentially shared among a wide audience. These modern methods of communication have emboldened Saudis to conduct their debates in more concrete ways. To be sure, Riyadh attempted to muzzle the level of this discourse, especially when it tried to "ban" satellite dishes, but that effort proved to be far more difficult to impose than originally thought. In short, Saudis are no longer shy in voicing their political opinions and, within elite circles, in emphasizing the need for orderly succession.

The Saudi body politic is also subjected to ideological and doctrinal polemics at all levels. Within the ruling family, a debate among senior and junior officials over the Kingdom's ideological foundations, and how well those have served the Al Saud, was initiated in the early 1990s. Having adopted the Holy Quran (Islam's most sacred scripture) as the Kingdom's constitution, junior Al Saud family members are evaluating its effectiveness as a modern political tool. As discussed above, a similar debate is under way among senior and junior members of the religious establishment. Young ulama (doctors of religious law) are challenging the traditional consensus that the Al Saud and the Al Shaykh have forged, calling for the adoption of strict guidelines in their relationships with the "state." At a time when calls for participation are strong, the Saudi leadership is chiming into this debate by cajoling junior princes, co-opting some, promoting others, and, in a radical move, creating a Ministry for Religious Affairs to respond (as well as control) potential rogue elements.

In addition to these developments, anachronistic promotions have been noted that could be explained only by the Al Saud's awareness of potential tensions. Jiluwi and Saud Al-Kabir junior princes, that is, individuals far from the first line of succession, have been critical of Khaled bin Sultan and Foreign Minister Saud bin Faysal. Having voiced their ideological or doctrinal challenges to potential successors, these junior officials were distanced from power. This phenomenon of voicing dissent has been used extensively throughout modern Saudi history (starting with King Abdul Aziz) and is likely to continue to be used in the future. Still, it is a rather disruptive method, as it antagonizes individuals that may be called upon to work together.

Whether a primogeniture system may be instituted to avoid a crisis entirely depends on how senior Al Saud members choose to resolve their myriad problems. Indeed, the family may opt to move in an open fashion or orchestrate a coup to ensure its survival or avoid a three-way confrontation between an ailing King Fahd, Heir Apparent Abdallah, and Defense Minister Sultan, and potentially between their offspring.

Military Opposition

Although coup attempts have failed in Saudi Arabia, notably in 1969 and 1977, they did not differ in scope and substance from similar changes elsewhere in the Arab world. In both known cases, Al Saud ruling family members rallied behind the monarch, received special favors in exchange for their renewed loyalties, and, almost in unison, agreed to purge the military whenever it was deemed appropriate. Indeed, the Saudi armed forces have experienced several coup attempts, much like other Middle East militaries.

In late 2000, with King Fahd bin Abdul Aziz's health in jeopardy, the Al Saud faced the potential for disruption and violence because of the discontent among ordinary citizens. The regular armed forces and the National Guard have not been passive participants in the Kingdom's anguish and may, in a serious crisis situation, take action. In the past, and since the 1950s, military officers have sympathized with various antimonarchical causes, which has led to numerous coup attempts and defections. Although no serious military uprising has been recorded in the past decade, largely the result of huge subsidies to the armed forces, Riyadh faces the prospect that its soldiers are becoming increasingly discontented with the ruling family. Old issues have reemerged to challenge the Al Saud: the scope, pace, and scale of weapons training and acquisitions plague the armed forces and the National Guard; younger princes no longer find military service to be an attractive alternative to bureaucratic positions in the government; and the ruling family's opponents are able to spread their influence among young Saudi recruits despite their relative isolation in the Kingdom's remote military installations.

The Challenge

In devising this response scenario, a nonclassic military coup could be envisaged for the Kingdom during the next decade. Unlike what Dr. Al Masaari believed, for example, the potential discontent in Saudi Arabia would not be over economic—and some social—issues within the military. Simply stated, the Al Saud have looked after the military rather well. Its officers and servicemen have received—and continue to receive—generous stipends and would have little to gain in rebelling against their main provider. Rather, the primary changes would most likely occur over religious and security policies that the ruling family may pursue.[2]

It has become widely known in recent years that members of the National Guard have a long tradition of religious orientation because of their tribal origins. Likewise, poorly educated army recruits have become easy targets for religious proselytizing, further alienating them from the government. Even the more elite air force has experienced a significant growth in religious extremist activities. These elements, led by tribal leaders opposed to the Al Saud, may well initiate uprisings at strategically located military facilities. Several well-equipped facilities throughout the Kingdom could provide the wherewithal that would allow a potential leader to force the regime's hand. Control over the Khamis Mushayt or Hafr al-Batin bases, for example, could easily provide a coup leader with the necessary force to bomb palaces, subdue large numbers of individuals, and impose law and order. A self-appointed "national salvation" coup leader could form a junta that would advocate the preservation of the Kingdom's resources for all Saudis. To put an end to perceptions of corruption and waste, the junta could be expected to call for a limit on oil production.[3]

The Response

Although the Al Saud subdued potential military uprisings in the 1950s and 1960s through a variety of purges, most senior members of the family knew that such tactics were outdated, at a time when Saudi Arabia was changing and the entire Persian Gulf area was preoccupied by both domestic and regional upheavals. In the aftermath of the War for Kuwait, Saudi leaders further reassessed their relations with the military, aware that they needed a stronger arm to defend the family as well as the country. This awareness has translated into the purchase of up-to-date and expensive systems, expert training whenever needed, and, more important, the expending (even mortgaging) of vast sums to entice Western powers to rush to their defenses. Future purges, therefore, would be far more difficult to rationalize.

Revolution and Disintegration

The ultimate nightmare scenario, either a revolution or a disintegration of the Kingdom, would mean that everything that could go wrong would. Unfortunately, it is a likely scenario due to the snowball effect, should the Al Saud fail to properly manage a minor crisis. Past examples have illustrated how senior family members could panic and commit blunders. Grave errors were committed in 1979, after extremist elements stormed and occupied the Holy Mosque in Makkah, when Riyadh panicked. At the time, close to 1,000 individuals perished due to tactical errors that were finally brought under control after Jordanian and French counterterrorist forces restored order. Had the Al Saud continued in their nonchalant attitudes toward this most serious rebellion, the Kingdom of Saudi Arabia in 2000 would indeed be a far more different country. It is important to note that this scenario assumes that central authority in Saudi Arabia would be intact but increasingly under acute stress because of religious tensions. Calls for organized opposition to the Al Saud were made by members of the *clergy*, mostly younger clerics who opposed senior ulama's close ties to the ruling family and, more important, demanded accountability. Riyadh faced a legitimacy crisis, because it certainly needed the support of the religious community. The result of this crisis scenario is that decision making within the Al Saud would grind to a halt, creating a high level of hesitation in all matters affecting the country's national security. Although an extreme case, with a minimal likelihood, the scenario should not be dismissed out of hand given the competition for power and various actors' inabilities to control evolving situations.

The Challenge

The disintegration of the Kingdom is a scenario in which the Al Saud have lost control over the state. Rebellions would erupt throughout the country against Riyadh because of perceptions of social decay, and, independently, young men would flock to mosques where they would preach violence against unjust authority. Under such circumstances, Makkah and Madinah could be in full turmoil, with large numbers of casualties. Paramilitary and military forces could desert in throngs, displaying Riyadh's utter military incoherence. The King's messages for calm would be ignored, and within a matter of days, radio and television centers would become occupied by extremist elements who would initiate a systematic propaganda war against the ruling family. Competing forces would emerge throughout Saudi Arabia, each claiming authority in their own cities or provinces. In the vital Eastern Province, multiple oil enterprises could offer their services to consuming states, thereby ending the Aramco monopoly of the country's petroleum resources. The King would be forced to abdicate, large numbers of Al Saud officials would be arrested, tried, and executed. Leading merchant families would transfer funds to European and American banks. Chaos would reign supreme and Saudi Arabia would be dismantled.

Again, it is important to underscore the influence of the religious opposition in this scenario. The crisis could well be initiated by an ordinary confrontation with a growing Islamist movement calling for sweeping changes in the Kingdom's political and social life. Although such a call may seem unnecessary in a country that bases its entire legitimacy on the Shariah (Islamic law)—maintaining that the Quran is its constitution and that "democracy" is an alien concept—what would be more unusual would be the regime's response to such calls. In the scenario, as in reality, there would be a religious challenge manifesting itself on two levels: first, within the clergy itself, and second, between the clergy and the Al Saud family, where several princes would be vocal and influential on the matter.

As discussed above, the nature of the Islamist challenge would also be traced to various "petitions" addressed to the monarch by groups of religious scholars and intellectuals—for equality before the law irrespective of rank and stature, for a redistribution of wealth, for the accountability of all officials, and for stricter adherence to Islamic values. Others could draw attention to public mismanagement and corruption, recommending remedial action, including granting the clergy a far greater role in the decision-making process and calling for severe cutbacks in government expenditures.

Like the two petitions of the early 1990s, the new ones could well be signed by religious leaders—preachers, jurists, and teachers—from the Najd, especially Riyadh, the cradle of the Muwahiddun movement and the traditional power base of the Al Saud. Yet, and unlike the *demands* made in the early 1990s, the new ones could entice ordinary Saudis to follow different leaders. In essence, under this scenario, the call would be to change Saudi Arabia's basic political structure, involving a major transfer of power from the ruling Al Saud family to a self-appointed elite of religious puritans. Again, and this point is worth repeating, most of these clerics would be young and would oppose senior ulama in the Kingdom because, they would allege, the old men had been co-opted a long time ago.

The Response

Although difficult to envisage, the current Saudi Arabia, that is, the third monarchy on the Arabian Peninsula, could succumb to strong forces challenging the status quo. To be sure, some Al Saud leaders would attempt to prevent the fall of the family, but it may be too little too late, and practically no one could prevent events taking their natural course. The disintegration could be accelerated by the regime response to the religious opposition factor.

The Al Saud's initial response to the Islamist challenge would be characterized by a blend of indecision and appeasement. After all, it would be in the monarchy's nature to avoid confrontation. The conspicuous consumption of the ruling family, against the pressures of severe budget problems, would also make the regime vulnerable to criticism. No matter how hard members of the ruling family try to buttress their Muslim credentials, dissident elements would successfully point out questionable behavior and offer a variety of objectionable inferences. When junior members of the religious establishment add their voices probing such behavior, Riyadh would have little choice but to take notice. Indeed, the response would resemble King Fahd bin Abdul Aziz's December 1992 response, when the ruler warned all religious activists to stop their antigovernment campaign, to voluntarily refrain from preaching anti–Al Saud sermons and producing anti–Al Saud pamphlets and cassettes. At the time, the monarch emphasized that the Kingdom adhered to the full tenets of Islam and that no one in Saudi Arabia could pretend to be more religious than those that looked after Islam's holiest shrines. At the same time, however, the authorities welcomed private commentaries that citizens wished to make. In other words, the King reiterated his ban on using the pulpit for political discourse, but entertained controlled discourse. Ironically, this element underlines a subtle trend toward separation of church and state, even if the reality does not match Riyadh's rhetoric. In the event, the monarch's December 1992 warning was placed in the public domain: all were warned. A future monarch would surely respond in a similar fashion if he were to preserve Al Saud rule.

An Assessment of the Three Responses

Riyadh's concerted efforts to control what was perceived as "radical" teachings, as well as the use of the mosque as a platform to oppose government policies, which began in earnest in 1993, prompted the Al Saud to enlarge the cabinet and establish the Shura Council. Starting in the early 1990s, a special effort was made to gain the upper hand on the Kingdom's Islamists. A Ministry of Islamic Affairs was created, whose varied purposes included responsibility over preachers, Friday sermons, and, most important, Saudi Arabia's Islamic universities. This first effort was supplemented with the establishment of a 14-member *Majlis al-Da'wa* (Religious Propagation Council) in October 1994, under the authority of the minister of Islamic affairs. The council was vested with the power to supervise Friday sermons—essentially faxing out a model weekly sermon outline that could be adapted to local circumstances—and, in a radical departure for Saudi Arabia, actually vetting prayer leaders. The council was also empowered to oversee educational programs designed to "protect youth from radical ideas." No matter how determined the Al Saud were in muzzling the growing junior religious clergy, the creation of the Da'wa reflected the failure of the senior ulama to keep peace among their ranks. In other words, Shaykh Bin Baz and his successor, Shaykh Abdul Aziz bin Abdallah, along with the other senior clergymen, have failed to bring dissident activists to heel, even if they have successfully maintained the balance of power with the Al Saud. Senior ulama are still the ultimate authorities insofar as theology is concerned, but few junior clergymen accept the idea that they are "independent" from the Al Saud.

In yet another illustration of the government's concern with the religious opposition, Riyadh announced the creation of a Supreme Council for Islamic Affairs (SCIA) in October 1994, under the chairmanship of Defense Minister Sultan. SCIA members included the ministers of the interior, higher education, finance, justice, and foreign affairs, as well as the secretary-general of the Muslim World League, the primary channel of Saudi financial aid to Islamic causes throughout the world. Ostensibly vested to coordinate all Saudi aid to Muslim societies abroad (to ensure that the precious assistance is denied to politically active groups operating under the mantle of Islam), the SCIA aimed to channel domestic anti–Al Saud sentiments to regional and international fora. In fact, because Riyadh was often accused of funding a variety of Islamic dissident groups around the world, as well as failing to prevent private financial support from reaching such groups, the government created yet another mechanism to collect all such donations and channel them through official bodies. That too failed to make a dent. Even when Riyadh stripped the citizenship of Usama bin Laden, allegedly for funding Egyptian and other extremist groups, such activities did not stop. Bin Laden, a member of one of the wealthiest merchant families in the Kingdom, was sacked to please Cairo—and, eventually, Washington—

but, irrespective of what this case represented, no changes were observed on the level of Saudi funding to religious opposition figures throughout the Muslim world.

To be sure, the Al Saud have maintained a skillful balancing act between the requirements of a modern state and religious traditions. They guaranteed loyalty by spreading wealth and neutralized both secular and religious dissent by creating a relatively well functioning welfare state. Since the War for Kuwait, however, a politically active group has emerged from the ranks of the loyal religious community, demanding a more accountable government and calling for the implementation of strict moral codes. Moreover, junior clergymen are also insisting that custodianship over Islam's holiest shrines is not a mere physical act, namely the preservation of the holy sites for pilgrimage purposes. Rather, for Islamists, custodianship over Islam's holy cities means that Riyadh must extend its active support to all Islamic causes around the world. They argue that Muslims should not tolerate that their brethren be mistreated the way they are, for example, in the Balkans. Because many Al Saud family members agree with such assessments, the government has become a hostage to its own claims of Islamic legitimacy.

Finally, and although dismissed as an unlikely possibility by many, a military takeover in Riyadh is also possible. To be sure, such an outcome would pose an acute dilemma for Western powers, many of whom have invested heavily in the Al Saud. Given that Saudi forces are, for the most part, equipped and trained by the United States, Britain, and France, any military involvement in the Kingdom's political life would present embarrassing situations for Washington, London, and Paris. More radical crisis scenarios, that is, the establishment of an Islamic government or the full disintegration of the monarchy, would prove to be far more difficult to cope with than generally acknowledged. Although these are not necessarily envisaged, neither can they be ruled out. All three crisis scenarios discussed above have, at any rate, the potential to affect the free flow of oil. Unimpeded access to Saudi Arabia's oil resources remains the primary objective of major Western powers, an objective that is not expected to change for the next few decades.

There is little doubt that the Al Saud ruling family has a very strong desire to rule over the Kingdom and that it has the capability to do so with relative success. Riyadh has displayed a will to power, and because credible alternative leaderships have not emerged, the Al Saud remain the prime point of reference. Moreover, the ruling family has sealed its right to rule by acquiring legitimacy through (a) an adherence to Hanbali Islam and (b) the well-established and time-tested alliance with the ulama. In short, an ideological compatibility is established between the staunchly conservative Najdis and the Kingdom's religious establishment, which ensures, at least in the immediate future, unitarian traditions. Still, the Al Saud face challenges and an erosion of power, a fact that some within the ruling family—especially among younger officials—are cognizant of. To avert outright confrontations, leading Al Saud officials have started to cultivate opposition figures, ranging from the CDLR to counterelites (junior ulama, businessmen, intellectuals, human rights or nongovernmental organizations). For all practical purposes, these new actors are changing the way the Kingdom is ruled and are rapidly acquiring strengths that cannot be neglected. They certainly require the formation of new alliances within the Al Saud family to maintain effective rule.

Chapter 5 ⌒

An Assessment of the New Alliances

A vast country with considerable wealth and a small population, Saudi Arabia is ruled by an ailing monarch who has seen his workload multiply exponentially since his accession to the throne in 1982. Given his unique background—King Fahd bin Abdul Aziz bin Abdul Rahman has held key posts for the better part of the past five decades—the monarch has become indispensable. To his credit, the King has become aware of the need to respond to rising internal challenges emanating not only from extremist groups bent on weakening the regime, but from educated technocrats searching to voice their neglected views in the country's decision-making process. Although the ruler has responded to some of these intrinsic political challenges, he has been engaged in a careful balancing act between conservative and modernist elements that has garnered both praise and opposition. Even if his immediate successor were to deal effectively with many of these emerging pressure points, how future successors will deal with the Saudi political pendulum is far more difficult to decipher, given internal family complexities.

This book aimed at examining the succession issue as well as some of the ruling family's political agenda. As such, it focused on politics among Al Saud members, rather than between the ruling family as a whole and the rest of Saudi society. It also identified leading members of the new generation, men with the capacity to rule over the Kingdom in the next few years, without actually predicting which one may be chosen to rule. Finally, and more important, it provided a paradigm for the formation of alliances within the large family. Indeed, this last phenomenon became something of a requirement for senior members of the family, who, for better rather than worse, positioned themselves and their offspring in sensitive but essential posts.

Ruling Family Politics

A focus on the Al Saud in studying the Kingdom of Saudi Arabia is justified, because the ruling family remain absolutely central to the political system of the country. At the highest levels, the internal politics of Saudi Arabia are essentially the internal politics of the "family." Perhaps the best evidence to buttress this claim is the reality that all key positions within the government are in the hands of Al Saud princes or members of cadet branches. In addition to the monarch, the posts of prime minister, deputy prime minister, minister of defense, minister of the interior, commander of the National Guard, director of intelligence, and most of the governorships, as well as a myriad other positions—ranging from the civil service to the military—are also held by Al Saud princes.

Still, and over the years, rivalry and factionalism have been an inherent aspect of family politics, not an occasional lapse of personal ambition or enmity. This has been the result of a number of factors, including the nature of Saudi political traditions and the family's large size, diverse composition, and complex internal structure. As described earlier, factions clustered around a combination of distinct "fault lines" embedded within the family. Importantly, the rivalry among these factions focused on the succession issue, the maintenance and distribution of power, and, after oil price increases, the benefits of financial largesse. Perhaps the best example to illustrate this point is associated with succession itself, which, in Saudi Arabia, is not determined by primogeniture. Traditions and circumstances have tended to favor the oldest and/or the most able relative of the King to succeed him. Given that disputes over ability were inevitable, the succession issue tended to produce competition among multiple claimants. Similarly, the King's hold on the throne depended on a continuous demonstration of ability that, after the mid-1970s, took on added technical demands when Saudi Arabia crossed the modernization Rubicon.

In recent years, some of these technical demands, including complex oil questions and the requirements of a rapidly growing population, translated into unpopular policies. In turn, these spawned challenges from princes armed with the entirely legitimate claim that they were more able to rule the Kingdom, even if their actions tended to be motivated by a variety of concerns. For example, the Free Officers movement of the early 1960s portended equipping Riyadh with more effective governance tools, even if family politics motivated several of the princes. For this reason, crises tend to aggravate family rivalries rather than unify princes, to the extent that the monarch can be blamed for causing the crisis or failing to meet it.

As stated above, the impact of oil wealth complicated rivalries, and the emerging factionalism as well. To be sure, "wealth" led to the development of new alliances seeking access to power, and the evolution of a state structure that multiplied the number of potential allies for princes. At the same time, "wealth" further expanded the sources of power in the hands of princes, especially those with effective inner-circle networks that could be mobilized to advance a particular line. To say that bureaucratic politics compounded family politics would, indeed, be an understatement. For example, the commander of the National Guard, Heir Apparent Abdallah bin Abdul Aziz bin Abdul Rahman, and Minister of Defense Sultan bin Abdul Aziz bin Abdul Rahman have fortified their respective controls over rival military forces in recent years. Although this imposed mutual "respect" in their rivalry for the throne, the consequences would be explosive if their contention were to lead to confrontation.

Nevertheless, persistent feuds and factions have not translated into outright violence, at least in most cases. This is because the pattern of family politics, and the distribution of power within the family, is not determined by a set of formal rules or institutionalized structures. Rather, family politics remained fluid, determined by the personalities and peculiarities of leaders at any given time. As a result, a diversity of opinion emerged, clearly demonstrated under the rules of the last four Kings. Family politics under King Saud (1953–1964) were marked by a sharp polarization of power between the monarch and his Heir Apparent, coupled with a bitter feuding that, ultimately, ended in a palace coup. Under King Faysal (1964–1975), there was a considerable centralization of power under a dominant monarch, and only latent feuds. Under King Khalid (1975–1982), a rough balance of multiple power centers emerged that contained feuds through shifting alliances. Finally, the present period, under King Fahd (1982-), has been characterized by a consolidation of particular alliances.

As discussed above, the political dynamics of each period and their implications for Saudi stability are very different indeed. When, for example, the ranks of the ruling family are broken by internal divisions over a specific issue, social groups that are normally excluded from the inner circle become involved in the contest. The same applies to foreign actors, particularly within the Arab world, who for various established reasons interject their pan-Arab perspectives. As rivalry between leading princes escalates, the reliance on raw force becomes more likely, a phenomenon that was best illustrated by the Saud and Fahd periods. The exception to this general observation has been the Faysal and Khalid periods, although the latter witnessed an intermediate pattern when rival princes appealed to outside groups without jeopardizing internal cohesion. To his credit, King Khalid retained control over the family, in part because he successfully held the various factions in balance.

Importantly, the same theme of continuity applied to the effects of family politics on the regime's behavior and, not a negligible point, to the effects that such continuity has had on politics. To be sure, Al Saud officials faced persistent dilemmas and constant choices in foreign and domestic policies, best illustrated in the need to balance their Western and Arab/Islamic relationships. This pattern was also evident in the need to combine internal development policies with conservative traditions. Still, the linkages between some of these dilemmas and family politics in general have been mixed.

Under King Saud, for example, Saudi policy choices became both polarized and politicized. Riyadh's behavior swung back and forth as the balance between the monarch and his highly motivated Heir Apparent shifted. Ineffectual policies were used by both to challenge each other, with disastrous consequences. Under King Faysal, policy dilemmas were resolved under the central direction of a strong monarch. Riyadh's behavior displayed "strategic" continuity, combined with "tactical" flexibility. Indeed, King Faysal's strong political base, nurtured and supported by a vast network of loyal princes, made relatively bold initiatives possible. Multiple power centers under King Khalid prevented any such bold initiatives. His rule was more of the caretaker variety. In fact, few novel ideas—which could propel the country at a time of substantial additional income—were introduced, which in turn encouraged the emergence of these multiple power centers. The independent power base of different princes allowed for independent initiatives in policy areas under their control. This was accomplished at the cost of contradicting other princes' initiatives, amply illustrating policy contradictions. In the end, the rough balance of multiple power centers required consensus and compromise on major policy issues, but at the cost of delay and indecision.

The theme of continuity under King Fahd's rule was characterized—at least throughout the 1980s and early 1990s—by a rough distribution of power between the monarch and his Heir Apparent. In fact, a protracted period of maneuvers and intrigues upset the family's balance of power for several years, but, to his credit, the monarch ruled effectively. He prevented a military coup and, after the advent of the 1979 Iranian Revolution, a spillover of that country's social upheavals into the Kingdom. For Riyadh, the more genuine threat to the monarchy was still the palace coup variety, although the Al Saud united against the external threat created by the 1990 Iraqi invasion and occupation of Kuwait. Still, King

Fahd aspired to become, like King Faysal, a dominant monarch, and at least until the late 1990s—when his health started to fail—succeeded in this endeavor. Working against any centralization, however, was the momentum of multiple power centers, which had developed during the Faysal period and fully emerged during Khalid's reign. The same factors that determined the line of succession after King Khalid apply to the distribution of power during the next accession. Both Princes Abdallah and Sultan can, and probably will, call on their firm military and bureaucratic bases, social alliances, and loyal supporters in the religious and business communities. Even on a personal level, their relative abilities and handicaps remain diverse, as some of the factors making for concentration of power appear to be evenly balanced. All indications point to the unlikelihood that the issue of the next Heir Apparent will be resolved quickly. Even King Faysal, who started from a stronger position than Heir Apparent Abdallah will, took a number of years to establish his dominant position. The major difference from the Faysal era, nevertheless, concerns the military, and a future monarch cannot but factor this reality into his equation. As long as the Saudi military establishment remains divided, with different sections under the control of rival princes, conditions for a palace coup are not ripe. Indeed, the Saudi military establishment may be said to be relatively united, especially in its capacity to reject any one actor from dominating the political arena. Nevertheless, a palace coup cannot be dismissed as a figment of one's imagination, because portions of the Saudi military are led by battle-tested officers who have a keen appreciation of what power is and what it can accomplish. Naturally, the future pattern of Saudi politics is most likely to be determined through prolonged maneuvers and intrigues, mixed with consensus and compromise, which certainly marks the Fahd reign to date.

Once Heir Apparent Abdallah accedes to the throne, several political issues that will help verify the direction of future family politics may also emerge. Perhaps the most pressing of these will be control over the National Guard, a critical post because it provides a check against the regular armed forces and an institutionalized link to traditional tribal groups. King Abdallah's supporters will surely argue that just as he retained control over the Guard during all the years when he was Heir Apparent and first deputy prime minister, he should continue doing so, particularly since he has no full brother to entrust his traditional power base to. Detractors will argue that Prince Abdallah should relinquish control over the Guard because, as monarch, all of the country's security institutions fall under his ultimate control. Unlike King Fahd, however, Heir Apparent Abdallah does not have the propensity to develop the deputy prime ministership into a strong position, particularly since Prince Sultan will probably control the Council of Ministers. Even if Prince Abdallah were to turn over full control of the National Guard to his son, Prince Mit'ab, the move would not be welcome by rivals, given that most will interpret it as a camouflaged attempt to retain independent control over one of the pillars of family power.

A second issue will be the designation of a second deputy prime minister once Defense Minister Sultan is elevated to the position of Heir Apparent and first deputy prime minister. The position implies seniority in the line of succession after the Heir Apparent and is, most probably, the most important within the ruling family. Although several older brothers linger in line, most appear to be unsuited for succession. Governor Salman bin Abdul Aziz—several years younger than most senior members—is generally held to be the most likely candidate for this post and, as will be discussed below, seems to be well positioned to fill the vacancy.

A third set of issues are the political fortunes of the next generation— the sons of the current leadership. If past family politics are any guide, Princes Abdallah and Sultan could be expected to push for the advancement of their sons to strengthen their own positions while in office. Even those that lack the patronage of a living father, including the sons of the late King Faysal, represent a particularly important dilemma. Divisions among uncles and cousins will surely provide greater opportunities for maneuver as family members position themselves on the evolving checkerboard. The political careers of several of these young princes raises the ultimate political question: At what point would the throne pass from Abdul Aziz's sons to a grandson?

To be sure, there are no indications that a public solution has been found, and even if the problem is not pressing, it will become more so as age and infirmity weakens the old guard. The danger is that these new issues, when combined with old rivalries, could undermine the established consensus and lead to an escalation in family feuding. Since these rules are based on tacit understandings, rather than formal procedures, there is an inherent risk that the complex balance would break down if no agreement could be reached on who would lead and whether all remaining members of the family would pledge their *bay'ah* (allegiance) to that ruler. If this were to occur, the likelihood that Saudi Arabia would experience a period of instability would increase dramatically, reminiscent of the Saud-Faysal struggle. Since that time, of course, the multiplication and expansion of sources of power—in the hands of dozens of more princes—has created a much greater potential for prolonged and intense struggle. Also increased are the numbers of foreign actors and social groups within

Saudi Arabia that seek to exploit family rivalries or make alliances with prince against prince.

These same considerations apply to future Saudi behavior. As long as a rough balance within the family is maintained, Saudi policies are likely to reflect a process of consensus and compromise, with all the characteristic strengths and weaknesses. If, however, political rivalries were to escalate, it is nearly certain that policy differences would harden. Similarly, internal and foreign events that potentially threaten to alter the standing of top princes and bring latent policy disputes to a head would aggravate underlying rivalries. The consequences for Saudi behavior, as well as for stability, are likely to be more profound than during King Saud's reign. At that time, Saudi oil policy was insulated from family politics by Aramco's dominant role in oil decisions. Since then, oil policy has been brought under the direct control of the family—the need and availability of technical expertise notwithstanding—and, without a doubt, would be directly affected by family feuds.

Thus, the implications of these differences for Al Saud behavior and its policymaking process are jumbled. While a certain diversity of views brings to bear the need to reconcile differences and ward off some inherent dilemmas faced by Saudi Arabia, the division of responsibilities tends to encourage the formation of competing alliances. Without a doubt, specialization requires the necessity to accommodate the more complex environment the country operates in, but in other respects, when different policy directions clash, Al Saud behavior is marked by indecision and vacillation. In fact, this is the result of compromises that attempt to accommodate as many as possible. In addition, the relative autonomy of different princes creates a certain inconsistency and lack of coordination, unless the monarch intervenes directly. These problems are especially evident when events demand both a quick and an unambiguous response, as in the aftermath of the Iranian Revolution or the Iraqi invasion of Kuwait.

As demonstrated by recent developments, the connections between policy and politics are most difficult to manage. Disagreeing princes are more likely to call on their core political allies, and the eventual policy decision is more likely to be seen as a reflection of underlying political standings rather than a clear, unified articulation of the national interest. In fact, under King Fahd's reign, the Al Saud have managed political competition and policy disputes within tolerable limits, although in large part because of the monarch's own involvement in key areas. In the post-Fahd period, several new factors will be introduced, including the influence of emerging alliances around the monarch and his Heir Apparent.

An Assessment of the New Alliances

When King Khalid acceded to the throne in 1975, he had the support of his full brother Muhammad, who by then was the family's *eminence grise.* A future King Abdallah bin Abdul Aziz bin Abdul Rahman will not have a full brother and, given his advanced age, might not have a lot of time to form alliances. His best bets are Princes Badr, Talal, Nawwaf, Majid, and Sattam, although the deputy governor of Riyadh is close to Prince Salman as well. Heir Apparent Abdallah's primary challenge will certainly come from the Sudayris who, from the next monarch's perspective, cannot remain a united cluster. Should the Sudayris remain a formidable alliance, and a crisis ensue because of the challenge to Abdallah, Governor Salman bin Abdul Aziz would most likely emerge as a compromise candidate to keep internal family stability. The weak point in this outlook is not Defense Minister Sultan, but Interior Minister Nayif, whose qualifications to lead may be questioned by leading members. The more interesting developments, however, are with the new generation of Saudi leaders.

As discussed above, suballiances are being established in Riyadh, although no clear lines exist as of yet. Positioning their offspring in critical posts throughout the government, prominent leaders are pushing their sons to assume leadership roles, and, in a remarkable way, many are. Abdul Aziz bin Salman, for example, is clearly emerging as a leader with significant knowledge of the oil factor in Saudi affairs. His brother Sultan, a former air force pilot and astronaut, is very much in the public eye, freely commenting in newspapers on how a minister should be accountable to the population, or what kinds of visions all should have in spending their hard-earned development riyals. Likewise, and although out of office, Prince Khaled bin Sultan is not shy in expressing views about Islamists, or Iraq and Iran. The consensus in Riyadh is that Prince Khaled is trying to demonstrate his unique military capabilities—some argue his strategic knowledge—of the Kingdom's long-term regional interests. Even if senior members of the family hold similar views, they would never consider discussing them in public, preferring instead to make oblique references in their majlises. Not so with the new generation, which is far more confident in expressing opinions. What is especially useful to note is that many share penetrating views of major Western powers, including the United States.

To be sure, almost all Al Saud family members know the immense contributions that Washington has made, and continues to make, in defending them. Nevertheless, new-generation leaders see a change in

Riyadh's relationship with Washington, arguing that the Saudi government cannot be dragged into America's disputes in the Persian Gulf region. In sharp contrast to their fathers' approach, most seem eager to distance themselves from U.S. policies toward the region, criticizing dual containment and hoping for wiser policies. It is to their credit that new interpretations—perhaps (blurry) visions—are emerging with respect to domestic and foreign policies as well. The new generation of Saudi leaders is poised to assume power and would probably do so far sooner than generally assumed.

Conclusion

Throughout Saudi Arabia's modern history, the Al Saud have faced numerous internal threats from tribal uprisings, Shia and Sunni extremism, and Arab nationalism. Their enemies sought to oust them from power but were unable to unite under a common banner. Far from being incompetent, the Al Saud ruled with savvy, tackling many difficult challenges to their authority. Still, and worse than any external threats, the ruling family has had to deal with internal opposition and, over the years, several succession crises. In fact, attempts to disrupt the political and social fabric in the Kingdom occurred within a four-year period after each succession, some resulting in "corrective" moves, others dealt with more harshly. Revolts within the military in 1954 and 1955, for example, as well as uprisings between 1958 and 1960 occurred during the troubled rule of King Saud. These were dealt with swiftly. Similarly, when a coup plot was discovered in the Royal Saudi Air Force (RSAF) in 1969—a few years after King Faysal acceded to the throne—systematic purges were organized to cleanse the military of "undesirable elements." Another RSAF coup plot was detected in 1977 when King Khalid ruled, with similar results. In short, the Kingdom has not been immune to classic military insurgencies so prevalent throughout the Middle East and the rest of the developing world, and, like elsewhere, Riyadh has aced them with a single-minded approach.

In late 2000, with King Fahd's health in jeopardy, the Al Saud faced the potential for disruption because of discontent among ordinary citizens—the result of severe economic shortcomings—and, more important, because of tensions within the ruling family. Moreover, the Al Saud faced a reinvigorated religious opposition that drew succor both from disenfranchised masses as well as from within the ruling family. Finally, the Al Saud leadership was much closer to a change at the highest levels, with an aging generation slowly positioning its offspring for the next round.

Throughout this study, an attempt has been made to identify individuals with the greatest leadership potential, examining their political, social, and religious perceptions, including views of major Western powers. This was accomplished in order to assess how the coming leadership changes in the Kingdom of Saudi Arabia may affect the younger generation of royals.

This study anticipates that Heir Apparent Abdallah bin Abdul Aziz will accede to the throne upon King Fahd's death. Still, while Defense Minister Sultan will be elevated to the position of Heir Apparent, that decision will most probably trigger a series of personal and policy clashes between a future King Abdallah and a future Heir Apparent Sultan. The positioning that both men practice—which is already an art form in the Kingdom—could have severe consequences for the Al Saud family and, consequently, for the Kingdom. Both Princes Abdallah and Sultan favor their offspring—by placing them in sensitive posts from where they can influence policy—in order to protect and preserve certain power fiefdoms for their children. Several of the key individuals identified above could play critical roles in future successions precisely because of how their fathers position them. In other words, a contention is made that Princes Abdallah as well as Sultan—and, of course, King Fahd—are keenly aware of which posts to allocate to their sons. Heated debates occur in closed chambers to push the appointment of a favorite son to a specific post.

Naturally, new alliances would emerge, which could easily lead to a family crisis. Under such circumstances, family leaders would alter their heretofore ironclad views, leading to a search for a compromise candidate who, in turn, would preserve and enhance Al Saud interests. If a crisis were to develop under King Abdallah, for example, Prince Salman could be that compromise candidate. This is not a prediction but a premonition. In turn, a future King Salman would face a slew of problems, including—insofar as the family is concerned—the need for discipline in dire fiscal times and, more important, the critical decision to alter the succession mode as practiced for over 50 years. Whether Governor Salman would rise above bitter internal debates—Sudayri versus Jiluwi or Thunayan branches—remains unclear. Although this is not a major concern here, the assumptions made are important, since they influence choices for key royals identified above.

It is important to repeat that a full-blown succession struggle which would polarize the Al Saud is not anticipated at this time. Chances are good that speedy and resolute action by the family will prevent events from ever reaching such a stage. As stated above, senior Al Saud family members—with the explicit support of several younger princes—would probably move to nominate Prince Salman bin Abdul Aziz precisely to avoid a drawn-out dispute that, left to its own course, would threaten internal stability. There are, of course, more senior princes—including Nayif and Turki bin Abdul Aziz—who could make a bid for power, but Governor Salman retains a more positive reputation and, as important, heads the powerful "family council," certainly a unique platform from which to bid for power. Nonetheless, the prospects for a stalemate, extreme rivalry, and instability within the Al Saud remain of concern for both Riyadh and its major Western allies. The implications of any such development for Washington, for example, would be serious, as family strife could hinder the monarchy's efforts to meet growing internal and external challenges to its continued rule and could potentially destabilize the regime.

The Al Saud family has dominated contemporary affairs in the Kingdom. Still, it differs considerably from its Arab counterparts, especially those that belong to the idealist school of thought, who dream of nationalism and make promises they could not possibly fulfill.[1] Saudi rulers assert their leadership in accordance with the religious, political, and geographical forces of the region. They do not—and probably never will—follow any secular ideological commitments. Increasingly, however, senior members have had to assess how their offspring would fare in the family balance of power. Few deny that growth within the ranks has created a substantial dilemma: Would existing alliances shift, and, in the process, would the Kingdom's political system be jeopardized?

Appendices

Appendix 1 ⌒

Interviews

[Unless otherwise stated, all interviews on or about Saudi Arabia were held in Riyadh; names are listed alphabetically; 14 additional interviews with Saudi officials were held on condition of nonattribution].

Al Saud Ruling Family

HRH Fahad bin Abdullah bin Mohammad Al Saud, Assistant to the Minister of Defense and Aviation, Chairman of the Economic Offset Committee, Ministry of Defense and Aviation (in Jeddah)
June 12, 1996

HRH Dr. Faysal bin Salman bin Abdul Aziz Al Saud, Assistant Professor, King Saudi University (in London)
February 4 and November 4, 1995; January 23, and March 2, 1997

HRH Naef bin Ahmed bin Abdul Aziz Al Saud, doctoral candidate, Cambridge University, United Kingdom
January 21, 1997

HRH Salman bin Abdul Aziz Al Saud, Governor of Riyadh
January 17, 1996

HRH Sultan bin Salman bin Abdul Aziz Al Saud, Royal Saudi Air Force (Ret.), former astronaut, head of several charitable organizations
January 18 and 21, 1997

HRH Turki bin Faysal bin Abdul Aziz Al Saud, Director, Directorate General of Intelligence
January 20, 1997

Other Saudi Officials

Dr. Abdulrahman Y. Al-Aali, Associate Professor, Department of Business Administration, King Saud University
January 16, 1997

Abdul Muhsin Al-Akkas, Member of the Board and Assistant to the Chairman, Saudi Research and Marketing Group
January 14, 1997

Dr. Ghazi A. Algosaibi, Ambassador of Saudi Arabia to the United Kingdom (in London)
January 23, 1997

Hussein M. Al-Askary, General Secretary, Islamic States Broadcasting Organization (ISBO-OIC) (in Jeddah)
November 15, 1994

Dr. Ibrahim Al-Awaji, Former Deputy Minister of the Interior
June 1, 1996; January 18, 1997

Dr. Saeed M. Badeeb, Directorate General of Intelligence
June 4, 1996; January 15, 1997

Dr. Omar S. Bagour, Assistant Professor, Department of Business Administration, King Abdul Aziz University (in Jeddah)
November 15, 1994; May 27, 28 and June 11, 13, 1996

Dr. Hassan A. Bahafzalah, Deputy General Secretary of Commission, Commission on Scientific Signs of Qur'an & Sunnah (in Jeddah)
June 12, 1996

Mohammed bin Ibrahim Basrawy, Director, Islamic Affairs Department, Ministry of Foreign Affairs
November 13, 1994

Ahmed Behery, General, Royal Saudi Air Force (Ret.)
June 1, 1996

Zein Al-Abedin Dabbagh, Director, Legal & Conferences Department, Ministry of Foreign Affairs
November 13, 1994

Dr. Fouad Al-Farsy, Minister of Information
January 17 and May 26 (in Jeddah) 1996

Dr. Abdul Aziz Al-Fayez, Member, Majlis al-Shura
January 17, 1997

Hassan Abdul-Hay Gazzaz, Founder and Former Chief Editor, *Arafat* and *Al-Bilad;* Author (in Jeddah)
May 28, 1996

Faheem Al-Hamid, Managing Editor-Foreign Affairs, *Ukaz* (Jeddah)
November 15, 1994; June 12, 1996

Dr. Turki Al-Hamad, Chairman of the Political Science Department, College of Administrative Sciences, King Saud University
November 13, 1994; June 10, 1996; January 17, 1997

Dr. Waheed Hamzah Hashem, Associate Professor and Assistant Dean for Graduate Studies and Scientific Research, King Abdul Aziz University (in Jeddah)
June 11, 1996

Hashem Abdo Hashem, Member, Majlis al-Shura; Editor; *Ukaz* (in Jeddah)
May 28, 1996

Shaykh Saleh Al-Lihaydan, President, Higher Justice Council
January 12, 1997

Jamil Ibrahim Al-Hujeilan, Secretary-General, Cooperation Council for the Arab States of the Gulf (Gulf Cooperation Council)
January 13, 1997

Dr. Khaled Ibrahim Jindan, Ambassador and Director, Western Affairs, Ministry of Foreign Affairs
November 13, 1994; January 13, 1997

Shaykh Muhammad bin Jubeir, President, Majlis al-Shura
June 11, 1996

Sherif Kandil, Managing Editor, *Al-Muslimoon* (in Jeddah)
June 11, 1996

Abdulwahab Kashef, Director, International Islamic News Agency (in Jeddah)
November 16, 1994

Dr. Rayed Krimly, Assistant Professor, Department of Political Science, King Saud University
November 13, 1994; January 16, 1997

Ridah M. Larry, Editor, *Saudi Gazette* (in Jeddah)
May 27, 1996

Dr. Mohammed Omar M. Al-Madani, Ambassador and Director-General, The Institute of Diplomatic Studies, Ministry of Foreign Affairs
November 13, 1994

Dr. Nizar Madani, Member, Majlis al-Shura
January 16, 1997

Khalid Maeena, Columnist, *Arab News,* and Executive Director, Saudi Public Relations Company (in Jeddah)
May 28, 1996

Dr. Abdullah Siraj Mansi, History Department, King Abdul Aziz University (in Jeddah)
June 11, 1996

Abdul Rahman Mansouri, Assistant Foreign Minister, Ministry of Foreign Affairs (in Jeddah)
June 12, 1996

Dr. Jamil M. Merdad, The Institute of Diplomatic Studies, Ministry of Foreign Affairs
November 13, 1994

General Saleh Al-Mohaya, Chief-of-Staff, Ministry of Defense
January 15, 1997

Dr. Majid A. Al-Moneef, Associate Professor, Department of Economics, King Saud University
January 16, 1997

Dr. Mazin Salah Motabbagani, Assistant Professor, Department of Orientalism, Faculty of Da'wa, Imam Muhammad bin Saud Islamic University, Madinah (in Jeddah)
November 16, 1994

Dr. Saleh M. Al-Namlah, Assistant Professor, Department of Political Science, King Saud University
November 13, 1994; January 15, 1996

Dr. Abdul Aziz M. Al-Rabghi, Vice Dean, King Abdul Aziz University (in Jeddah)
November 13, 1994

Abdallah Al-Rashid, Economic Adviser to Brigadier General Ali Muhammad Khalifa, Prince Sultan's Office, Ministry of Defense (in Jeddah)
June 12, 1996

Dr. Othman Y. Al-Rawaf, Professor, Department of Political Science, King Saud University
November 13, 1994; January 16, 1996; January 13, 1997

Dr. Abdulrahman bin Muhammad Al-Sadhan, Assistant Secretary-General, Council of Ministers (in Jeddah)
May 29, 1996

Mohammed Ibrahim A. Sattar, Editor in Chief, *Muslim World* (in Jeddah)
November 14, 1994

Dr. Fahd Al-Semmari, Deputy Director, Ministry of Higher Education; Director, King Abdul Aziz Research Center
January 14, 1997

Mansour M. bin Shalhoub, Political Analysis Department, Office of HRH Minister of Foreign Affairs
November 13, 1994

Abdallah Al Shaykh, Manager, Business Development, Hughes Aircraft (Saudi Arabia)
January 13, 1997

Dr. Abdul Aziz A. Turkistani, Abdul Latif Jameel Company, Limited
November 16, 1994

Shaykh Abdul Aziz Al-Tuwayjiri, Deputy Assistant Commander, National Guard
January 12, 1997

Non-Saudi Officials

Dr. Abdulhamid Abdulghani, Director of the International Organization Department, later Director, Department of Information, Cooperation Council for the Arab States of the Gulf
November 13, 1994; June 3, 1996; January 13, 1997

Dr. Jasim Muhammad Abdulghani, Office of the Secretary-General, Cooperation Council for the Arab States of the Gulf
November 13, 1994; June 3, 1996

James E. Akins, United States Ambassador to the Kingdom of Saudi Arabia (1972–1974) (in Washington, D.C.)
November 19, 1999

Willis Brown, President, Hughes Aircraft (Saudi Arabia)
January 19, 1997

Charles L. Daris, Consul General, Embassy of the United States of America (in Jeddah)
November 15, 1994

Chas. W. Freeman, Jr., United States Ambassador to the Kingdom of Saudi Arabia (1989–1992) (in Washington, D.C.)
November 19, 1999

Fred M. Hofstetter, Hughes Aircraft (Saudi Arabia)
January 19, 1997

Michel Jobert, Former Foreign Minister of France (in Paris)
February 1, 1993; March 21, 1994; March 17, 1995

Jessica E. Lapenn, Second Secretary, Political-Military Affairs, Embassy of the United States of America
January 19, 1997

Saif bin Hashil Al-Maskari, Undersecretary for Tourism, Ministry of Commerce and Industry (former Assistant Secretary-General of the Gulf Cooperation Council, 1981–1992)
September 25, 27, and 29, 1993; March 22 and 25, 1995

David McClain, Second Secretary-Economic Affairs, Embassy of the United States of America
January 19, 1997

Kenneth McKune, Political Counselor, Embassy of the United States of America
November 13, 1994

Colonel Gary Nelson, Defense Attaché, Embassy of the United States of America
November 13, 1994

Guy Ruediger, First Secretary, Embassy of Australia
January 19, 1997

David C. Welch, Deputy Chief of Mission, Embassy of the United States of America
November 14, 1994

Appendix 2 ✐

Chronology

1720   Saud bin Muhammad reigns as a local shaykh (ruler) around Dir'iyah in central Arabia.

1745   Muhammad bin Saud campaigns for religious piety and order with Muhammad bin Abdul Wahhab. "First" Saudi state initiated.

1800   Al Saud forces capture Buraimi and begin series of incursions into Oman lasting until 1860s.

1818   First Saudi state ends after most of Arabia falls to the Ottoman Empire. Great-grandson of Muhammad bin Saud, Abdallah bin Saud bin Abdulaziz bin Muhammad bin Saud, is executed by Ottoman conquerors.

1824   Turki bin Abdallah bin Muhammad bin Saud, a grandson of Muhammad bin Saud, seizes Riyadh from Egyptian forces, marking the beginning of the "second" Saudi state. The seventh Saudi ruler, and probably the most powerful in the nineteenth century, Turki rules until 1834. He is succeeded by his son Faysal, who is exiled to Cairo in 1837.

1843   Faysal bin Turki bin Abdallah escapes from his Cairo prison and returns to power to usher in a period of prosperity and stability. He unifies Riyadh and rules until 1865.

1865   Start of two-decade-long Al Saud family feud over succession matters; increasingly the Al Rashid dominate Riyadh and its surroundings.

1891   "Second" Saudi state ends when Abdul Rahman bin Faysal bin Turki flees to Kuwait. His eleven-year-old son, Abdul Aziz, escapes with him.

1902   Abdul Aziz bin Abdul Rahman leads a small group of men in attack on Riyadh and seizes control.

1912   The Ikhwan, a religious brotherhood of tribesmen, are established to provide Abdul Aziz bin Abdul Rahman with shock troops.

1913   Abdul Aziz bin Abdul Rahman gains control of Gulf coast.

1920s   Widespread rivalry and takeovers on the Arabian Peninsula.

1926   Abdul Aziz bin Abdul Rahman gains control of Makkah and Madinah as well as all of the Hijaz (western region of the Kingdom). He declares himself King of the Hijaz.
Establishment of a General Education Department. Primary and secondary education starts.

1927   Abdul Aziz bin Abdul Rahman declares himself King of the Hijaz and Najd.

1929   Rebellious Ikhwan forces are defeated.

1930   Establishment of the Ministry of Foreign Affairs in Jeddah. Prince Faysal bin Abdul Aziz bin Abdul Rahman is appointed minister.

1932   Abdul Aziz bin Abdul Rahman establishes the Kingdom of Saudi Arabia. Establishment of the Ministry of Finance.

1933   Abdul Aziz bin Abdul Rahman appoints eldest son, Saud, Heir Apparent and declares that the next eldest, Faysal, will be Heir Apparent when Saud is King.

1937   Oil is discovered in Saudi Arabia.

1944   Establishment of the Ministry of Defense.

1945   Abdul Aziz bin Abdul Rahman meets U.S. President Franklin D. Roosevelt on the *USS Quincy* in the Red Sea.
Saudi Arabia is founding member of the League of Arab States.

1951   Establishment of the Ministry of the Interior.

1952   Saudi Arabia occupies the Buraimi oasis at the Oman-Abu Dhabi border.
Establishment of the Saudi Arabian Monetary Agency (SAMA) and introduction of paper currency in the Kingdom.

1953   Establishment of the Council of Ministers. Heir Apparent Saud bin Abdul Aziz bin Abdul Rahman heads the cabinet.
Abdul Aziz bin Abdul Rahman dies. Crown Prince Saud bin Abdul Aziz succeeds him and Faysal bin Abdul Aziz is declared Heir Apparent.
Aramco workers go on strike in October.
The General Education Department is transformed into a Ministry of Education.

1956   Aramco workers strike. King Saud issues a royal decree banning strikes.

1957   Establishment of the University of Riyadh (later King Saud University).

1958   Heir Apparent Faysal bin Abdul Aziz takes over executive powers after King Saud surrenders his authority under pressure from the ruling family. Serious internal disagreements on governance surface.

1960   Prince Faysal bin Abdul Aziz bin Abdul Rahman resigns. King Saud bin Abdul Aziz regains full executive powers. Prince Talal bin Abdul Aziz bin Abdul Rahman is appointed minister of finance and Shaykh Abdallah Tariqi is appointed minister of petroleum. Prince Talal bin Abdul Aziz bin Abdul Rahman proposes constitutional reforms for the Kingdom.
Establishment of seven primary schools, and three teacher training facilities, for female students.

1961   Government shuffle in September. Prince Talal bin Abdul Aziz bin Abdul Rahman leaves the cabinet. Prince Faysal bin Abdul Aziz bin Abdul Rahman is appointed vice president of the Council of Ministers.

1962   Ruling family split leads to the rise of the so-called liberal princes. Princes Talal, Badr, and Fawwaz present themselves as liberal backers of King Saud against the so-called conservatism of Heir Apparent Faysal. Their "cause" is supported by President Gamal Abdel Nasser of Egypt. Heir Apparent Faysal promises to establish a Majlis al-Shura and abolish slavery in the Kingdom following family contest. Shaykh Ahmad Zaki Yamani replaces Shaykh Abdallah Tariqi as minister of petroleum and mineral resources.
Monarchy overthrown in Yemen (September). Egypt and USSR support revolutionary government.
Heir Apparent Faysal is named head of the Council of Ministers in October and announces a ten-point reform plan including the abolition of slavery.
Saudi Arabia is founding member of the Muslim World League in Makkah.

1963   The Egyptian Air Force, supporting Yemeni revolutionaries, initiates bombing raids on Saudi Arabia. Attempt by King Saud to retake power against sustained family opposition.

1964   Members of the ruling family gain the support of senior ulama (religious leaders) to force a change of power. Saud is deposed after he is declared "unfit to rule," and Faysal is proclaimed King.

1965   Khalid bin Abdul Aziz is named Heir Apparent.

1966   Establishment of the University of Petroleum and Minerals in Dhahran (later King Fahd University of Petroleum and Minerals).

1967   Six-day Arab-Israeli war.
Egypt withdraws troops from Yemen at start of civil war.

1968   Britain announces that treaties with nine Arab emirates would be terminated by the end of 1971 when it plans a "withdrawal" from east of Suez.

1969   Deposed King Saud bin Abdul Aziz dies in exile in Greece.
Coup attempt within Royal Saudi Air Force. Purges follow.

1971   Iran occupies Abu Musa and Greater Tunb and Lesser Tunb islands, a day before six emirates (Abu Dhabi, Ajman, Dubai, Fujairah, Sharjah, Umm al-Qaiwain) issue a proclamation (December 2) announcing the establishment of the state of the United Arab Emirates. Saudi Arabia does not extend recognition.
First five-year economic plan is introduced.

1972   Riyadh purchases 25 percent of Aramco.

1973   October Arab-Israeli war. King Faysal bin Abdul Aziz proposes an Organization of Arab Petroleum Exporting Countries (OAPEC) oil embargo (which Iraq refuses to honor) against the United States and the Netherlands after an arms resupply air bridge is opened between the United States and Israel (via the Netherlands).

1974   Riyadh purchases 60 percent of Aramco.

1975   King Faysal bin Abdul Aziz is assassinated by his American-educated nephew. Heir Apparent Khalid bin Abdul Aziz is proclaimed monarch after his older brother, Muhammad, renounces his place in line of succession. Fahd bin Abdul Aziz is Heir Apparent (the latter decision skips over Princes Nasir and Saad, who step aside as well). Prince Fahd assumes additional responsibilities to manage the government.
Iran-Iraq Shatt al-Arab border agreement signed in Algiers.

1976   Second five-year economic plan is adopted.

1977   King Khalid bin Abdul Aziz is unwell. Defense Minister Sultan bin Abdul Aziz attempts to prevent Prince Abdallah bin Abdul Aziz from becoming Heir Apparent when the monarch dies.

1979   Shah of Iran overthrown by Ayatollah Khumayni (February 11).
Egypt and Israel sign Camp David Accords (March). Baghdad Summit expels Cairo from League of Arab States.
Seizure of the Makkah Grand Mosque. Uprising by several hundred followers of Sunni extremists Juhayman Al Utaybi and Muhammad Al Qahtani. Rebels surrender after a two-week siege. Shia Muslims riot in Eastern Province.
USSR invades and occupies Afghanistan (December 25).

1980   A nine-member Constitutional Commission is established to draft a definitive text for the Kingdom.
Riyadh purchases 40 percent of remaining Aramco holdings. The company is renamed Saudi Aramco.
Iran-Iraq war starts (September 20).

1981   Gulf Cooperation Council (GCC) established in Abu Dhabi (May 25–26). Saudi Arabia is founding member (along with Bahrain, Kuwait, Oman, Qatar, and the United Arab Emirates) of the Riyadh-based regional organization.
People's Democratic Republic of Yemen, Ethiopia, and Libya establish tripartite treaty organization. Observers label it the "anti-GCC body."
Bahrain coup plot uncovered. Riyadh deploys military assets to the island state and signs a bilateral security agreement.

1982   Saudi Arabia signs bilateral security agreements with the UAE, Qatar, and Oman.
King Khalid bin Abdul Aziz dies. Heir Apparent Fahd bin Abdul Aziz is proclaimed monarch. Next oldest son of Abdul Aziz bin Abdul Rahman, Prince Abdallah bin Abdul Aziz, is chosen Heir Apparent.
Israel invades Lebanon. Saudi Arabia convenes a GCC emergency meeting to discuss Sabra and Shatilla Palestinian camp massacres.

1983   Saudi military units participate in the first GCC *Dara al-Jazirah* (Peninsula Shield) maneuvers, held near Abu Dhabi, UAE.

1984   Saudi military units participate in the second GCC *Dara al-Jazirah* maneuvers, held near Hafr al-Batin, Saudi Arabia.

1985   Two explosions, for which Islamic Jihad claims responsibility, take place in Riyadh, coinciding with a visit to Iran by Saudi Foreign Minister Prince Saud bin Faysal. The visit is the first by a high-ranking Saudi official to Teheran since the 1979 revolution.

1986   King Fahd bin Abdul Aziz changes his title from "Majesty" to "Custodian of the Two Holy Mosques."

1987   More than 400 Muslims, mostly Shia pilgrims from Iran, die in riots—allegedly instigated by Iranian pilgrims—in Makkah after National Guard units open fire on demonstrators.

1988   U.S. intelligence discovers that Saudi Arabia has purchased medium-range missiles from China, with the capability to reach Israel and Iran. U.S. Ambassador Hume Horan delivers a formal protest, after which King Fahd bin Abdul Aziz demands his replacement, and Washington obliges.

Iran-Iraq war cease-fire (Baghdad on the 17th and Teheran on the 18th of August—in effect on the 20th).

1989   Riyadh does not react to the establishment of the Arab Cooperation Council on February 16, when Egypt, Iraq, Jordan, and the Republic of Yemen join in the ACC.

Ayatollah Ruhollah Khumayni dies (June 3).

1990   At the ACC Amman Summit, Saddam Hussein warns that Israel might embark on "new stupidities" in the wake of the recent U.S. supremacy in international affairs.

Iraqi invasion of Kuwait (August 1). Western forces deploy to Kingdom and other Gulf Cooperation Council states.

A "secular" petition, calling for political reforms in the Kingdom, is signed by 43 prominent Saudi public figures and delivered to King Fahd.

1991   Kuwait liberated by UN-backed international coalition forces operating, for the most part, from the Kingdom of Saudi Arabia.

A "religious" petition, calling for political reforms in the Kingdom, is signed by prominent Saudi religious figures, several judges, preachers, and university professors. It too is delivered to King Fahd.

King Fahd announces that the old system of ministerial appointments for life would be changed to an appointment period of four years.

Demonstrations occur in Burayda against the ban preventing two prominent religious preachers from delivering sermons that, in the past, were critical of the autocratic ways of the Saudi ruling family and the presence of U.S. troops in the Kingdom.

1992   King Fahd bin Abdul Aziz issues edicts defining principles of succession and a basic law of government, and establishes a new Consultative Council.

In a joint interview with the Kuwaiti *Al-Siyasa* and Emirati *Al-Ittihad* dailies, King Fahd declares that Riyadh would not hold "free elections" and that Islam would continue to provide the social and political laws for the Kingdom. The King posits that "the nature of [the Saudi] people is different," which consequently requires values different from those espoused in the West.

The Washington Post reports (September 28) that in July 1992, 107 religious scholars had submitted a 45-page memorandum to King Fahd criticizing Saudi foreign policy as well as its human rights record and its failure to follow Shariah law.

King Fahd dismisses seven members of the Supreme Authority of Senior Scholars, the country's highest-level religious body, after they refuse to denounce religious figures who earlier criticized the government. They are replaced by ten younger, more "progressive" scholars.

King Fahd demands that Saudi Islamists cease the distribution of antigovernment materials and the use of mosques in spreading antigovernment sentiment. He accuses foreign influences of backing an alleged antigovernment campaign.

USSR abolished (December 25).

1993   Six Saudis headed by Shaykh Abdallah Al Masaari announce the creation of the Committee for the Defense of Legitimate Rights (CDLR), whose goal is to "alleviate injustice and defend the right secured by Islamic Law." The CDLR claims to be the first Saudi human rights organization, as some of its founders are vocal advocates of a strictly Islamic political structure.

Riyadh dismisses Abdallah bin Abdul Rahman Jibrin, Abdallah bin Humud Tuwayjiri, Abdallah Hamid, Hamad Sulayqih, as well as Sulayman bin Abdallah Rushudi, from their university positions and closes the offices of two Islamist lawyers, ostensibly because all were founders of the CDLR. The government-appointed Senior Muslim Scholars Authority condemns the group as "superfluous" and "illegitimate."

King Fahd decrees the formation of a Ministry of Islamic Affairs, headed by Shaykh Abdallah bin Abd al-Muhsin al-Turki, and a Ministry of the Hajj, headed by Mahmud bin Muhammad al-Safar.

Prince Saad bin Abdul Aziz dies in July, making King Fahd bin Abdul Aziz the oldest surviving son of Abdul Aziz bin Abdul Rahman.

King Fahd bin Abdul Aziz appoints 60 male citizens not belonging to the ruling family to four-year terms on the Majlis al-Shura (August).

A gunman drives into the grounds of King Fahd's al-Salam Palace in Jeddah and opens fire. A security guard is injured but the gunman is killed.

Riyadh and the Shia Reform Movement announce an agreement whereby the group will suspend publication of its monthly newsletter, *Al-Jazirah Al-Arabiyah,* and cease its various attacks on government policies. In return, the interior ministry agrees to allow the safe return of dissidents, the release of an undetermined number of imprisoned group members, and the issue of passports to members who wish to travel.

Members of first Majlis al-Shura are sworn in (December 29).

1994   Muhammad Al Masaari, the spokesman for the banned Committee for the Defense of Legitimate Rights, disappears while on a business trip to al-Qasim. He was detained by Riyadh for six months in 1993.

Widespread demonstrations occur after the arrest of Shaykh Salman Al-Awda, a religious figure in Burayda, for "antigovernment activities."

Approximately 270 Muslim worshippers are killed when crowds surge toward the Mina cavern near Makkah during the annual pilgrimage.

Saudi diplomat Muhammad al-Khilewi seeks asylum in the United States (June 13) and accuses Riyadh of financial improprieties, human rights violations, and funneling money through Jordan to the Islamic Resistance Movement (Hamas). He is granted asylum in August.

King Fahd bin Abdul Aziz appoints a Supreme Council of Islamic Affairs led by Prince Sultan bin Abdul Aziz, the defense minister, to "widen the government's authority over religious interpretation."

The British home office rejects Muhammad Al Masaari's bid for asylum (November 28).

Riyadh dismisses Shaykh Ibrahim Al-Akhdar as imam of the Madinah Mosque, reportedly because he criticizes government policies.

1995   Riyadh arrests Shaykh Hammud bin Abdallah al-Shaabi, a leading cleric, reportedly for criticizing alleged government human rights abuses.

King Fahd bin Abdul Aziz acknowledges new ruler of Qatar after the latter overthrows his father (June 28).

King Fahd bin Abdul Aziz shuffles the cabinet, replacing 16 ministers, including those of finance, oil, and information (August 2).

A car bomb in Riyadh on November 13 kills seven, including five U.S. military advisers assigned to National Guard training duties, and wounds more than 60. The Tigers of the Gulf, Islamic Movement for Change, and Ansar Allah [Partisans of God] all claim responsibility.

King Fahd bin Abdul Aziz suffers a minor stroke; court sources report a "temporary health emergency."

1996   King Fahd bin Abdul Aziz, citing a temporary need to rest due to work overload, voluntarily turns control of the government over to Heir Apparent Prince Abdallah bin Abdul Aziz.

After two months of rulership by Heir Apparent Abdallah bin Abdul Aziz, King Fahd bin Abdul Aziz announces that he is resuming full control of the government, on February 21.

Muhammad Al Masaari is granted a four-year "permit" to remain in Britain (April) after his safety could not be guaranteed on Dominica.

Four Saudis are executed after being sentenced to death for the November 1995 Riyadh bombing, although U.S. officials are refused permission to interview them before the public executions.

A powerful bomb explodes at the Khobar Towers barracks near Dhahran (June 25). Nineteen U.S. servicemen are killed and 400 individuals of various nationalities are wounded. Two previously unknown groups, the Legion of the Martyr Abd al-Huzayfi and Hizballah-Gulf, according to the London *Times,* claim responsibility a few days later. The U.S. Federal Bureau of Investigation (FBI) acknowledges "difficulties in conducting its investigation because Saudi officials refuse to cooperate with the U.S. agency."

The "Grouping of Clergymen of Hijaz" reports that security forces have arrested a Shia cleric, Shaykh Hashim Muhammad Shakshi, in Hasa.

King Fahd bin Abdul Aziz is ill. Heir Apparent Abdallah temporarily assumes authority.

1997   American and Canadian counterterrorism officials link the Khobar bombing to Hani Abd al-Rahim Al-Sayegh, who confesses that Ahmad Ibrahim Mughassil, another Saudi citizen, is the mastermind and head of Hizballah-Gulf. Al-Sayegh further links an Iranian officer, Brigadier Ahmad Sharifi, to terrorist plots against U.S. targets in the Gulf.

An estimated 217 die and 1,290 others are wounded outside Makkah when a fire breaks out in a pilgrimage tent.

King Fahd approves the establishment of an Internet system.

1998   The U.S. Immigration and Naturalization Service (INS) announces that it plans to deport Hani al-Sayegh, a suspect in the bombing of the Khobar Towers in 1996, to Saudi Arabia. INS officials claim that al-Sayegh backed out of an arrangement to help instigate the bombing.

In an interview with the Kuwaiti daily *Al-Ray al-'Am,* Interior Minister Prince Nayif bin Abdul Aziz recognizes that the Khobar Towers bombing was "carried out by Saudi hands."

An estimated 750,000 expatriate workers are expelled for violating residency regulations.

The London *Financial Times* reports that the Kingdom received a $5 billion loan from the United Arab Emirates.

1999   Iranian President Mohamed Khatami visits Saudi Arabia in May. King Fahd and senior Saudi officials extend a red-carpet welcome.

King Fahd spends several months in Marbella, Spain.

The London-based publication *Al Hayat* reports that women attended a session of the Consultative Council (October 4) for the first time. The 20 women in attendance sat in the balcony.

2000   King Fahd established the Supreme Council for Petroleum and Mineral Affairs (January 4) to devise strategic oil policies.

The Saudi Press Agency reports (April 23) that in Najran Province, after the closing of an Ismaili mosque and the arrest of an alleged sorcerer, demonstrators had opened fire on security forces in front of the residence of Governor Prince Mish'al bin Saud, killing one policeman and injuring three others.

Saudi Arabia and Yemen sign a historic border agreement (June 12), although a full demarcation is not announced.

Sources: *FBIS-Middle East and Africa, 1977–1987; FBIS-Near East and South Asia, 1987–1996,* Anders Jerichow, *The Saudi File: People, Power, Politics,* New York: St. Martin's Press, 1998, pp. 330–331; Simon Henderson, *After King Fahd: Succession in Saudi Arabia,* Washington, D.C.: The Washington Institute for Near East Policy, 1994, pp. 61–64; *The Middle East Journal,* chronology sections, 1985–2000.

Appendix 3 ⌐

Mainline of Succession and Cadet Branches

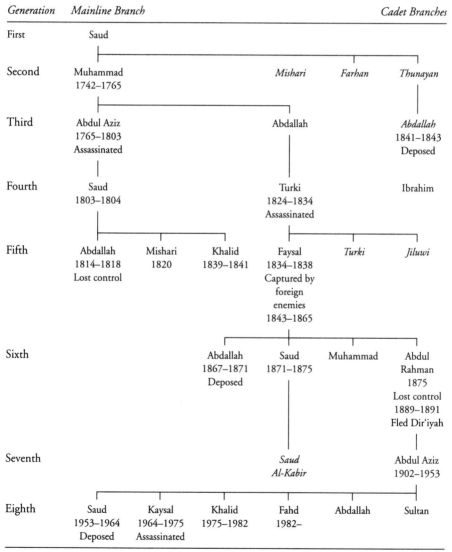

Generation	Mainline Branch				Cadet Branches	

First — Saud

Second — Muhammad 1742–1765 | Mishari | Farhan | Thunayan

Third — Abdul Aziz 1765–1803 Assassinated | Abdallah | Abdallah 1841–1843 Deposed

Fourth — Saud 1803–1804 | Turki 1824–1834 Assassinated | Ibrahim

Fifth — Abdallah 1814–1818 Lost control | Mishari 1820 | Khalid 1839–1841 | Faysal 1834–1838 Captured by foreign enemies 1843–1865 | Turki | Jiluwi

Sixth — Abdallah 1867–1871 Deposed | Saud 1871–1875 | Muhammad | Abdul Rahman 1875 Lost control 1889–1891 Fled Dir'iyah

Seventh — Saud Al-Kabir | Abdul Aziz 1902–1953

Eighth — Saud 1953–1964 Deposed | Kaysal 1964–1975 Assassinated | Khalid 1975–1982 | Fahd 1982– | Abdallah | Sultan

Sources: Simon Henderson, *After King Fahd: Succession in Saudi Arabia,* Washington D.C.: The Washington Institute for Near East Policy, 1994, p. 57; and Alexander Bligh, *From Prince to King: Royal Succession in the House of Saud in the Twentieth Century,* New York and London: New York University Press, p. 105.

Appendix 4 ~

Twentieth-Century Al Saud Leaders

Generation	Name	Life Span	Rule Period
Sixth	Abdul Rahman	1850–1928	1875–1876
			1889–1891
Seventh	Abdul Aziz	1880–1953	1902–1953
Eighth	Saud	1902–1969	1953–1964
	Faysal	1906–1975	1964–1975
	Khalid	1912–1982	1975–1982
	Fahd	1921–	1982–
	Abdallah	1923–	
	Sultan	1924–	

Source: Alexander Bligh, *From Prince to King: Royal Succession in the House of Saud in the Twentieth Century,* New York and London: New York University Press, p. 108.

Appendix 5 Maternal Linkages Among Sons of King Abdul Aziz

DOB	1	2	3	4	5	6	7	8	9	10	11	12	13	14	15	16	17
1900	*Turki*																
1902	Saud																
1904		*Faysal*															
1910			*Muhammad*														
1912			Khalid														
1920				Nasir													
1921					Saad												
1922						Fahd											
1923					Musaid		Mansur										
1924						Sultan		Abdallah									
1925					A. Mohsin												
1926							Mish'al		Bandar								
1928							Mit'ab										
1931						A. Rahman				Talal							
1932											Mishari						
1933						Nayif				Nawwaf							
1934						Turki			Fawwaz			Badr					
1935												A. Illah					
1936						Salman											
1937						Ahmad							Majid				
1940												A. Majid		*Thamir* Mamduh			
1941															Hidhlul		
1942														Mashhur			
1943													Sattam				
1947																Miqrin	Hamud

Source: Simon Henderson, *After King Fahd: Succession in Saudi Arabia*, Washington, D.C.: The Washington Institute for Near East Policy, 1994, p. 58. This chart lists the sons of King Abdul Aziz and indicates their fraternal relationship with one another. Each number along the horizontal axis represents a different mother; names in the same column are thus full blood brothers. Sons in the same row were born in the same year. Names in italics are deceased. In several cases, dates and relationships are in dispute.

Appendix 6 ⌒

The Sons of Abdul Aziz

King Abdul Aziz bin Abdul Rahman bin Faysal Al Saud (1880–1953) fathered 36 sons and 21 daughters. Only the male offspring are listed here.

Number/Name	Years	Maternal Origin	Full Brothers	Political Career
1. Turki	1900–1919	Wahba of the Bani Khalid tribe	Saud	Court education. Eldest son. Commanded Saudi forces against Rashids (1918). Died in 1919 Spanish Flu epidemic.
2. Saud	1902–1969	Wadhba of the Bani Khalid tribe	Turki	Court education. Fought in several Najdi battles, including defeat of Rashids (1921) and Ikhwan rebellion (1929). Viceroy of Najd (1932–53), Heir Apparent (1932–53), regent (1950–53), King (1953–64), prime minister (1953–54, 1960–62), foreign minister (1960–62). Deposed in 1964 and died in exile in 1969.
3. Faysal	1906–1975	Tarfah bint Abdallah Al Shaykh	None	Court education. Fought conquest of Asir (1920) and Hijaz (1924–26). Viceroy of Hijaz (1926–53). Foreign minister 1930–60, 1962–75), prime minister (1954–60, 1962–75), Interior (1959–60), Defense (1959–60), Finance (1958–60), Commerce (1958–60), Heir Apparent (1953–64), regent (1953–64), King (1964–75). Assassinated by nephew in 1975.
4. Muhammad	1910–1988	Jauhara bint Musaid bin Jiluwi	Khalid	Court education. Fought in conquest of Hijaz and defeat of Ikhwan rebellion. Honorary governor of Madinah (1926–54) after he liberated it in 1925. Played key role in Saud-Faysal struggle. Voluntarily renounced succession in favor of younger full brother Khalid, but influential family elder and adviser to Faysal and Khalid.
5. Khalid	1912–1982	Jauhara bint Musaid bin Jiluwi	Muhammad	Court education. Fought in Ikhwan rebellion and Yemen war (1934). Early career as deputy to

(continued)

Number/Name	Years	Maternal Origin	Full Brothers	Political Career
				Faysal, including acting viceroy of Hijaz (1932). Played key role in Saud-Faysal struggle. Deputy prime minister (1962–75), Heir Apparent (1965–75), prime minister and King (1975–82). Died of natural causes in 1982.
6. Nasir	1920–1984	Bazza (Moroccan concubine)	None	Court education. Early career as deputy to Saud including acting deputy of Najd (1944). First governor of Riyadh (1944–47), but forced to resign in scandal. Held no further office. Supported Saud and refused to sign 1964 decision against him. Bypassed for succession in favor of Fahd.
7. Saad	1920–1993	Jauhara bint Said Al Sudayri	Musaid Abdulmuhsin	Court education. Son of Jauhara bint Saad Al Sudayri, widow of Abdul Aziz's brother Saad. Has never held office. Bypassed in succession in favor of Fahd.
8. Fahd	1921–	Hassa bint Ahmad Al Sudayri	Sultan Abdulrahman Nayif Turki Salman Ahmad	Court education. Eldest son of Hassa bint Ahmad Al Sudayri after her remarriage to Abdul Aziz. Early career as assistant to Faysal. Key supporter during Saud-Faysal struggle. Governor of Jawf (1949–53), minister of education (1953–60), minister of the interior (1962–75), second deputy prime minister (1967–75), Heir Apparent and first deputy prime minister (1975–82), appointed regent during King Khalid's illnesses. Prime minister and King since 1982.
9. Mansur	1921–1951	Shahida (Armenian wife)	Mish'al Mit'ab	Court education. First Saudi minister of defense (1940). Considered rising prince until death due to kidney illness in 1951. Succeeded as minister of defense by younger full brother Mish'al.
10. Abdallah	1923–	Fahda bint Asi Al Shammar	None	Court education. Obscure early career, but emerged a key supporter of Faysal in last years of Saud-Faysal struggle. Commander of National Guard since 1963. Second deputy prime minister (1975–82), first deputy prime minister and Heir Apparent since 1982.
11. Bandar	1923–	Bazza (unknown origins. Moroccan concubine?)	Fawwaz	Court education. Noted for strict religious observance. Never held office. Recluse.

(continued)

Number/Name	Years	Maternal Origin	Full Brothers	Political Career
12. Musaid	1923–	Jauhara bint Said Al Sudayri	Saad Abdulmuhsin	Court education. Never held office; supported Saud and refused to sign 1964 decision deposing the latter. Considered an eccentric. His son assassinated King Faysal.
13. Sultan	1924–	Hassa bint Ahmad Al Sudayri	Fahd Abdulrahman Nayif Turki Salman Ahmad	Court education. Early career as commander of Royal Guard (?–1947) and governor of Riyadh (1947–53). Key supporter of Faysal and later one of his chief lieutenants. Minister of agriculture (1953–55), minister of communications (1955–60), minister of defense since 1962. Second deputy prime minister since 1982. Considered next in line for throne after Heir Apparent Abdallah.
14. Abdulmuhsin	1925–1985	Jauhara bint Saad Al Sudayri	Saad Musaid	Court education. Early career as court figure under his father. Supported Faysal in 1958 crisis, but switched to Saud and appointed minister of the interior (1960–61) in Saud-Talal coalition. After Saud-Faysal reconciliation, joined Talal in exile as free prince (1962–64). Rehabilitated by Faysal to governor of Madinah (1965–85). Said to have challenged Sultan's claim to seniority.
15. Mish'al	1926–	Shahida (Armenian wife)	Mansur Mit'ab	Court education. Succeeded full brother Mansur as defense minister (1951–56). Made royal adviser (1957–60) by King Saud. Appointed governor of Makkah in 1963, but removed by King Faysal in 1971. Extensive business interests.
16. Mit'ab	1928–	Shahida (Armenian wife)	Mansur Mish'al	Court education. Deputy minister of defense (1951–56). Governor of Makkah (1959–60), deputy governor of Makkah (1963–69) when removed by Faysal. Returned to office as minister of housing and public works since 1975.
17. Abdul Rahman	1931–	Hassa bint Ahmad Al Sudayri	Fahd Sultan Nayif Turki Salman Ahmad	First son to study abroad, B.A. (USA). Major businessman for years; appointed deputy minister of defense (1983-), under his full brother Sultan.
18. Talal	1931–	Munaysir (Armenian wife)	Nawwaf	Court education. Commander of Royal Guard (1950–52), minister of communications (1953–55), until removed by King Saud.

(continued)

Number/Name	Years	Maternal Origin	Full Brothers	Political Career
				Supported Faysal in 1958 crisis, but later led "liberal princes" in alliance with Saud and appointed minister of finance (1962–64). Business interests. Special envoy to UNESCO since 1979.
19. Mishari	1932–	Bahra(unknown origins)	None	Court education. Never held office. Business interests. Shot dead British consul in Jeddah (1951).
20. Badr	1933–	Haiya bint Saad Al Sudayri	Abdul Illah Abdul Majid	Court education. Joined Saud-Talal coalition as minister of communications (1960–61) and later joined Talal in exile as Free Prince (1962–64). Rehabilitated by Faysal to deputy commander of National Guard (1968–).
21. Nayif	1933–	Hassa bint Ahmad Al Sudayri	Fahd Sultan Abdulrahman Turki Salman Ahmad	Court education. Career pattern has followed close association with older full brothers, Fahd and Sultan. Deputy governor of Riyadh (1951–53), governor of Riyadh (1953–54), governor of Madinah (1954–60), remained in business until deputy minister of the interior (1970–75). Minister of interior since 1975.
22. Nawwaf	1933–	Munaysir (Armenian wife)	Talal	Court education. Commander of Royal Guard (1952–56) when removed by Saud, later supported Saud as chief of Royal Diwan (1961) and minister of finance (1961–62), served as adviser on Gulf affairs to Faysal (1968–75) and retired to business in 1975.
23. Turki	1934–	Hassa bint Ahmad Al Sudayri	Fahd Sultan Abdulrahman Nayif Salman Ahmad	Court education. Deputy minister of defense (1969–78) when forced to resign in marital scandal. Later in business.
24. Fawwaz	1934–	Bazza (unknown origins. Moroccan concubine?)	Bandar	Court education. Joined in Saud-Talal coalition as governor of Riyadh (1960–61) and later joined Talal in exile as Free Prince (1962–64). Rehabilitated by Faysal as governor of Makkah (1971–79) but forced to resign following Makkah Mosque takeover. Now in business.
25. Abdul Illah	1935–	Haiya bint Saad Al Sudayri	Badr Abdul Majid	Court education. Appointed governor of Qasim (1980–92) after Makkah Mosque takeover.
26. Salman	1936–	Hassa bint Ahmad Al Sudayri	Fahd Sultan	Court education. Governor of Riyadh (1954–60, 1962-). Said to

(continued)

Number/Name	Years	Maternal Origin	Full Brothers	Political Career
			Abdulrahman Nayif Turki Ahmad	be possible future candidate for succession.
27. Majid	1937–	Mudhi (Armenian concubine)	Sattam	Court education. Considered one of the young "liberal princes," but broke with Talal in 1960 and entered business. First appointed to office as minister of municipal and rural affairs (1975–80) and transferred to governor of Makkah in 1980 after the Makkah Mosque takeover. His deputy, Saud bin Abdul Muhsin, has been acting governor since 1992. Retired in 1999.
28. Thamir	1937–1958	Nouf bint Al Ruwalah	Mamduh Mashhur	Committed suicide in 1958.
29. Ahmad	1940–	Hassa bint Ahmad Al Sudayri	Fahd Sultan Abdulrahman Nayif Turki Salman	B.A. (USA). Entered business with older brother Abdulrahman until appointed deputy governor of Makkah (1971–75) and transferred to deputy minister of the interior (1975–).
30. Mamduh	1940–	Nouf bint Al-Ruwalah	Thamir Mashhur	Never held public office, but extensive business interests. Chairman of Strategic Studies Bureau.
31. Abdul Majid	1940–	Haiya bint Saad Al Sudayri	Badr Abdul Illah	Court education. Appointed governor of Tabuk (1980–1985) after Makkah Mosque takeover, then governor of Madinah.
32. Hadhlul	1941–	Baraka (Yemeni concubine)	Miqrin	Never held public office, but extensive business interests.
33. Mashhur	1942–	Nouf bint Al-Ruwalah	Thamir Mamduh	Never held public office, but extensive business interests.
34. Sattam	1943–	Mudhi (Armenian concubine)	Majid	B.A. (USA). Deputy governor of Riyadh since 1968.
35. Miqrin	1943–	Baraka (Yemeni concubine)	Hadhlul	Military training in USA and UK. Air force major, retired to become governor of Hail (1980–99) after Makkah Mosque takeover. Governor of Madinah (1999–). Married to a member of the Al Rashid tribe.
36. Hammud	1947–	Futayma (Yemeni concubine)	None	Never held public office, but extensive business interests providing transport for military programs. Lives in Paris, France.

Sources: Alexander Bligh, *From Prince to King: Royal Succession in the House of Saud in The Twentieth Century,* New York and London: New York University Press, 1984, p. 109; Gary Samuel Samore, *Royal Family Politics in Saudi Arabia (1953–1982),* doctoral dissertation, Cambridge, Massachusetts: Harvard University, 1984, pp. 528–532; and Simon Henderson, *After King Fahd: Succession in Saudi Arabia,* Washington, D.C.: The Washington Institute for Near East Policy, 1994, pp. 65–71.

Appendix 7 ～

Leading Grandsons of Abdul Aziz

Father/Son (Years)	Political Career
1. Turki (1900–1919)	
1. Faysal (1920–)	Supporter of King Saud during the Saud-Faysal struggle, minister of labor and social affairs (1961–62), and minister of the interior (1962). Adviser to the minister of petroleum and mineral resources. His eldest son, Abdallah (b. 1946), is director of the Yanbu and Jubayl Industrial Project.
2. Fahd (xxxx–)	Major in army special forces.
3. Khalid (xxxx–)	Businessman.
4. Sultan (xxxx–)	N/A
2. Saud (1902–1969)	
1. Fahd (1923–)	King Saud's eldest son. Chief of the Diwan (1953–56) and minister of defense (1956–60). Later in business.
2. Musaid (xxxx–)	Commander of the Royal Guard (1956–58).
3. Muhammad (1934–)	Early favorite to succeed Saud, married to King Faysal's daughter. Chamberlain (1953–59), chief of the Diwan (1959–60), and minister of defense (1960–62). Later in business along with sons Faysal and Mish'al (1951-). Now governor of Baha Province.
4. Abdallah (xxxx–)	Chief of Royal Gardens and Farms (1953–?), and governor of Makkah (1960–62).
5. Faysal (1945–)	B.A., M.B.A. (USA), director of overseas education, director-general of education, and assistant deputy minister of education.
6. Khalid (xxxx–)	Commander of National Guard (1957–61) and chief of the Diwan (1962–63). Joined his father in exile.
7. Mansur (1946–)	Commander of Royal Guard (1961–63) and chief of the Diwan (1963–64). Joined his father in exile.
8. Saad (1948–1968)	Commander of personal bodyguard (1958–61) and commander of National Guard (1961–63). Joined his father in exile.
9. Badr (xxxx–)	Commander of Royal Guard (1958–61) and governor of Riyadh (1962–63). Joined his father in exile. Later in business.
10. Sultan (xxxx–)	Commander of Royal Guard (1963–64). Joined his father in exile.
11. Abdulrahman (xxxx–)	B.A. (USA). One of the first of Saud's sons to declare loyalty to King Faysal. Director-general at Ministry of Finance.
12. Salman (xxxx–)	B.A. (USA). President of Saudi Direction Company for Trading and Construction.
13. Moataz (xxxx–)	Captain in the National Guard, now assigned to the Saudi National Guard office in Washington, D.C., while studying at Johns Hopkins University's School of Advanced International Studies.
3. Faysal (1906–1975)	
1. Abdallah (1921–)	Son of Sultana bint Ahmad Al Sudayri. Eldest son who was deputy to his father as viceroy of Hijaz minister of health (1951–54) and minister of the interior (1951–59). Supported his father during

(continued)

Father/Son (Years)	Political Career
	Saud-Faysal struggle. Retired to extensive business interests. Poet. His own sons include Khalid (B.S., business interests), Muhammad (B.A., assistant deputy minister of education), and Saud (army officer).
2. Muhammad (1937–)	Son of Iffat Al Thunayan. B.A. (USA), deputy in SAMA (1963–65), director-general (1965–71) and deputy minister of agriculture (1971–75), director of saline water conversion company (1975–77). Now in business. Heads the Faysal Islamic Bank Group, headquartered in Switzerland.
3. Khalid (1941–)	Son of Haya bint Turki bin Abdallah Al Jiluwi. B.A. (UK). Director-general of youth welfare (1969–71) and governor of Asir (1971–).
4. Saud (1941–)	Son of Iffat. B.A. (Princeton, USA). Deputy at Petromin (1965–70), deputy governor at Petromin (1970–71), and deputy minister of Petroleum (1971–75). Minister of state for foreign affairs (1975) and minister of foreign affairs since 1975.
5. Abdulrahman (1942–)	Son of Iffat. Sandhurst Academy (UK). Army Lt. colonel, commander of an armored brigade.
6. Saad (1942–)	Son of Haya. B.A. (UK). Deputy governor at Petromin (1971–74). Later in business. Head of the Faysal Foundation.
7. Bandar (1943–)	Son of Iffat. Cranwell RAF Academy (UK) and RAF Staff College (UK). Lt. colonel in charge of air force intelligence.
8. Turki (1945–)	Son of Iffat. B.A. (USA), Ph.D (UK). Deputy director (1973–78) and director—since 1978—of the Directorate General of Royal Intelligence. Commander of Saudi forces at 1979 Makkah Mosque takeover.
4. Muhammad (1910–1988)	No sons known to hold office, but several in business (Bandar, Saud).
5. Khalid (1912–1982)	No sons known to hold office, but several in business (Bandar [1935–], Faysal).
6. Nasir (1920–1984)	
1. Muhammad (xxxx–)	Son of Mudhi bint Ahmad Al Sudayri. Army officer.
2. Turki (xxxx–)	Son of Mudhi bint Ahmad Al Sudayri. Air force Lt. colonel. Commands Dhahran air wing.
7. Saad (1920–1993)	No sons known to hold public office. Muhammad in business.
8. Fahd (1921–)	
1. Faysal (1945–1999)	Son of Anud bint Abdul Aziz bin Musaid Al Jiluwi. B.A. (USA). Director-general of youth welfare (1971–99), director-general at the Ministry of Planning, and minister of state (1977–99). Sometime emissary for King Fahd to Iraq. Married to Munirah bin Sultan bin Abdul Aziz.
2. Khalid (1947–)	Runs Al-Bilad Company. Deputy head of youth welfare and head after his older brother passed away in 1999.
3. Muhammad (1950–)	B.A. (USA). Major businessman. Married to Nura bint Nayif bin Abdul Aziz. Governor of the Eastern Province since 1985.
4. Saud (1950–)	B.S. (USA). Major businessman, copublisher of *Who's Who in Saudi Arabia*. Married to daughter of Turki bin Abdul Aziz. Deputy head of External Intelligence since 1985. Elevated to minister rank in September 1997.
5. Sultan (1951–)	Sandhurst Academy (UK). Army officer. Elevated to minister rank in November 1997.
6. Abdulaziz (1973–)	King Fahd's youngest—and allegedly favorite—son. Involved in business ventures with the Al-Ibrahim brothers, whose sister is King Fahd's wife.

(continued)

Father/Son (Years)	Political Career
9. Mansur (1921–1951)	
1. Talal (xxxx–)	B.A. (USA). Businessman.
10. Abdallah (1923–)	
1. Khalid (xxxx–)	B.A. (UK). Eldest son. Director of planning and administration in National Guard, appointed deputy head of National Guard for the Western Province after 1979 Makkah Mosque takeover. Deputy governor of the Western region until 1992.
2. Mit'ab (1943–)	Sandhurst Academy (UK). National Guard officer. Deputy head of the National Guard since 1984. Local representative for the Ford Motor Corporation.
3. Abdulaziz (1964–)	Adviser to his father's court.
4. Faysal (xxxx–)	Dropped out of Sandhurst Military Academy. Later in business.
5. Mish'al (xxxx–)	N/A
6. Turki (xxxx–)	Sandhurst Academy (UK). National Guard officer.
11. Bandar (1923–)	
1. Faysal (1943–)	Eldest son. Appointed governor of Asir after 1979 Makkah Mosque takeover. Now governor of Qasim Province.
2. Mansur (xxxx–)	Air force Lt. colonel. Commands Jeddah Air Base squadron.
12. Musaid (1923–)	
1. Khalid (xxxx–65)	Shot in 1965 protest against Riyadh's first television transmitter.
2. Faysal (1944–75)	B.A. (USA). Assassinated King Faysal. Tried and executed.
13. Sultan (1924–)	
1. Khaled (1949–)	Eldest son. Sandhurst Academy (UK), U.S. Army Command General Staff College (Fort Leavenworth, Kansas), Air War College (Maxwell AFB, Alabama), M.A. (Naval Postgraduate School, Monterey, California). Commander, Royal Saudi Air Defense Forces (1986–90), commander of the Joint Forces after the Iraqi invasion of Kuwait (1990–91). Resigns commission at forty-two. Author of *Desert Warrior: A Personal View of the Gulf War by the Joint Forces Commander* (1995). Owner and publisher of London-based *Al-Hayat* (daily) and *Al-Wasat* (weekly). Extensive business interests.
2. Fahd (1950–)	B.A. (USA). Director of research (1969–70) and director-general of social welfare (1970–) at the Ministry of Labor and Social Affairs. Governor of Tabuk since 1988.
3. Faysal (1950–)	Ministry of Planning official.
4. Bandar (1950–)	Cranwell RAF College (UK). Air Force major. Director of Asad Military City at Al-Kharj (1978–83). Ambassador to Washington since 1983. Married to Haifa bint Faysal bin Abdul Aziz.
5. Nayef (xxxx–)	N/A
6. Muhammad (xxxx–)	N/A
7. Turki (xxxx–)	Director of the press department at the Ministry of Information.
14. Abdul Muhsin (1925–)	
1. Saud (1947–)	Sandhurst Academy (UK), B.A. (USA). Director of health and housing in Central Planning Organization (1970–73), director-general of planning at the Ministry of Health (1973–76), and deputy governor of Makkah (1976–92). Acting governor of Makkah since 1992. Governor of Hail since 1999. Married to Lu'lua bint Faysal bin Abdul Aziz.
2. Badr (xxxx–)	B.A. (USA). President of the Saudi Arts Association.
15. Mish'al (1926–)	
1. Mansur (1951–)	B.A. (USA). President of the Saudi-American Modern Agriculture Company.
16. Mit'ab (1928–)	No sons known to hold public office.

(continued)

Father/Son (Years)	Political Career
17. Abdul Rahman (1931–)	No sons known to hold public office, but Turki in business.
18. Talal (1931–)	
1. Walid (1955–)	Major investor. Starting in 1991, when he invested $590 million in Citicorp—making him the bank's largest individual shareholder—he accumulated an estimated $15 billion, which by 1999 ranked him as *Forbes* magazine's eighth richest person in the world. His Lebanese mother is former president Riad Solh's daughter.
19. Mishari (1932–)	No sons known to hold public office.
20. Badr (1933–)	
1. Khalid (xxxx–)	Lt. colonel in army.
2. Faysal (xxxx–)	Son of Haya bint Saad Al Sudayri. B.A. (USA). Director-general of training, Ministry of Posts, Telegraphs and Telecommunications.
21. Nayif (1933–)	
1. Saud (xxxx–)	Eldest son. B.A. (USA). Major businessman, including president of Saudi-French road construction company. Deputy governor of the Eastern Province since 1993.
2. Muhammad (xxxx–)	Extensive business holdings.
22. Nawwaf (1933–)	No sons known to hold public office.
23. Turki (1934–)	
1. Faysal (xxxx–)	Ministry of Petroleum and Mineral Resources official.
2. Fahd (xxxx–)	N/A
3. Khalid (xxxx–)	B.A. (USA). Businessman, cofounder of Arab National Bank.
4. Sultan (xxxx–)	N/A
24. Fawwaz (1934–)	Has no sons.
25. Abdul Illah (1935–)	No sons known to hold public office.
26. Salman (1936–)	
1. Ahmad (xxxx–)	Army officer. Director of firm that owns *Al-Sharq Al-Awsat* daily.
2. Fahd (xxxx–)	B.A. (USA). Deputy governor of the Eastern Province until February 1993. Businessman. Keen on racing horses.
3. Abdulaziz (xxxx–)	B.A. (USA). Ministry of Petroleum and Mineral Resources official. Businessman.
4. Sultan (xxxx–)	Lt. colonel in Royal Saudi Air Force. Former astronaut on a *Discovery* mission.
5. Faysal (xxxx–)	Ph.D (Oxford, UK). Assistant professor, King Saud University.
27. Majid (1937–)	
1. Mish'al (xxxx–)	B.A. (UK). Businessman, partner in Saudi-Danish dairy company.
28. Thamir (1937–1958)	No sons known to hold public office.
29. Ahmad (1940–)	
1. Nayef (xxxx–)	Army special forces; promoted to ministry of defense post in 1999.
2. Abdulaziz (xxxx–)	Partially blind. Active in the Saudi Blind Society.
30. Mamduh (1941–)	No sons known to hold public office.
31. Abdulmajid (1940–)	No sons known to hold public office.
32. Hadhlul (1941–)	No sons known to hold public office.
33. Mashur (1942–)	No sons known to hold public office.
34. Sattam (1943–)	No sons known to hold public office.
35. Miqrin (1943–)	No sons known to hold public office.
36. Hammud (1947–)	No sons known to hold public office.

Sources: Alexander Bligh, *From Prince to King: Royal Succession in the House of Saud in The Twentieth Century,* New York and London: New York University Press, 1984; and Gary Samuel Samore, *Royal Family Politics in Saudi Arabia (1953–1982),* doctoral dissertation, Cambridge, Massachusetts: Harvard University, 1984, pp. 528–532.

Appendix 8 ~

Provincial Governors

Except for the Jizan post, which is held by a cadet family branch member, all governors are members of the Al Saud ruling family (November 1999).

Governor	Province
Salman Bin Abdul Aziz Al Saud	Riyadh
Khalid Bin Faysal Bin Abdul Aziz Al Saud	Asir
Abdul Majid Bin Abdul Aziz Al Saud	Makkah
Muhammad Bin Fahd Bin Abdul Aziz Al Saud	Eastern Province
Abdallah Bin Abdul Aziz Bin Musaid Bin Jiluwi Al Saud	Northern Territories
Faysal Bin Bandar Bin Abdul Aziz Al Saud	Qasim
Miqrin Bin Abdul Aziz Al Saud	Madinah
Mish'al Bin Saud Bin Abdul Aziz Al Saud	Najran
Muhammad Bin Saud Bin Abdul Aziz Al Saud	Baha
Muhammad Bin Turki Al Sudayri	Jizan
Fahd Bin Sultan Bin Abdul Aziz Al Saud	Tabuk
Abdul Ilah Bin Abdul Aziz Al Saud	Jawf
Saud Bin Abdul Muhsin bin Abdul Aziz Al Saud	Hail

Source: Kingdom of Saudi Arabia, Ministry of Information. Updated by *Reuters* on November 25, 1999.

Appendix 9 ～

The Cabinet (June 1999)

Royal Decree
2/3/1420H/16 June 1999

(Protocol List)

The Custodian of the Two Holy Mosques, Head of State, Prime Minister
   HRH Fahd bin Abdul Aziz Al Saud

First Deputy Prime Minister and Commander of the National Guard
   HRH Heir Apparent Abdallah bin Abdul Aziz Al Saud

Second Deputy Prime Minister, Minister of Defense and Aviation, and Inspector General
   HRH Prince Sultan bin Abdul Aziz Al Saud

Minister of Public Works and Housing
   HRH Prince Mit'ab bin Abdul Aziz Al Saud

Minister of the Interior
   HRH Prince Nayif bin Abdul Aziz Al Saud

Minister of Foreign Affairs
   HRH Prince Saud bin Faysal bin Abdul Aziz Al Saud

Minister of State (no portfolio)
   HRH Prince Abdul Aziz bin Fahd bin Abdul Aziz Al Saud

Minister of Justice
   Dr. Abdallah bin Muhammad bin Ibrahim Al Shaykh

Minister of State (no portfolio)
   Dr. Abdul Aziz bin Abdallah al-Khuweiter

Minister of Higher Education
   Dr. Khalid bin Muhammad al-Angari

Minister of State (no portfolio)
   Dr. Muhammad bin Abdul Aziz Al Shaykh

Minister of Islamic Affairs, Endowments and Guidance
Shaykh Saleh bin Abdul Aziz bin Ibrahim Al Shaykh

Minister of Civil Service
Muhammad bin Ali al-Fayez

Minister of Commerce
Osama bin Jaafar bin Ibrahim al-Faqih

Minister of Health
Dr. Osama bin Abdul Majeed al-Shobokshi

Minister of Agriculture and Water
Dr. Abdallah bin Abdul Aziz bin Muammar

Minister of Petroleum and Mineral Resources
Ali bin Ibrahim al-Naimi

Minister of Post, Telegraph and Telecommunications
Dr. Ali bin Talal al-Juhani

Minister of Information
Dr. Fouad bin Abdul Salaam bin Muhammad al-Farsy

Minister of Municipal and Rural Affairs
Dr. Muhammad bin Ibrahim al-Jarallah

Minister of Education
Dr. Muhammad bin Ahmad al-Rashid

Minister of Communications
Dr. Nasir bin Muhammad al-Salloum

Minister of Industry and Electricity
Dr. Hashim bin Abdallah bin Hashim al-Yamani

Minister of Finance and National Economy
Dr. Ibrahim bin Abdul Aziz al-Assaf

Minister of Pilgrimage
Dr. Iyad Amin Madani

Minister of Planning
Dr. Khalid bin Muhammad al-Ghosaibi

Minister of Labor and Social Affairs
Dr. Ali bin Ibrahim al-Namlah

Minister of State (no portfolio)
Dr. Mutlib bin Abdallah al-Nafissa

Minister of State (no portfolio)
Dr. Abdul Aziz bin Ibrahim al-Manie

Minister of State (no portfolio)
Dr. Musaid bin Muhammad al-Ayban

Minister of State (no portfolio)
   Dr. Madani bin Abdul Qadir Alaqi

Secretary-General of the Cabinet
   Abdul Aziz bin Abdallah al-Salem

Assistant Secretary General of the Cabinet
   Abdul Rahman bin Muhammad al-Sadhan

Source: Kingdom of Saudi Arabia, Ministry of Information.

Appendix 10 ⤳

Leading Religious Figures
in the Kingdom of Saudi Arabia

Shaykh Abdallah bin Humaid
Shaykh Abdul Aziz bin Abdallah (Chief Theologian)
Shaykh Abdul Aziz bin Nasir bin Rashid
Shaykh Abdallah bin Abdallah bin Aqil
Shaykh Rashid bin Salih bin Khinnin
Shaykh Umar bin Abdul Aziz bin Mutriq
Shaykh Abdul Aziz bin Abdul Rahman al-Rabi'a
Shaykh Abdul Rahman Al-Rabi'a
Shaykh Abdul Rahman bin Muhammad bin Faris
Shaykh Nasir bin Hamad al-Rashid
Shaykh Ali bin Sulayman al-Rumi
Shaykh Sulayman bin Abdul Aziz bin Sulayman
Shaykh Muhammad bin Abdallah al-Amir
Shaykh Abdallah bin Abdul Aziz bin Rashid
Shaykh Muhammad bin Sulayman al-Badr
Shaykh Muhammad bin Ibrahim bin al-Jubair
Shaykh Salih bin Ali bin Ghassan
Shaykh Ghunaym bin Mubarak al-Ghunaym
Shaykh Nasir bin Abdul Aziz al-Shatari
Shaykh Abdallah bin Sulayman bin Mani'
Shaykh Abdul Aziz al-'Isha al-Shaykh
Shaykh Muhammad 'Alawi Maliki
Shaykh Salih bin Muhammad bin Lahidan
Shaykh Muhammad bin Sabil
Shaykh Sulayman bin Ubaid
Shaykh Abdul Rahman Hamza al-Marzuqi
Shaykh Muhammad bin Ibrahim al-Bashar
Shaykh Muhammad Ibrahim al-'Isha

⤳ ⤳ ⤳

There are many younger religious figures throughout the Kingdom who articulate points of view that are sometimes diametrically opposed to the establishment perspective. Among these are:

Shaykh Hamud Al-Uqla
Shaykh Safar al-Hawali
Shaykh Nasir al-Umar
Shaykh Ali bin Said Al-Ghamidi
Shaykh Salman Al-Awda

∼ ∼ ∼

Many respected religious authorities have been arrested and/or received "visits" from interior ministry officials. Most have strong followings throughout the Kingdom.

Appendix 11 ⌒

"Secular" Petition to King Fahd (December 1990)

In the Name of God, the Merciful, the Compassionate.
The Guardian of the Two Holy Mosques, King Fahd bin Abdul Aziz, may God support him.

Preamble

One of the favors bestowed by God upon you is that you held, during the past forty years, the most momentous and delicate responsibilities. That provided you an unadulterated acquaintance with the workings of the State as well as a fine knowledge of the various exigencies of state reforms. Your open-doors policy and your open-heartedness with regard to all peoples' appeals, your care and concern for the requests submitted to you, created truthfulness and encouraged your subjects to speak freely.

A number of your loyal subjects have prepared the enclosed memorandum about the ways of affecting certain reforms as they see them. They are concerned with the safety of the entity we are proud of. They address you out of their desire to enhance its safety and stability, progress and prosperity, out of their obligation to their rulers, and out of their obedience to God with regard to the religious duty of offering advice to God, His Messenger, the leaders of the community as well as all Muslims.

They put this memorandum before you, the Guardian of the Two Holy Mosques, in expression of their deep conviction that you are best qualified to turn their hopes [into] reality and sanction their loyalty.

May God preserve and support you in your search for the right path.

Proposed Landmarks of the Way of Reforms and Development

The critical conditions and painful events unfolding in this region for the Muslim Nation—with our country in the foreground—that emerged in the wake of the invasion of Kuwait and the scattering of its people, are in fact ominous forerunners which make the citizens duty-bound to give their advice to rulers. Citizens are obliged to share with their rulers, in words and deeds, what they deem to be advantageous to the country that belongs to all of them. All are responsible to build it and share in its benefits as well as losses.

The Holy Quran stresses this great religious duty in the following words: "And from amongst you there should be a party who invite to good and enjoin what is right and forbid the wrong, and these it is that shall be successful. And be not like those who became divided and disagreed after clear arguments had come to them, and these it is that shall have a grievous chastisement." This passage makes it quite clear that refraining from calling to good and keeping away from enjoining good and forbidding evil inevitably leads to the emergence of rifts between people and spreads confusion in their affairs, as well as scatters them in opposing fronts.

The Prophetic Holy Sunnah had explained the grades of this duty and identified the parties to whom Muslims should offer advice. The Messenger of God (peace and the blessings of God be upon him) is reported to have said: "Faith is advice." Muslims who were present asked him: "To whom should we offer our advice." "To God (that means to be obedient to Him), to His Messenger, and to the leaders of the Community and to all Muslims," he replied.

Advice is then the soul of faith. It is obligatory on the Muslim to give his advice first to God and His Messenger, expressed in obeying them and abiding by their orders. Secondly, to the leaders of the Community, to emphasize his loyalty out of his duty to help them and bless their efforts. Thirdly, to the faithful out of his concern for their interests, care for their affairs and truthful desire in exhausting all means of serving them.

Thus, according to the holy traditions, there are three pillars on which the Muslim Nation is built:

1. The Shariah that governs people, regulates society's movement and is, in itself, the decisive word that settles all affairs.
2. The rulers who shoulder the responsibility of implementing the Shariah, do their utmost to secure the interests of the people, and serve the Ummah.
3. The believers who represent the whole Muslim Nation, the faithful party who are addressed by divine words.

Throughout Islamic history, Muslim communities progressed as long as these three pillars were in harmony. The power of the Shariah was extended and implemented as rulers did their duties and complied with God's orders. The whole Ummah were completely aware of their responsibilities and were forthcoming. But when these three pillars were shaken, the lives of all Muslims were thrown into chaos.

If the Holy Shariah had made it compulsory on rulers to advise their people, it had made it similarly obligatory on wise and fair-minded believers to advise their leaders as well. We are from this section of the faithful. If offering advice is an ordained duty observed at any time, it becomes more necessary during critical times of hardships and desperation, like those we are going through today. The momentous and horrid events we are witnessing, that make us stop at crossroads, are banging the doors of the region and the world violently and relentlessly. Out of our obedience by the Shariah, our love for the rulers and fidelity to this country and its citizens, we felt it was our duty to put before you this concise summary of opinions, views and frameworks, with the aim of solidifying the bases of this country, which lead it towards further achievements and keep it abreast of events. We have two prime goals in mind:

1. A full implementation of the blessed Shariah, as it has been the Kingdom's policy right down from its formation, for the purpose of fulfilling the sublime ob-

jectives of the Shariah, including establishing justice, achieving equality, carrying out reforms and restoring peoples' rights. That would make our society a noble image of the modern Islamic state and an example followed by others in implementing Islam.

2. Retaining the present rule and keeping the noble Royal family, the symbol of loyalty, the axis of unity and the just rule that serves the country and Ummah. It is the rule that keeps the interests of the country and Ummah above differences as well as criticisms, and prevents them from being a means of abandoning laws or ignoring them.

Accordingly, we propose the following:

First. Setting up an organized framework for the religious fatwa [decree], taking into consideration the Holy Shariah—that is never erroneous or immune from being changed—expressed in the texts from the Book as well as the Sunnah. Apart from these texts, we believe that all the fiqh [jurisprudence] presented by the Fuqaha [Islamic legal scholars], the religious schools of thought, the commentaries of Quranic exegetes and the fatwas of the jurisprudent, are only human attempts at grasping the full meaning of the religious texts, likely to be affected by the grade of human power of understanding and the concerned people's knowledge. Usul al-Fiqh is also influenced by the times and surroundings. In other words, such interpretations are likely to be either flawless, or erroneous, and subject to lengthy discussions. That is why scholars unanimously agree that no one, no matter how high his status is, can monopolize the explanation of the true meaning of the words of God and His Messenger, nor can he impose his religious views as binding on the whole Ummah.

In our life, it is decisively necessary to draw a distinction between Divine Law, that is infallible and binding, and the views put forth by the ulama that must be seriously examined beforehand. They are subject to boundless discussions. We must adopt the opinions of the ulama and that of the prominent religious men, be they in the past or present, that may make our country the true image of the modern Islamic state and a good example adopted by other Muslims.

Second: Viewing the conditions of the main system of rule, and in light of the statements and addresses given by officials on various occasions, we call for:

Third: The immediate setting up of a consultative assembly comprising a group of competent, learned and fair-minded people, known to be honest and impartial, well-bred and hardworking, who perform in the interests of the country, and hail from different parts of the Kingdom. One of the assembly's duties is to study, develop and approve the laws and regulations related to all economic, political, educational and other matters, as well as keep watch on the workings and duties of the executive.

Fourth: Reviving the municipal councils, implementing the system of provinces and opening trade chambers in the provinces.

Fifth: Examining the judiciary at all levels and powers, to modernize its working methods, re-examining the system of forming judges and their assistants, and taking all measures to secure their independence. These are necessary so that justice may be served in an effective way, and the judiciary power be solidified. Judicial institutions should open their doors to all citizens, without bias toward a certain section of the population, on the basis of granting equal chances to all. That is what the Shariah calls for.

Sixth: Establishing total equality between all citizens, in all domains, without discrimination against any group due to race, lineage, sect or social status, and implementing the principle of noninterference in any citizen's affairs without lawful and religious justification.

Seventh: Re-examining the media on the basis of a comprehensive and precise criterion that reflects the most modern technology and planning available in the world. The Saudi media is free to exercise its freedom in enjoining good and forbidding evil and enriching free discussions in an open society.

Eighth: Affecting a comprehensive reform of the *Bodies of Enjoining Good and Forbidding Evil* and laying down an exact system for their assignments, a religious framework for their duties, and stern standard with respect to the process of choosing their members and directors in a way that stresses the method of calling to Islam with wisdom and goodly exhortation, as well as achieving the outlined goals set for this important and sensitive apparatus.

Ninth: Notwithstanding our belief that caring for the new generations is the most sacred duty of the Muslim woman, we believe that there are various scopes for her participation in social activities. These spheres can be opened to the noble women within the limits of the Shariah, as a token acknowledging their role in building society and as a way of honoring them.

Tenth: All divine books and God's messengers had come to teach and nurture human beings. This fact emphasizes the great importance of teaching as an indispensable ground for the revival of the people and the progress of nations. We hold the opinion that teaching in our country is in need of deep and all-out reforms to prepare faithful, committed generations that can positively and effectively take part in building the present and future of the country, face contemporary challenges, and foster the Ummah to catch up with other nations that are quite ahead of us in every sphere.

These are broad lines that need detailed examination. You undoubtedly look at these demands as being pressing, exactly as we do, and take them into consideration, as we do. We made a covenant with God that we only tell you the truth and open our hearts to you as God had ordered us, and as a sign of our love and loyalty to you. We believe that the Arab and Islamic World and the whole World are entering a new era in which much of the old concepts have given way to new ones, where conditions changed and the equations of forces altered. This fact makes it necessary for us to review some of our affairs without bias, re-study the whole of our conditions actively and honestly, so that we are able to weather what events the future will bring and what troubles it may cause us.

It is worth mentioning that the signatories are the elite of your subjects, your brothers, and sons. You know very well that they are neither ill-meaning or spiteful, nor are they in pursuit of private interests or whims. Their sole motivation is, InshAllah, to seek the good and right, and their goal is to secure the highest interests of the country. Their first and foremost objective is the preservation of this great entity, the continuation of its stability, security and safety.

Certainly God alone can grant us success.

Signatories:

1. Ahmad Salah Jamjoon
2. Muhammad Abduh Yamani
3. Abdul Maqsud Khujah
4. Muhammad Salahuddin
5. Dr. Rashid al-Mubarak
6. Ahmad Muhammad Jamal
7. Salih Muhammad Jamal

8.   Abdallah al-Dabbagh
9.   Muhammad Hassan Faqi
10. Dr. Abdallah Manna'
11. Muhammad Said Tayyib
12. Muhammad Ali Said al-'Audi
13. Abdallah bin Abdul Rahman Al-Ibrahim
14. Dr. Abdul Rahman al-Mari'i
15. Yusuf Muhammad al-Mubarak
16. Dr. Marzuq bin Manitan
17. Dr. Ibrahim bin Abdul Rahman al-Mudaybigh
18. Adil Jamal
19. Fahd Ali al-Urayfi
20. Salih Abdul Rahman al-Ali
21. Abdallah Hamad al-Sabkhan
22. Salih Abdallah al-Ashqar
23. Aql Rajih al-Bahili
24. Dr. Ahmad Mahdi al-Shuwaykhat
25. Ali Jawad al-Khurs
26. Isa Fahd
27. Dr. Saad al-Abdallah al-Soyan
28. Dr. Abdul Khaliq Abdallah Aal Abdul-Hay
29. Abdul Karim Hamad al-Odah
30. Abdallah Yusuf al-Kuwaylit
31. Hamad Ibrahim al-Bahili
32. Abdul Jabbar Abdul Karim al-Yahyah
33. Ibrahim al-Hamdan
34. Ishaq al-Shaykh Ya'qub
35. Muhammad Obaid al-Harbi
36. Shakir Abdallah al-Shaykh
37. Abdul Ra'uf al-Ghazal
38. Ali al-Dumayni
39. Muhammad al-Ali
40. Abdul Rahman Abdul Aziz al-Husayn
41. Ibrahim Fahid al-Aql
42. Jam'an Abdallah al-Waqidi
43. Abdallah Bukhayt al-Abdul Aziz

Source: "A Memorandum to the King," translated from the original Arabic, in author's hands. According to *Middle East Watch,* this so-called secular petition, believed to have been first written in October 1990 and presented to the monarch in December of that same year, was written by Dr. Abdallah Manna', a physician and writer known for voicing critical views of the government.

Appendix 12 ⌒

"Religious" Petition to King Fahd (February 1991)

In the Name of God, the Merciful, the Compassionate.

To the Custodian of the Two Holy Mosques: May God help you. May the peace and blessings of God be upon you.

This state has distinguished itself by announcing its adherence to Islamic Shariah, and the ulama and those capable of offering guidance have always fulfilled their divine obligation in offering sound advice to those in power. We therefore find that the most pressing task, at this critical juncture and at a time when all have realized the necessity of change, is to direct our energies to reforming the situation which put us in our present predicament. For this reason, we request the ruler to look into the matters which need to be addressed by reform in the following areas:

1. The establishment of a consultative council to decide on internal and external affairs. The members of this body should be selected so as to include individuals of diverse specialization, and who must be known for their sincerity and upright conduct. The council must be fully independent and free from any pressures that could affect the discharging of its full responsibilities.

2. Examining all political, economic and administrative laws and regulations to ascertain their conformity to Shariah. This task should be conducted by fully mandated, competent and trustworthy Shariah committees. All laws not conforming to the Shariah should then be abrogated.

3. Ensuring that all state officials and their representatives internally and abroad must be competent and suitably specialized. They must also be dedicated, upright and honest. Failure to fulfill any of these requirements must be deemed as betrayal of trust and a major threat to the country's interest and its reputation.

4. Granting justice and equality for all members of society to safeguard full rights and exacting duties without any favoritism to the privileged or condescension towards the disadvantaged. It should also be realized that taking advantage of one's influence to shirk one's duties or usurp the rights of others could cause the disintegration of society and lead to the dire fate against which the Prophet (peace be upon him) had warned.

5. Establishing justice in distributing the public wealth among all classes and factions of society. Taxes must be abolished and government fees must be decreased

as they have overburdened people. The financial assets of the state must be safeguarded against waste and exploitation, and priority must be given to the dire needs of the country. All forms of monopoly and illegitimate types of ownership must be removed. The ban on Islamic banks must be lifted, and all public and private financial institutions must be cleaned of usury (interest), which is an assault against God and His Messenger and a reason for the vanishing of God's bounties and blessings.

6. Building strong and integrated armed forces fully equipped from diverse sources. Special attention should be paid to the development of military industries. The aim of the army should be to protect the country and its sacred values.

7. Reconstructing the media to bring them in line with the Kingdom's policy of serving Islam. The media should reflect the values of society and enhance and advance its culture, and they must be purified from all that contradicts the above goals. Freedom of the media to educate and inform, through the propagation of true stories and constructive criticism, must be safeguarded in accordance with legitimate safeguards.

8. Directing foreign policy to safeguard the interests of the nation, away from illegitimate alliances. The state must champion Muslim causes, while the status of our embassies abroad must be rectified to reflect the Islamic character of this country.

9. The development of religious and missionary institutions in this country, and providing them with all the necessary human and material resources. All obstacles preventing them from fulfilling their tasks properly must be removed.

10. Unifying judicial organs, according them full and real independence, and ensuring that the authority of the judiciary extends to all. An independent body must be set up to follow the implementation of all judicial decisions.

11. Safeguarding the individual and collective rights, and lifting all traces of pressures against the will and rights of people in a way that preserves human dignity and that accords with the acceptable legal rules and regulations.

Signatories [partial list]

1. Shaykh Abdul Aziz bin Baz
2. Shaykh Muhammad bin Salih al-Uthaymin
3. Shaykh Hamudah bin Abdallah al-Tuwayjiri
4. Shaykh Abdallah bin Jibrin
5. Shaykh Abdul Muhsin al-Ubaykan
6. Shaykh Safar al-Hawali
7. Shaykh Said al-Qahtani
8. Shaykh Salman al-Audah
9. Shaykh Abdallah al-Jalali
10. Shaykh Muhammad al-Shihah
11. Dr. Ahmad al-Tuwayjiri
12. Dr. Tawfiq al-Qaseer
13. Shaykh Said bin Zuayr

Note and Sources: Known as the Shawwal Document, or more commonly, the Letter of Demands (sometimes also referred to as the Letter of the Ulama), this petition was probably written in February 1991, although various sources give an April 1991 date as well. This so-called religious petition may well have been a response to the December 1990 "secular" petition or, as claimed by opposition groups, was in the making long before the latter surfaced. See Saad al-Faqih, *The Rise and Evolution of the Modern Islamic Reform Movement in Saudi Arabia,* London: The Movement for Islamic Reform in Arabia (MIRA), 1996? (on-line at http://www.miraserve.com/HistoryOfDissent.htm). MIRA maintains that an estimated 400 individuals signed this petition, although it does not reproduce any names. The facsimile copy in my hands reproduces 52 signatures, although most are illegible (the 13 signatures above are the names that are relatively legible). Shaykh Abdul Aziz bin Baz added this phrase: "On the basis of Islamic Law," before giving his support to the demands. Shaykh Muhammad bin Salih al-Uthaymin also gave his support to this memorandum. Together, the support of these two senior religious scholars must have caught King Fahd and other Al Saud officials by surprise. Signatories included religious scholars, judges, university professors, and members of the intelligentsia. Translated from the original Arabic, in author's hands, and adapted to the MIRA text (reproduced as an appendix on the home page edition).

Appendix 13 ❧

King Fahd bin Abdul Aziz
Address to the Nation on the New Laws
March 1, 1992

In the name of God, the merciful, the compassionate. Thanks be to God, the lord of all universe, and prayers and peace be upon the most noble of prophets, our Lord Muhammad, and upon all his family and companions.

Fellow citizens:

If God intended good to come to a people He will guide them to what is most appropriate. God bestowed on us countless bounties, and the greatest favor of all is Islam. If we fully adhere to this religion, we shall never go astray. Rather, we shall be guided and be pleased by it because Almighty God has told us this, as has His Messenger (peace be upon him). The facts of history and reality are the best witness to this.

Muslims have been happy with the Islamic Shariah ever since it came to rule their affairs and daily lives. In modern history, the first Saudi state was established, based on Islam, more than two and a half centuries ago when two pious reformers—Imam Muhammad bin Saud and Shaykh Muhammad bin Abdul Wahhab (may God have mercy on their souls)—committed themselves to it. This state was established on a clear course of politics and government. It was committed to propagating Islam and to fostering a sense of community. This is the course of Islam—the Creed and the Shariah. Ever since the establishment of this righteous State, Saudis have enjoyed happiness, security and unity of opinion. They have been living in harmony and fraternal cooperation, after a prolonged period of fear and division.

The Creed and the Shariah being the basic principles on which this State has risen, the application of these principles has manifested itself in full adherence to the correct Islamic course in the Creed, its doctrine, in the Propagation of Islam (Da'wa), in the enjoining of good and the forbidding of evil, in its judicature and in the relationship between the ruler and the ruled. As such, the Saudi State has become a distinguished model of politics and government in modern political history. The adoption of this course has continued in all subsequent stages as successive rulers have continued to adhere to the Islamic Shariah. And it is that bounty of God that He grants to whom He wishes.

This continuous upholding of the course of Islam is based on three facts:

1. The fact that the basis of the course of Islam is fixed and is not subject to change or alteration. God Almighty said: "Lo! We, even We, reveal the Reminder [Message], and lo! We verily are its Guardian [from corruption]" [XV:9].
2. The fact that upholding the course of Islam should be continuous. God Almighty said: "Warn them (O Muhammad) of the Day of the approaching (doom), when the hearts will be choking the throats, (when) there will be no friend for the wrong-doers, nor any intercessor who will be heard" [XL:18].
3. The fact that the rulers of this State remain loyal to Islam under all circumstances and conditions. Loyalty to Islam, the Creed and the Shariah, continued during the era of King Abdul Aziz (may God have mercy on him). He founded the Kingdom of Saudi Arabia and unified it on the same course, despite difficult historical circumstances and the problems he faced during the process of unifying the country.

In accordance with this course, the Kingdom of Saudi Arabia was founded on the following grounds:

1. The unity of faith that encourages believers to worship God alone, with no partners, and live in dignity and honor.
2. Islamic Shariah that protects life, preserves rights, and regulates the relationship between ruler and ruled, regularizes dealings among members of the community, and safeguards public security.
3. Undertaking the propagation of the faith (Da'wa) because spreading the Islamic call for God is among the most important responsibilities of an Islamic state.
4. The founding of an environment free of evil deeds and deviations that helps believers to act honestly and righteously. This task is achieved by encouraging good and discouraging evil.
5. Achieving the "unity" of faith that is the basis of political, social, and geographic unity.
6. Adopting the means of progress and achieving an "overall awakening" that directs peoples' lives and their livelihood, and looks after their interests in light of Islam's guidance and standards.
7. Achieving "Shura" just as Islam has commanded, and praised whoever undertakes it, since Islam has ranked practicing consultation among the qualities of believers.
8. The two holy mosques shall remain inviolate for visitors and worshippers—as they were intended by God—far away from all that which hinders the performance of the minor and major pilgrimage and worship in the best way. The Kingdom shall carry out this duty in fulfillment of God's right and to serve the Islamic community.
9. To defend the faith and the holy shrines, the homeland, the people, and the State.

These are the grand bases on which the Kingdom of Saudi Arabia has been established.

〜   〜   〜

During the reign of King Abdul Aziz, political systems based on this course emerged, due to the development of modern life. In the year 1373H, in view of the evolution of the State and the expansion of its responsibilities, King Abdul Aziz—may God have mercy on him—issued a decree for the formation of a Council of Ministers. This Council is in operation in accordance with the law issued then and the amendments that followed. This course is still followed to this day, with the grace and guidance of God. Therefore, the Kingdom of Saudi Arabia has never known the so-called "constitutional vacuum." The literal meaning of "constitutional vacuum" is that the State has no guiding principles, or binding frames of reference, in the sphere of legislation and regulations. The Kingdom of Saudi Arabia has never witnessed such a phenomenon in its entire history because it has been ruled according to the guiding principles, the binding rules, and the clear fundamentals to which judges, ulama, and all those employed by the State refer.

All the organs of the State currently function according to laws that stem from Islamic Shariah and are regulated by it. Thus, it is not from a vacuum that we are today enacting the following laws in new forms: the Basic Law of Government, the Law of the Majlis al-Shura, and the Law of the Provinces. These three laws codify existing practices and embody what is already in operation. These statutes are subject to reconsideration and amendments in accordance with what the Kingdom's circumstances and interests require. The three laws were formed on the basis of the Islamic Shariah, reflecting our genuine traditions, righteous values and cherished customs.

∼　∼　∼

Compatriots:

The source of the Basic Law of Government as well as its foundation is the Islamic Shariah. This law has been guided by the Islamic Shariah in defining the nature, objectives, and responsibilities of the State, as it has been in defining the relationship between ruler and ruled on the basis of brotherhood, consultation, friendship and cooperation.

The relationship between citizens and state officials is founded on solid and deep-rooted traditions, compassion, mutual respect and loyalty stemming from the sincere and firm convictions in the hearts of this country's people, generation after generation. There is no difference between the ruler and the ruled. They are equal before God, and they are all equal in their love of this homeland and in their eagerness to preserve its safety, unity, pride and progress. Whoever is in charge has obligations as well as rights. The relationship between the ruler and the ruled is first and foremost governed by the Shariah of God as it has come to us in His Holy Book and in the traditions of His Messenger (peace be upon Him). The Basic Law of Government has been inspired by these sources. It has sought to apply them fully in the relationship between the ruler and the ruled, in compliance with all that has been revealed through our true religion in this respect.

As for the Majlis al-Shura Law, it is based on Islam both in name and content, in response to God's words, "Those who respond to their Lord, and establish regular prayer, who (conduct) their affairs by mutual consultation; who spend out of what we bestow on them for sustenance" [XL:38]. "It is part of the mercy of God that thou dost deal gently with them. Wert thou severe or harsh-hearted, they would have broken away from about thee: so pass over (their faults) and ask for (God's) forgiveness for them; and consult them in affairs (of moment). Then, when thou hast taken a decision, put thy trust in God. For God loves those who put their trust (in Him)" [III:159].

∼　∼　∼

We have already mentioned on several occasions that the country witnessed the establishment of Majlis al-Shura long ago. Throughout this period, Shura (consultation) activities continued in many and various ways. The rulers of the Kingdom maintained consultations in times of need with ulama and advisers.

The new Law of the Majlis al-Shura provides for the modernization and development of an existing system through the consolidation of the Majlis' framework. It also provides vehicles for more efficiency, better organization and vitality in order to achieve the desired objectives. The capable members of this Majlis will be carefully chosen so as to contribute to the development of the Kingdom of Saudi Arabia and its progress, taking into consideration the public interest of the Homeland and its citizens. While the Majlis al-Shura undertakes, God willing, general consultation at the level of the State, we ought not to ignore the consultations currently practiced within the State's organs through specialized councils and committees. These structures ought to remain active so that their work will complement that of the Majlis al-Shura.

The country has recently witnessed tremendous developments in various fields. These developments have called for a renewal of the general administrative system in the country. To meet this need and interest, the Law of the Provinces has come to allow for more organized action through appropriate administrative measures, and to upgrade the level of administration in the provinces of the Kingdom.

ﻢ   ﻢ   ﻢ

O Compatriots:

These laws have been drawn up after a meticulous and patient study carried out by a select group of learned men of sound knowledge and experience. Full consideration was given to the Kingdom's distinguished position in the Islamic world, and to its traditions and customs, as well as its social and cultural conditions. Therefore, these laws have sprung from our realities, taking into account our traditions and customs, while adhering to our true religion. We are confident that these laws will, with the help of God, assist the State in realizing every Saudi citizen's hopes for the welfare and progress of his homeland and his Arab and Islamic nation. The Saudi citizen is the base for the advancement and development of this homeland, and we shall not spare any effort to ensure his happiness and well-being.

The world, that is following the development and progress of this country, greatly admires its domestic policy, which safeguards the citizen's security and well-being. It also admires this country's foreign policy, that seeks to establish relations with other countries, and contribute to world peace.

The Kingdom of Saudi Arabia is the sanctuary of the Muslim Shrines and a site for the Hajj, the Umrah and the visit to the Prophet's Mosque. It has a special place in the hearts of all Muslims. God has honored this State with the custody of the Two Holy Mosques, to facilitate the performance of the pilgrimages and the visit to the Mosque of the Prophet (peace be upon Him). We have done our utmost to expand the Two Holy Mosques and develop the other holy sites. The State offers full assistance to all guests bound for the Holy Places. We thank God and ask Him to continue granting us more grace to go on serving these places and all Muslims wherever they may be.

The Kingdom of Saudi Arabia has adhered constantly to the Islamic course in government, in judicature, in the Propagation of Islam (Da'wa), in education, in enjoining good and forbidding evil, as well as in the performance of God's rites. The rulers and state officials have adhered to that course. The people, too, have adhered to it in their daily lives.

〜   〜   〜

Islam is a way of life. There can be no neglecting what has been included in God's Book (The Holy Quran), what has been authenticated of the Prophet's traditions, or what Muslims have unanimously agreed on. Our constitution in the Kingdom is the Book of God, that is infallible, and the Traditions (Sunnah) of His Messenger, who does not speak irresponsibly. Whatever we disagree on we refer back to them. They both are arbiters on all laws issued by the State.

Rulers and ulama in the Kingdom of Saudi Arabia have cooperated, and are still cooperating and helping each other. Similarly, the people have been, and still are, supportive of, cooperative with, and obedient to their leadership according to the legal pledge of allegiance (*bay'ah*) rendered by the ruled to the rulers.

The ruler fulfills his obligations with regard to the implementation of the Shariah, the establishment of justice among the people and the defense of legitimate individual rights. The society, therefore, enjoys security, stability and prosperity.

In the past and present, the Kingdom has been and is committed to the Shariah and to implementing it vigorously and firmly in all its domestic and foreign affairs. With the help of God, it will remain keenly committed to the Shariah.

With the help of Almighty God, we hold firm to Islam and advise each other, generation after generation, ruler after ruler. As promised by God, there can be no harm done to us by those who oppose us. We do not close the door on any aspect of modernization, so long as it does not conflict with our Islamic heritage and identity.

The Kingdom of Saudi Arabia is an Arab, Islamic, State. All matters that concern Arabs and Muslims will be its concerns. The State promotes their solidarity and their unity of opinion and contributes, with all its capabilities, to their welfare. Past events and circumstances have indeed witnessed the truth of its stances and the fulfillment of its commitments towards the Arab nation and the Islamic nation as well as towards other international obligations.

〜   〜   〜

Compatriots:

With the help of God, we will continue upon our Islamic course, cooperating with those who want good for Islam and Muslims, and is determined to consolidate and disseminate the religion of God and to ensure progress for this country and happiness for its people. We ask Almighty God to bestow on our people and on the Arab nation and the Islamic nation goodness, righteousness, progress, prosperity and welfare. Praise be to God, by whose grace all righteous deeds are done.

Fahd bin Abdul Aziz
Custodian of the Two Holy Mosques

Source: Kingdom of Saudi Arabia, Majlis al-Shura, *The Basic Law of Government*, Riyadh: n.d. (translated and adapted from the Arabic), pp. 6–14.

Appendix 14 ⌒

The Basic Law of Government

Royal Decree Number A/90
Dated 27 Shaaban 1412H/1 March 1992

In the name of God, the merciful, the compassionate.

With the help of God, we, Fahd bin Abdul Aziz Al Saud, Monarch of the Kingdom of Saudi Arabia, having taken into consideration the public interest, and in view of the progress of the State in various fields and out of the desire to achieve the objectives we are pursuing, have decreed the following:

1. The promulgation of the Basic Law of Government as the attached text;
2. That all regulations, orders and decrees in force shall remain valid when this Basic Law comes into force, until they are amended to conform with it;
3. That this decree shall be published in the Official Gazette, and shall come into force on the date of its publication.

Fahd bin Abdul Aziz Al Saud
Custodian of the Two Holy Mosques

The Basic Law of Government

Chapter One: General Principles

Article 1
The Kingdom of Saudi Arabia is a sovereign Arab Muslim State. Its religion is Islam. Its constitution is Almighty God's Book, the Holy Quran and the Sunnah (Tradition) of the Prophet (Peace be upon Him). Arabic is the language of the Kingdom. The city of Riyadh is the capital.

Article 2
The State's public holidays are 'Id al-Fitr [the Feast of Ramadan] and 'Id al-Adha [The Feast of the Sacrifice]. Its calendar follows the Hijri [lunar] year.

Article 3
The flag of the State is as follows:

    a. Its color is green.
    b. Its width equals two thirds of its length.
    c. The words "There is no God but God and Muhammad is His Messenger" are inscribed in the center with a drawn sword underneath. The flag should never be inverted.

The Law will specify the rules pertaining to the flag.

Article 4
The State's emblem represents two crossed swords with a palm tree in the middle of the upper space between them. The Law will define the State's anthem and its medals.

Chapter Two: The Law of Government

Article 5
    a. Monarchy is the system of rule in the Kingdom of Saudi Arabia.
    b. Rulers of the country shall be from amongst the sons of the founder, King Abdul Aziz bin Abdul Rahman al-Faysal Al Saud, and their descendants. The most upright among them shall receive allegiance according to the Holy Quran and the Sunnah of the Prophet (Peace be upon Him).
    c. The King shall choose the Heir Apparent and relieve him by a Royal Decree.
    d. The Heir Apparent shall devote himself exclusively to his duties as Heir Apparent and shall perform any other duties delegated to him by the King.
    e. Upon the death of the King, the Heir Apparent shall assume all Royal powers until a pledge of allegiance [bay'ah] is given.

Article 6
In support of the Holy Quran and the Sunnah of His Messenger (Peace be upon Him), citizens shall give the pledge of allegiance [bay'ah] to the King, professing loyalty in times of hardship as well as ease.

Article 7
The Government of the Kingdom of Saudi Arabia derives its authority from the Holy Quran and the Sunnah of the Prophet (Peace be upon Him), which are the ultimate sources of reference for this Law and the other laws of the State.

Article 8
The Government of the Kingdom of Saudi Arabia is based on justice, Shura [consultation], and equality according to Islamic Shariah.

Chapter Three: The Values of Saudi Society

Article 9
The family is the nucleus of Saudi society. Members of the family shall be raised in the Islamic Creed, that demands allegiance and obedience to God, to His Prophet (Peace be

upon Him), and to the rulers; respect for and obedience to the laws; and love for, as well as pride in, the Homeland and its glorious history.

Article 10
The State shall aspire to promote family bonds and Arab/Islamic values. It shall take care of all individuals and provide the right conditions for the growth of their talents and skills.

Article 11
Saudi society is based on full adherence to divine guidance. Members of this society shall cooperate amongst themselves in charity, piety, and cohesion.

Article 12
The consolidation of national unity is a duty. The State shall forbid all activities that may lead to disunity, sedition, and partition.

Article 13
The aim of education is to instill the Islamic Creed in the hearts of the young generation, to help them acquire knowledge and skills, to prepare them to become useful members in their society, to love their homeland and take pride of its history.

Chapter Four: Economic Principles

Article 14
All natural resources that God has deposited underground, on the surface, or in national territorial waters, or within the land and maritime domains under the authority of the State, together with revenues of these resources, shall be the property of the State, as provided by the Law. The law shall specify means for the exploitation, protection and development of these resources in the best interests of the State, its security and economy.

Article 15
No concessions or licenses to exploit any public resources of the country shall be granted unless authorized by provisions of the Law.

Article 16
Public funds are sacrosanct. They shall be protected by the State and safeguarded by all citizens and residents.

Article 17
Ownership, capital and labor are basic components of the economic and social entities of the Kingdom. They are personal rights which perform a social function in accordance with Islamic Shariah.

Article 18
The State shall guarantee private ownership and its sanctity. No one shall be deprived of his private property, except when this serves the public interest, in which case a fair compensation is due.

Article 19
General confiscation of assets is prohibited. No confiscation of an individual's assets shall be enforced without a judicial ruling.

Article 20
No taxes or fees shall be imposed, except in need, and on a just basis. Imposition, amendment, cancellation or exemption shall take place according to the provisions of the Law.

Article 21
Tithes [*Zakat*] shall be collected and dispersed for legitimate expenses.

Article 22
Economic and social developments shall be carried out according to a just and scientific plan.

Chapter Five: Rights and Duties

Article 23
The State shall protect the Islamic Creed, apply the Shariah, encourage good and discourage evil, and undertake its duty regarding the Propagation of Islam (Da'wa).

Article 24
The State shall develop and maintain the Two Holy Mosques. It shall provide care and security to pilgrims to help them perform their Hajj and Umrah [pilgrimage] and visit the Prophet's Mosque in ease and comfort.

Article 25
The State shall nourish the aspirations of the Arab and Muslim nations, in solidarity and harmony, and strengthen relations with friendly states.

Article 26
The State shall protect human rights in accordance with the Shariah.

Article 27
The State shall guarantee the rights of citizens and their families in cases of emergency, illness, disability, and old age. The State shall support the Social Insurance Law and encourage organizations and individuals to participate in philanthropic activities.

Article 28
The State shall facilitate job opportunities for every able person, and enact laws to protect both employees and employers.

Article 29
The State shall patronize the sciences, letters and the arts. It shall encourage scientific research, protect the Islamic and Arab heritage, and contribute towards Arab, Islamic and human civilization.

Article 30
The State shall provide public education and commit itself to the eradication of illiteracy.

Article 31
The State shall promote public health and provide medical care to all citizens.

Article 32
The State shall work towards the preservation, protection and improvement of the environment, as well as prevent pollution.

Article 33
The State shall form the armed forces and equip them to defend the Islamic Creed, the Two Holy Mosques, society and the homeland.

Article 34
It shall be the duty of every citizen to defend the Islamic Creed, society and the homeland. The Law shall specify rules for military service.

Article 35
The Law shall specify rules pertaining to the Saudi nationality.

Article 36
The State shall provide security for all citizens and residents alike. No one may be confined, arrested or imprisoned without reference to the Law.

Article 37
Dwellings are inviolable. Access is prohibited without their owners' permission. No search may be carried out except in cases specified by the Law.

Article 38
No one shall be punished for another's crimes. No conviction or penalty shall be inflicted without reference to the Shariah or the provisions of the Law. Punishment shall not be imposed ex post facto.

Article 39
Mass media and all other vehicles of expression shall employ civil and polite language, contribute towards the education of the nation and strengthen unity. It is prohibited to commit acts leading to disorder and division, affecting the security of the State and its public relations, or undermining human dignity and rights. Details shall be specified in the Law.

Article 40
The privacy of telegraphic, postal, telephone and other means of communication shall be inviolable. There shall be no confiscation, delay, surveillance or eavesdropping, except in cases provided for by the Law.

Article 41
Foreign residents in the Kingdom of Saudi Arabia shall abide by its laws, observe the values of the Saudi community, and respect Saudi traditions, values and feelings.

Article 42
The State shall grant the right of political asylum provided it is in the public interest. International agreements and laws shall define the rules and procedures for the extradition of common criminals.

Article 43
Councils held by the King and the Heir Apparent shall be open to all citizens and to anyone else who may have a complaint or a grievance. A citizen shall be entitled to address public authorities and discuss matters of concern to him.

Chapter Six: The Authority of the State

Article 44
The authority of the State shall consist of:

   a. Judicial Authority;
   b. Executive Authority; and
   c. Organizational Authority.

Officials shall cooperate in performing their duties according to this Law and other regulations. The King is the ultimate arbiter of these authorities.

Article 45
The Holy Quran and the Sunnah of the Prophet (Peace be upon Him) shall be the sources for fatwas [religious advisory rulings] in the Kingdom of Saudi Arabia. The law shall specify hierarchical organizations for the composition of the Council of Senior Ulama, the Research Administration of Religious Affairs, and the Office of the Mufti, together with their jurisdictions.

Article 46
The judiciary is an independent authority. In discharging their duties, judges bow to no authority, other than that of Islamic Shariah.

Article 47
Both citizens and foreign residents have an equal right to litigation. The necessary procedures are set forth by the Law.

Article 48
Courts shall apply the provisions of Islamic Shariah to cases brought before them, according to the Holy Quran and the Sunnah of the Prophet (Peace be upon Him), as well as other regulations issued by the Head of State in strict conformity with the Holy Quran and the Sunnah of the Prophet (Peace be upon Him).

Article 49
Subject to the provisions of Article 53 of this law, the courts shall have jurisdiction to deal with all disputes and crimes.

Article 50
The King, or whosoever he may deputize, shall be concerned with the implementation of judicial rulings.

Article 51
The law shall specify the composition of the Supreme Judiciary Council and its functions, as well as the organization and jurisdiction of all courts.

Article 52
Judges shall be appointed and relieved by Royal Decree, based on a proposal by the Supreme Judiciary Council, in accordance with provisions of the Law.

Article 53
The Law shall specify the hierarchy of the Board of Grievances and its functions.

Article 54
The law shall specify the relation between the Commission of Inquiry and the General Prosecutor, and their organizations and prerogatives.

Article 55
The King shall rule the nation according to the Shariah. He shall also supervise the implementation of the Shariah, the State's general policy, as well as the protection and defense of the country.

Article 56
The King shall be the Prime Minister and shall be assisted in the performance of his duties by members of the Council of Ministers according to the rulings of this Law and other laws. The Council of Ministers Law shall specify the powers of the Council with regard to internal and external affairs, organizing government bodies and coordinating their activities. Likewise the Law shall specify the conditions that the Ministers must satisfy, their eligibility, the method of their accountability along with all other matters related to them. The Law of the Council of Ministers may be amended according to this Law.

Article 57
  a. The King shall appoint the Deputy Prime Minister and Cabinet Ministers and may relieve them of their duties by a Royal Decree.
  b. The Deputy Prime Minister and Cabinet Ministers shall be jointly responsible before the King for the implementation of Islamic Shariah, the laws and the State's general policy.
  c. The King shall have the right to dissolve and reconstitute the Council of Ministers.

Article 58
The King shall appoint ministers, deputy ministers and other senior officials, and may dismiss them by a Royal Decree in accordance with the rules of the Law. Ministers and heads of independent authorities shall be responsible before the Prime Minister for their ministries and authorities.

Article 59
The law shall prescribe the provisions pertaining to civil service, including salaries, bonuses, compensation, privileges and retirement pensions.

Article 60
The King shall be the Supreme Commander of the armed forces, and shall appoint military officers, as well as terminate their services in accordance with the Law.

Article 61
The King shall have the right to declare a state of emergency, a general mobilization, and war. The Law shall specify rules for this purpose.

Article 62
If danger threatens the safety of the Kingdom, the integrity of its territory, the security of its people and their interests, or impedes the performance of State institutions, the King shall take all necessary and speedy steps to confront such a danger. If the King concludes that these measures may better be permanent, he then shall take whatever legal actions he deems necessary in this regard in accordance with the Law.

Article 63
The King shall receive Kings and Heads of States, appoint his representatives to other countries, and accept accreditation of the representatives of other countries to the Kingdom.

Article 64
The King shall award medals according to provisions of the Law.

Article 65
The King may delegate parts of his authority to the Heir Apparent by a Royal Decree.

Article 66
In the event of his traveling abroad, the King shall issue a Royal Decree deputizing the Heir Apparent to run the affairs of the State, and protect the interests of the people as stated in the Royal Decree.

Article 67
Acting within its terms of reference, the "Regulatory Authority" shall draw up regulations and bylaws to safeguard the public interest, and eliminate corruption in the affairs of the State, in accordance with the rulings of Islamic Shariah. It shall exercise its authority in compliance with this Law and the two other laws of the Council of Ministers and the Majlis al-Shura [Consultative Council].

Article 68
The Majlis al-Shura shall be established. Its law shall determine the structure of its formation, the method by which it exercises its special powers, and the selection of its members. The King shall have the right to dissolve and reconstitute the Majlis al-Shura.

Article 69

The King may summon the Council of Ministers and Majlis al-Shura to hold a joint session to which he may invite whomsoever he wishes for a discussion of whatsoever issues he may wish to raise.

Article 70

Laws, treaties, international agreements and concessions shall be approved and amended by Royal Decrees.

Article 71

Laws shall be published in the Official Gazette and they shall take effect as from the date of their publication unless another date is stipulated.

Chapter Seven: Financial Affairs

Article 72

a. The Law shall determine the management of State revenues, and the procedures of their delivery to the State Treasury.
b. Revenues shall be accounted for and expended in accordance with the procedures stated in the Law.

Article 73

No commitments for funds from the State Treasury shall be made except in accordance with the provisions of the budget. Should the provisions of the budget not suffice to meet said obligations, a Royal Decree shall be issued for their settlement.

Article 74

State property may not be sold, leased or otherwise disposed of, except in accordance with the Law.

Article 75

The regulations shall define the provisions governing legal tender and banks, as well as standards, measures and weights.

Article 76

The Law shall determine the State's fiscal year. The budget shall be issued by a Royal Decree which shall spell out revenue and expenditure estimates for the year. The budget shall be issued at least one month before the beginning of the fiscal year. If, owing to overpowering reasons, the budget is not issued on time and the new fiscal year has not yet started, the validity of the old budget shall be extended until a new budget has been issued.

Article 77

The competent authority shall prepare the State's final accounts for the expired fiscal year and submit it to the Prime Minister.

Article 78

The budgets and final accounts of corporate authorities shall be subject to the same provisions applied to the State budget and its final accounts.

Chapter Eight: Auditing Authorities

Article 79

All State revenues and expenditures shall be audited to ascertain that they are properly managed. An annual report thereon shall be submitted to the Prime Minister. The Law shall define its terms of reference and accountability.

Article 80

Government institutions shall be audited to ensure proper administrative performance and implementation of laws. Financial and administrative violations shall be investigated and an annual report thereon shall be submitted to the Prime Minister. The Law shall specify the authority to be charged with this task and shall define its accountability and terms of reference.

Chapter Nine: General Provisions

Article 81

The implementation of this Law shall not violate the treaties and agreements the Kingdom has signed with other countries or with international organizations and institutions.

Article 82

Without prejudice to the provisions of Article 7 of this Law, none of the provisions of this Law shall, in any way, be obstructed unless it is a temporary measure taken during the time of war or in a state of emergency as specified by the Law.

Article 83

No amendments to this law shall be made except in the same manner in which it has been promulgated.

Source: Kingdom of Saudi Arabia, Majlis al-Shura, *The Basic Law of Government,* Riyadh: n.d. (translated and adapted from the Arabic), pp. 15–34.

Appendix 15 ⌒

The Majlis al-Shura Law

Royal Decree Number A/91
Dated 27 Shaaban 1412H/1 March 1992

In the name of God, the merciful, the compassionate.

With the help of God, we, Fahd bin Abdul Aziz Al Saud, Monarch of the Kingdom of Saudi Arabia, in compliance with the words of God, "Consult them on the matter," and His other words, "Their affairs are carried out in consultation among themselves," and following the Sunnah of His Messenger (peace be upon him) who consulted his companions, and after taking cognizance of the previous Shura [Consultative] Council of 1347H, decree the following:

1. The promulgation of the Majlis al-Shura Law in the attached text;
2. That this Law shall replace the Majlis al-Shura Law issued in 1347H and that the affairs of the Council shall be arranged according to Royal Decree;
3. That all laws, orders and resolutions in force at the time of promulgation shall remain valid until they are amended to comply with this Law;
4. That this Law shall come into force within a period not exceeding six months effective from the date of its publication;
5. That this Law shall be published in the Official Gazette.

Fahd bin Abdul Aziz Al Saud
Custodian of the Two Holy Mosques

The Majlis al-Shura Law

Article 1

In compliance with the words of Almighty God:

It was by the mercy of God that thou wast lenient with them (O Muhammad), for if thou hadst been stern and fierce of heart they would have dispersed from round about thee. So pardon them and ask forgiveness for them and consult with them upon the conduct of affairs. And when thou art resolved, then put thy trust in God. Lo! God loveth those who put their trust (in Him) [III: 159];

and in compliance with the words of Almighty God:

> And those who answer the call of their Lord and establish worship, and whose affairs are a matter of counsel, and who spend of what We have bestowed upon them [XLII: 38]

and following the Sunnah of His Messenger (peace be upon him) who consulted his Companions and urged the Nation [*Ummah*] to engage in consultations, the Majlis al-Shura shall be established to exercise all tasks entrusted to it according to this Law, and the Basic Law of Government, while adhering to the Book of God and the Sunnah of His Messenger (peace be upon him), maintaining brotherly ties and cooperating in righteousness and piety.

Article 2

The Majlis al-Shura shall be established in adherence to God's bonds and commitment to the sources of Islamic jurisprudence. All Members of the Majlis shall serve the public interest, preserve the unity of the jamaa [community], the entity of the State, and the interests of the Ummah.

Article 3

The Majlis al-Shura shall consist of a Chairman and sixty members chosen by the King from amongst scholars and men of knowledge and expertise. Their rights, duties and all other affairs shall be defined by Royal Decree.

Article 4

It is stipulated that every member of the Majlis al-Shura shall be:

   a. A Saudi national by birth and descent;
   b. A competent individual of proven integrity;
   c. Not younger than 30 years old.

Article 5

A member of the Majlis al-Shura may submit a request to resign his membership to the Chairman of the Majlis, who in turn shall refer the matter to the King.

Article 6

If a member of the Majlis al-Shura has neglected his duties, an investigation shall be conducted, and, if warranted, he shall be tried according to rules and procedures issued by Royal Decree.

Article 7

If, for any reason, the seat of a Majlis al-Shura member becomes vacant, the King shall name a substitute by Royal Decree.

Article 8

A member of the Majlis al-Shura may not use his membership to serve his own interests.

Article 9

A membership in the Majlis al-Shura may not be combined with any other government post, or with the management of any company, unless the need for such an exception arises and the King deems it necessary.

Article 10

The Chairman of the Majlis al-Shura, his Deputy and a Secretary-General shall be appointed and relieved by Royal Decrees. Their grades, rights and duties, as well as other affairs, shall be defined by Royal Decrees.

Article 11

Prior to the assumption of their duties, the Chairman, members, and the Secretary-General of the Majlis al-Shura shall take the following oath before the King:

> I swear by God Almighty to be loyal to my religion, then to my King and my country; I swear not to divulge any State secrets; to protect its interests and laws; and to perform my duties with sincerity, integrity, loyalty and fairness.

Article 12

The city of Riyadh shall be the headquarters of the Majlis al-Shura. The Majlis may meet in another place inside the Kingdom of Saudi Arabia if the King deems this necessary.

Article 13

A Majlis al-Shura term shall be four Hijira calendar years beginning from the date specified in the Royal Decree establishing it. A new Majlis shall be constituted at least two months before the previous body's term expires. If a term expires before a new Majlis is constituted, the outgoing Majlis shall continue to function until the successor institution is formed. When a new Majlis is established, new members shall account, at least, for one half of the total.

Article 14

The King, or his deputy, shall deliver an annual royal address before the Majlis al-Shura on the State's domestic and foreign policies.

Article 15

The Majlis al-Shura shall express its opinions on the general policies of the State referred to it by the Prime Minister. In particular, it shall have the right to:

a. Discuss and express its opinion of the general economic and social development plan;
b. Study laws, regulations, treaties, international agreements and concessions, and make whatever suggestions it deems appropriate;
c. Interpret laws;
d. Discuss annual reports submitted by various ministries and other government bodies and offer whatever suggestions it deems appropriate.

Article 16

Majlis al-Shura meetings shall not be valid if a quorum of at least two thirds of its members, including the Chairman or he his deputy, are not present. Resolutions shall not be valid unless approved by a majority of Majlis members.

Article 17

Majlis al-Shura resolutions shall be forwarded to the Prime Minister for consideration by the Council of Ministers. If the views of both councils are concordant, the resolutions shall come into force following the King's approval. If the views differ, the King may decide what he deems appropriate.

Article 18

Laws, international treaties, agreements and concessions shall be issued and amended by Royal Decrees, after being reviewed by the Majlis al-Shura.

Article 19

The Majlis al-Shura shall form specialized committees from amongst its members to exercise its various functions. It shall also have the right to form temporary committees to discuss any item on its agenda.

Article 20

Majlis al-Shura committees may, with the Chairman's consent, enlist the assistance of anyone from among nonmembers.

Article 21

The Majlis al-Shura shall have a General Commission composed of the Chairman, his two deputies, and the heads of specialized committees.

Article 22

The Chairman of the Majlis al-Shura shall submit to the Prime Minister a request to summon any government official to attend Majlis meetings, when matters within the area of his jurisdiction are discussed. The official shall have the right to debate but not the right to vote.

Article 23

Any group of ten Majlis al-Shura members may make a motion for the enactment of a new regulation, or the amendment of one already in effect, and present it to the Chairman, who shall forward it to the King.

Article 24

The Chairman of the Majlis al-Shura shall submit a request to the Prime Minister for access to governmental documents and statements deemed necessary by the Majlis to facilitate its tasks.

Article 25

The Chairman of the Majlis al-Shura shall submit an annual report to the King detailing the activities carried out by the Majlis in accordance with its bylaws.

Article 26

Civil service regulations shall apply to the personnel of the Majlis al-Shura, unless its bylaws stipulate otherwise.

Article 27

The Majlis al-Shura shall have a special budget approved by the King, and dispensed in accordance with rules issued by Royal Decree.

Article 28

Majlis al-Shura financial matters, auditing and closing accounts shall be organized in accordance with special rules issued by Royal Decree.

Article 29

Majlis al-Shura bylaws shall define the prerogatives of the Chairman, his deputy, the Secretary-General, and defines the Majlis Secretariat, the methods of holding its sessions, the management of its activities, the work of its committees and its voting methods. Likewise it organizes the rules of debate, rejoinder and other matters that could enhance order and discipline, and enable it to perform its duties in a manner that is beneficial to the Kingdom of Saudi Arabia and the probity of its people. The bylaws shall be issued by Royal Decree.

Article 30

This law shall be amended in the same manner in which it was promulgated.

The Rights and Duties of Majlis al-Shura Members

Article 1

Membership in the Majlis al-Shura shall take effect from the beginning of a term, specified in the order for its formation, according to Article 13 of the Law of the Majlis. A substitute member's term shall commence from the date specified in the Royal Decree nominating him and shall expire at the end of the Council's term. If the Council term ends prior to the formation of the new Majlis, the membership shall continue until the creation of a new Council, except if specifically terminated.

Article 2

A Majlis al-Shura shall receive a monthly remuneration of SR 20,000 (twenty thousand Saudi Riyals) while in office. The member shall be treated in accordance with the rules governing government officials of Grade 15 for his compensations, benefits and other privileges, all of which shall not affect any pensions to which the member may be entitled.

Article 3

A full-time member shall retain the position and grade he held before joining the Majlis al-Shura. His term of office in the Majlis shall be taken into consideration with respect to merit increases, promotions and retirement benefits, to which he is entitled. A member shall pay, during his membership term, his pension premiums imposed on the salary of his original employment.

A member shall not receive both the allowance and benefits assigned to members of the Majlis al-Shura and the salary and benefits from his original post simultaneously.

A member shall not receive both the Majlis al-Shura remuneration and the salary from his original post simultaneously.

In case a member's salary from his original post exceeds his remuneration in the Majlis al-Shura, the Council shall pay the member the difference. If the post he was holding entitled him to greater benefits than the benefits assigned to the membership, he shall continue to receive the former.

Article 4

As an exception to Article 2 hereof, the member of the Majlis al-Shura shall be entitled to a 45-day annual leave. The Chairman of the Majlis al-Shura shall determine its timing to ensure that leaves do not affect the quorum needed for Majlis meetings.

Article 5

A Majlis al-Shura member shall be completely impartial and objective in all his functions at the Majlis. He shall not raise any matter before the Majlis that may serve a private interest or that may conflict with the public's interest.

Article 6

A Majlis al-Shura member shall regularly attend the meetings of the Majlis and its committees. He shall notify the Chairmen of both the Majlis and the committee, in writing, of any forced absences. Members shall not leave Majlis al-Shura or committee meetings prior to their adjournment, except with the consent of the Chairmen.

Terms of Reference for the Chairman, Vice Chairman and Secretary-General

Article 1

The Chairman shall supervise the entire activities of the Majlis, represent it in its relations with other authorities and act as its spokesman.

Article 2

The Chairman shall chair the Majlis sessions and the meetings of its General Assembly as well as the committee meetings he attends.

Article 3

The Chairman shall declare the sessions open and closed. He shall manage and participate in debates, give permission to speak, determine the topic of the discussion, draw the speaker's attention to the need to bind himself to the subject and time limits, terminate the discussion and put the subjects to the vote. He shall take whatever action he deems appropriate to keep order during sessions.

Article 4

The Chairman shall call the Majlis al-Shura, or the General Assembly, or any other committee to hold an emergency session to discuss any given matter.

Article 5

The Vice Chairman shall give assistance to the Chairman when he is available, and shall deputize for him in his absence.

Article 6

The Vice Chairman shall chair the Majlis sessions and the meetings of the General Assembly in the absence of the Chairman. If both are absent, the chairmanship shall be taken up by whomever the King may choose. The one thus designated shall enjoy, in respect to sessions management, the same powers vested in the Chairman.

Article 7

The Secretary-General, or whoever may deputize for him, shall attend the sessions of the Majlis and meetings of the General Assembly, supervise the details of the minutes of meetings, notify members of the timetable of sessions and agendas, in addition to any other duties assigned to him by the Majlis, the General Assembly or the Chairman.

He shall answer to the Chairman for the financial and administrative affairs of the Majlis.

Article 8

The General Assembly of the Majlis shall consist of the Chairman, the Vice Chairman and the heads of specialized committees of the Majlis.

Article 9

The meetings of the General Assembly shall not be considered valid unless attended by at least two thirds of its members. Resolutions shall be passed by approval of the majority present, and in case of a tie vote, the Chairman of the meeting shall have the casting vote.

Article 10

For each meeting of the General Assembly, minutes shall be drawn up listing the date and place of the meeting, names of present and absent members, a summary of debates and the texts of recommendations. The minutes shall be signed by the Chairman and the participating members.

Article 11

The General Assembly shall have the following functions:

    a. To draw up a general plan for the Majlis and its committees in order to help it discharge its duties and realize its objectives;
    b. To prepare agendas for Majlis meetings;
    c. To decide on objections to the contents of minutes of the meeting, or balloting results, or separation of votes, or any other objections which may be raised during the meetings. Its decision in this regard shall be final;
    d. To issue the necessary rules needed to organize the activities of the Majlis and its committees in a manner that shall not conflict with the Majlis Law and its by-laws.

Article 12

The Majlis shall hold at least one ordinary session every two weeks. The date and time of the session shall be decided by the Chairman, who shall have the right to advance or set back the time of the session if necessary.

Article 13

The agenda shall be distributed to the members prior to the sessions. Reports and other documents, deemed by the General Assembly to be related to the subjects on the agenda, shall be attached thereto.

Article 14

A member of the Majlis shall study the agenda at the Majlis headquarters. Under no circumstance shall he take away with him outside the Majlis building any papers, laws or documents relating to his work.

Article 15

A member who may wish to speak during the sessions shall put his request in writing. Requests to speak shall be listed in order of submission.

Article 16

The Chairman shall give permission to speak to those who have requested to do so, taking into account the sequence of their requests and their relevance to a fruitful debate.

Article 17

A member may not speak for more than ten minutes on any one subject, except upon permission from the Chairman. A speaker may address himself to no one other than the Chairman. Only the Chairman may interrupt the speaker.

Article 18

The Majlis may decide to postpone the debate or reconsider a subject. The Chairman may suspend the session for a period not exceeding one hour.

Article 19

Each session shall have its own minutes, which make a note of the venue and date of the session, opening and closing times, name of Chairman, number of present and absent members, and the cause of absence, if any. They shall also include a summary of debates, the number of affirmative and negative votes, voting results, text of resolutions, session's adjournment or suspension and any other matters which the Chairman may decide to put on record.

Article 20

The Chairman and the Secretary-General, or whoever may deputize for them, shall sign the minutes after reading them out to the Majlis. All members shall have access to the minutes.

Article 21

The Majlis shall appoint, from among its members, at the start of its term, the specialized committees required for the implementation of its functions.

Article 22

Each specialized committee shall consist of a number of members as specified by the Majlis, provided that such number may not be less than five. The Majlis shall choose these members and nominate the head of the committee and his deputy with due regard to the member's line of specialization and the requirements of the committees. It may set up ad hoc committees from among its members. In turn each committee may set up one ad hoc subcommittee or more from among its members.

Article 23

The Majlis shall have the right to re-form its specialized committees or form new ones.

Article 24

A committee head runs the activity of his own committee and represents it at the Majlis. His deputy takes over in his absence. If both the committee head and his deputy are absent, the eldest member of the committee takes charge.

Article 25

The committee shall meet at the invitation of its head, the Majlis, or the Chairman of the Majlis.

Article 26

Committee meetings shall not be held in public and shall not be considered valid except when a minimum of two thirds of the members are present.

Article 27

Committees shall consider matters referred to them by the Majlis or the Majlis Chairman. If a matter is of concern to more than one committee, the Chairman of the Majlis shall decide which of them is more entitled to deal with the said matter, or shall refer it to a committee consisting of members from among all committees concerned. The said committee shall hold meetings under the chairmanship of the Chairman of the Majlis or the Vice Chairman.

Article 28

Each member of the Majlis may proffer his opinion on any subject referred to any committee, even if he is not a member thereof, provided that the said opinion is submitted in writing to the Chairman of the Majlis.

Article 29

Minutes shall be drawn up for each committee meeting, and shall indicate the date and venue of the meeting, the names of those members present and absent, a summary of debates and the text of recommendations. The minutes shall be signed by the chairman of the meeting and members present.

Article 30

Upon consideration of a given matter by the committee, a report shall be filed detailing the essentials of the referred subject, the committee's point of view and its recommendations relative to it, the fundamentals on which such recommendations are based and the opinion of the minority, if any.

Article 31

The Resolutions of the Majlis shall be passed by the majority stipulated in Article 16 of the Law of the Majlis al-Shura. If such a majority is not realized, the subject shall be rescheduled for voting at the next meeting.

If the majority is not obtained at this second meeting, the subject shall be brought before the King along with the study that has already been made thereon and the voting results at the two meetings.

Article 32

No debates or new points of view shall be accepted during voting. In all cases the Chairman of the Majlis shall vote after the completion of voting by members.

Article 33

The Chairman of the Majlis shall present the annual report, provided for in Article 5 of the Law of the Majlis al-Shura, within three months, after the end of the year.

Article 34

Financial and functional affairs of the Majlis shall be determined in accordance with the financial and functional bylaws.

The Chairman of the Majlis shall issue rules required to organize financial and administrative affairs of the Majlis, including the organizational structure and duties of the various departments of the Majlis, in a manner consistent with the Law of the Majlis and its bylaws.

Financial and Staffing Affairs of the Majlis al-Shura

Article 1

The fiscal year of the Majlis shall be the same fiscal year of the State.

Article 2

The Chairman of the Majlis shall prepare the draft of the annual budget of the Majlis and shall present it to the King for approval.

Article 3

Following approval, the budget shall be deposited with the Saudi Arabian Monetary Agency (SAMA). Expenditure of funds shall require the signature of the Chairman of the Majlis or the Vice Chairman.

Article 4

If the amounts allocated in the budget are outstripped by the expenditures of the Majlis, or if an emergency outlay arises which could not have been foreseen while the budget was being prepared, the Chairman shall submit a statement of the needed amounts to the King for possible endorsement.

Article 5

Titles and grades of the Majlis posts shall be included in its budget. Titles of posts may be amended and their grades scaled down during the fiscal year at the discretion of the Chairman.

Article 6

The posts of Grades 14 and 15 shall be filled with the approval of the King. Other posts of the Majlis shall be filled in accordance with the Civil Service Law and bylaws and shall be exempted from the provisions of the competitive examination.

Article 7

The General Assembly of the Majlis shall establish rules governing allowances of government officials and other individuals, other than the Majlis members, whose work with the Majlis may be needed.

Article 8

The Majlis shall not be subject to control by any other authority. The Majlis administration shall include a department for pre-disbursement financial control. The General Assembly of the Majlis shall undertake post-disbursement control. The Majlis Chairman shall have the right to request a financial or administrative expert to prepare a report on any financial or administrative matter related to the Majlis.

Article 9

At the end of the fiscal year, the general secretariat of the Majlis shall prepare the final accounts, which the Majlis Chairman shall forward to the King for possible approval.

Article 10

Without prejudice to the provisions of this bylaw, the Majlis financial affairs and accounts shall be organized in accordance with the same rules observed in organizing the accounts of ministries and government services.

Rules Governing the Investigation and Trial of the Majlis Member

Article 1

If a member of the Majlis betrays any of his duties, he shall be subject to one of the following penalties:

a. A censure in writing;
b. The deduction of one month's salary;
c. The forfeiture of membership.

Article 2

Investigation of a member of the Majlis shall be conducted by a committee consisting of three members of the Majlis nominated by the Chairman.

Article 3

The committee shall inform the member of the violation ascribed to him. It shall hear his testimony and record his justification (defense) in the investigation minutes. The committee shall submit a report on the outcome of the investigation to the General Assembly.

Article 4

The General Assembly of the Majlis shall form a committee consisting of its members, provided that none of them shall be the Chairman or the Vice Chairman of the Majlis, to prosecute the member to whom the violation is ascribed. The committee shall have the right to impose the penalty of censure or salary deduction.

If the committee decides to strip him of membership, the matter shall be submitted to the Chairman to forward to the King.

Article 5

Imposition of any of the foregoing penalties shall not impede the filing of a public or private suit against the member.

Source: Kingdom of Saudi Arabia, Majlis al-Shura, *The Basic Law of Government*, Riyadh: n.d. (translated and adapted from the Arabic), pp. 61–86.

Appendix 16 ⌒

The Law of the Provinces

Royal Decree Number A/92
Dated 27 Shaaban 1412H/1 March 1992

In the name of God, the merciful, the compassionate.

With the help of God, we, Fahd bin Abdul Aziz Al Saud, Monarch of the Kingdom of Saudi Arabia, having taken into consideration the public interest, and wishing to modernize and improve the performance of government institutions in various provinces, have decreed the following:

1. The promulgation of the Law of the Provinces in the attached text;
2. That this Law shall come into force within a period not exceeding one year effective from the date of its publication;
3. That this Law shall be published in the Official Gazette.

Fahd bin Abdul Aziz Al Saud
Custodian of the Two Holy Mosques

The Law of the Provinces

Article 1

The aim of this statute is to improve administrative operations in the provinces of the Kingdom and ensure their overall development. It further aims at maintaining law and order, guaranteeing the rights and liberties of citizens, all within the framework of Islamic Shariah.

Article 2

The provinces of the Kingdom and the headquarters of the governorates shall be organized by Royal Decree upon the recommendation of the Minister of the Interior.

Article 3

Administratively, each province shall consist of a number of governorates, districts and localities, created after taking into account demographic, geographic, and environmental conditions, as well as security needs and available communications facilities. The governorate is organized by Royal Decree on the recommendation of the Minister of the Interior. The districts and centers are created and linked by a decision of the Minister of the Interior upon the recommendation of the Provincial Governor.

Article 4

Each province shall have a Governor with the rank of Minister, and a Vice-Governor at a distinguished grade to assist him in discharging his duties, as well as to substitute for the Governor during the latter's absences. Provincial governors and vice-governors are appointed and relieved by Royal Decree upon the recommendation of the Minister of the Interior.

Article 5

The Governor of a province is accountable to the Minister of the Interior.

Article 6

Provincial governors and vice-governors shall take the following oath before the King prior to the assumption of their duties: I swear by Almighty God to be loyal to my religion, to my King and my Country, not to disclose any State secrets, to protect its interests and respect its laws, and to discharge my duties with honesty, trust, loyalty and justice.

Article 7

Each provincial governor shall administer his province according to the general policy of the State, in compliance with the provisions of this Law, as well as other laws and regulations. He must in particular:

   a. Maintain security, order and stability, and take necessary measures in accordance with this Law and other regulations;
   b. Implement judicial rulings;
   3. Protect the rights and liberties of individuals, and refrain from any actions that may compromise these rights and freedoms, except within the limits prescribed by the Shariah and this Law;
   4. Endeavor for the social, economic and urban development of the province;
   5. Attempt to develop and promote public services in the province;
   6. Administer governorates, districts and localities; supervise the work of administrators, district directors, and heads of localities; to ascertain their capabilities to perform assigned duties;
   7. Protect State assets and property and prevent any transgressions against them;
   8. Supervise governmental institutions and their personnel in the province to ascertain proper performance of their duties with honesty and loyalty, taking into account the ties of employees within ministries and within various services in the province with competent authorities;

9. Have direct contact with ministers and heads of departments to discuss the affairs of the province with them in order to improve the performance of organs under his authority; and inform the Minister of the Interior accordingly;
10. Submit annual reports to the Minister of the Interior on the efficiency of public services in the province according to the executive provisions of this Law.

Article 8

An annual meeting of provincial governors shall be held under the chairmanship of the Minister of the Interior to discuss issues related to the provinces. The Minister of the Interior shall submit a report hereon to the Prime Minister.

Article 9

At least two meetings shall be held every year for administrators and district directors to discuss matters of interest to the province. The Governor shall submit a report thereon to the Minister of the Interior.

Article 10

a. At least one undersecretary with a rank of not less than 14 is to be appointed to each province, in accordance with a decision by the Council of Ministers, based upon a recommendation from the Minister of the Interior.
b. Upon the recommendation of the Minister of the Interior, a governor shall be appointed by the Prime Minister, and shall have a grade not less than 14. Each province shall have a vice-governor at a grade not less than 12 who shall be appointed by the Minister of the Interior upon the recommendation of the provincial governor.
c. Each governorate shall have an administrator with a rank not less than 12 who shall be appointed by the Minister of the Interior upon the recommendation of the provincial governor.
d. Each district shall have a director, whose rank is not less than 8, who shall be appointed by the Minister of the Interior upon the recommendation of the provincial governor.
e. Each locality shall have a head, whose rank is not less than 5, who shall be appointed by the provincial governor upon the recommendation of the district director.

Article 11

Provincial governors, vice-governors, administrators, district directors and heads of localities shall reside within the province, and shall not leave it without authorization from immediate superiors.

Article 12

Administrators, district directors, and heads of localities shall assume their responsibilities within their jurisdictions, and within the limits of the powers vested in them.

Article 13

Administrators shall administer their provinces within the limits of the authorities stipulated in Article 7, with the exception of provisions (f), (i), and (j). They shall supervise the performance of district directors and heads of localities, to ascertain their ability to perform duties efficiently, and submit periodic reports to the provincial governor on the performance of public services and other matters with which the governorate is concerned, in accordance with the stipulations under the executive regulations of this Law.

Article 14

Every ministry or government agency providing services to the province shall appoint an official at the head of its bodies in the province with a rank not less than 12. He shall report directly to the parent ministry or agency and shall operate in close coordination with the governor of the province.

Article 15

Each province shall have a Provincial Council with offices at the headquarters of the governorate.

Article 16

The provincial council shall consist of:

a. The provincial governor as Chairman;
b. The vice governor as Vice Chairman;
c. The Commissioner (Wakil) of the Province;
d. The Heads of governmental institutions in the province as specified by an order issued by the Prime Minister upon the recommendation of the Minister of the Interior.
e. Not less than ten men from the local community who are eligible in terms of their knowledge, expertise and specialization. They are appointed by order of the Prime Minister, upon the provincial governor's recommendation, and with the approval of the Minister of the Interior. Their renewable term of office shall be four years.

Article 17

A member of a provincial council shall satisfy the following requirements:

a. Be of Saudi nationality both by birth and upbringing;
b. Be of recognized integrity and capability;
c. Be no younger than 30 years of age;
d. Be a resident of the province.

Article 18

A member shall be entitled to submit written proposals to the Chairman of the provincial council on matters pertaining to the council's jurisdiction. The Chairman shall place each proposal on the council's agenda for consideration.

Article 19

A member of a provincial council shall not attend deliberations, or the deliberations of any of its committees, if the subject under discussion shall involve personal gains, or benefit individuals for whom his testimony would be unacceptable, or individuals who have appointed him a guardian, proxy or a representative.

Article 20

If a council member wishes to resign, he shall submit his resignation to the Minister of the Interior, through the provincial governor. The resignation shall not be considered valid until approved by the Prime Minister upon the recommendation of the Minister of the Interior.

Article 21

In all cases other than those specified in this Law, an appointed member may not be dismissed during his term, except by order of the Prime Minister, acting on a recommendation from the Minister of the Interior.

Article 22

Should a vacancy arise for any specific reason, a successor shall be appointed within three months, effective from the vacancy date. The term of the new member shall be equal to the remaining period of his predecessor's term, in accordance with Article 16 (e) of this Law.

Article 23

The provincial council shall discuss any issue that may improve the standard of services in the province. Its prerogatives shall be as follows:

a. Determine the needs of the province and propose their inclusion into the State's development plans;
b. Determine useful projects according to a scale of priorities, and propose their endorsements in the State's budget;
c. Analyze the province's urban and rural organizational layouts, and implement changes once adopted;
d. Follow up and coordinate the implementation of allocations from the development plan as well as the budget.

Article 24

The provincial council shall propose and submit to the Minister of the Interior any move calculated to serve the general good of the province's population and shall encourage citizens' contribution thereto.

Article 25

The provincial council shall limit its deliberative scope to subjects that fall within its prerogatives as stipulated in this Law. Its decisions shall be considered null and void if its powers are misused. A resolution to this end shall be issued by the Minister of the Interior.

Article 26

Provincial councils shall hold ordinary sessions every three months at the invitation of their Chairmen. Under his discretion, a Chairman shall also convene extraordinary sessions. Ordinary sessions shall include one or more meetings that are held upon a single summons. The sessions may not be adjourned until all issues on the agenda have been examined and discussed.

Article 27

Attendance at the meetings of provincial councils shall be considered a function-related duty for members identified in Article 16, clauses (c) and (d) of this Law. Members must attend meetings in person or appoint substitutes when they cannot. For members identified in clause (e) of said Article, unexcused nonattendance at two successive sessions shall be considered grounds for dismissal from a council. In this case, the dismissed member shall not be eligible for reappointment, except after the lapse of two years from the date of dismissal.

Article 28

Provincial council meetings shall be considered in order only if attended by at least two thirds of council members. Council resolutions shall be issued by absolute majority of cast votes. Deadlocked votes shall be settled by the Chairman's ballot.

Article 29

Provincial councils shall form special committees, as needed, to examine any decrees falling within their jurisdictions. They may seek the assistance of specialists and invite whoever they wish to attend their meetings and participate in deliberations without having the right to vote.

Article 30

The Minister of the Interior shall have the right to summon a council to meet under his chairmanship at any venue he chooses. Likewise he shall have the right to preside at any meeting he attends.

Article 31

A provincial council may convene only at the request of its Chairman or his deputy or by order of the Minister of the Interior.

Article 32

The Chairman of a provincial council shall submit a copy of its resolutions to the Minister of the Interior.

Article 33

The Chairman of a provincial Council shall inform ministries and governmental agencies of any resolutions concerning them that are voted upon in the affirmative.

Article 34

Ministries and government agencies shall take into consideration resolutions voted by provincial councils in accordance with provisions of Article 23, clauses (a) and (b) of this Law. If a ministry or governmental institution rejects any such resolutions, it shall explain the reasons to the said provincial council. In case of disagreement, said provincial council shall refer the matter to the Minister of the Interior for reconsideration by the Prime Minister.

Article 35

Each ministry or governmental agency that maintains services of its own in the province shall inform the provincial council of projects allocated to it in the State budget. It will also notify the council about development plan allocations for the province.

Article 36

Every minister and head of service may seek the views of a provincial council about any subject pertaining to its jurisdiction. Said provincial council shall give its opinion as requested.

Article 37

The Prime Minister, acting upon a proposal from the Ministry of the Interior, shall set the remuneration of the Chairmen and members of provincial councils, taking into account transportation and residence costs.

Article 38

A provincial council shall only be dissolved by order of the Prime Minister based on a proposal from the Minister of the Interior. New members shall be appointed within three months from the date of dissolution. In the interim, members specified in Article 16, clauses (c) and (d) of this Law, shall perform the duties of the dissolved council under the chairmanship of the provincial governor.

Article 39

Provincial councils shall have a secretariat at their respective governorates, entrusted with the preparation of agendas, extending timely invitations, keeping records of all deliberations and meetings, counting ballots, preparing the minutes of meetings, drafting resolutions, maintaining order at council meetings, and registering council decisions.

Article 40

The Minister of the Interior shall issue the necessary regulations for the implementation of this Law.

Source: Kingdom of Saudi Arabia, Majlis al-Shura, *The Basic Law of Government*, Riyadh: n.d. (translated and adapted from the Arabic), pp. 48–60.

Appendix 17 ⌒

Heir Apparent Abdallah
Address to Majlis al-Shura
January 13, 1996

Brothers:

May the peace, mercy and blessings of God be upon you.

It gives me great pleasure to convey to you on this auspicious occasion the greetings of my brother the Custodian of the Two Holy Mosques and his best wishes for your council. I also bring you the good news that his health is constantly improving, thanks be to God.

⌒   ⌒   ⌒

Brothers:

Prior to my coming here, I recalled past speeches delivered by my brother the Custodian of the Two Holy Mosques to this revered council, realizing that they gave detailed accounts of our internal and external policies—Arab, Islamic and international relations—and of the benefits of consultation [Shura] in Islam, in addition to brief histories of this modern state of ours and its founder King Abdul Aziz. Let us remember these speeches and follow their advice, as I draw this address from their spirit and from the objectives and legitimacy of this revered council, whose activities are seen to reflect the dire need for its sincere opinions. I hope that you will continue to voice them, because this is your trust and responsibility, bearing in mind that sincere opinions like these have achieved social justice among various peoples in many an era of Islamic history. Thanks to God, we are governed by a gracious Islamic creed that has honored man with a just law capable of solving mankind's problems until the day of judgment when the Almighty inherits the earth and all that is on it.

⌒   ⌒   ⌒

Brothers:

If we look today to have others see us through this humane concept of the message of Islam, we have to protect this great message from flaws and concepts which do not measure up to its wisdom and justice, for it is indeed a lofty message and a just and divine law.

ᶜ᷉   ᶜ᷉   ᶜ᷉

Brothers:

On this occasion I say to you, that many questions have been raised with the establishment of this council and many things have been said; but our reply to all inquirers who seek the truth is that Shura in Islam can only be granted to those who have honesty in words, actions, and opinions, and in the proclaimed vision of what is true. This is what we understand and want to protect, to safeguard from faults and errors in an era of change, political and economic, in security and in information. We also say to you, brothers and citizens, that there is no room for hesitation in advice and consultation. We speak out, and remain committed, within the service of God, His religion, our homeland and its citizens, and we will, God willing, be sincere in performing this service.

As my brother the Custodian of the Two Holy Mosques has said, the doors are open, and the hearts and minds are vigilant, God willing, for all citizens and those in need.

May the peace, mercy and blessings of Allah be upon you.

Source: Press release, Royal Embassy of Saudi Arabia, Washington, D.C., January 15, 1996.

Notes

Introduction

1. Salah Nasrawi, "Saudi Prince Urges Changes," *The Associated Press,* June 6, 1999.
2. Prince Abdallah's remarks were first published on August 18, 1962, in *al-Safa* and *al-Hayat,* two leading Beirut dailies. See Gerald De Gaury, *Faisal: King of Saudi Arabia,* New York: Frederick A. Praeger Publishers, 1966, pp. 107–108.
3. Stanley Reed, "A Princely Power Struggle Could Shake the House of Saud," *Business Week,* December 25, 1995, p. 56; see also Kathy Evans, "Saudi Arabia: Shifting Sands at the House of Saud," *The Middle East Magazine,* number 253, February 1996, pp. 6–9.
4. An altered version of this introduction was first published in Joseph A. Kechichian, "Saudi Arabia's Will to Power," *Middle East Policy* 7:2, February 2000, pp. 47–60.
5. The body of water that separates the Arabian Peninsula and Iran is known as the Persian Gulf in Western sources and Arabian Gulf in Arab references.
6. Among the more useful introductory volumes on Saudi Arabia, see Hassan Abdul-Hay Gazzaz, *Al-Amn Allazi Na'ishuha* [The Security We Enjoy], 2 volumes, 3rd edition, Jeddah, Saudi Arabia: Dar Al-'Ilm Printing and Publishing Co., 1993 (a one-volume summary was published in English under the same title in 1992). See also H. St. John Philby, *Sa'udi Arabia,* London: Ernest Benn Limited, 1955; John S. Habib, *Bin Sa'ud's Warriors of Islam: The Ikhwan of Najd and Their Role in the Creation of the Sa'udi Kingdom, 1910–1930,* Leiden, the Netherlands: E. J. Brill, 1978; and Joseph Kostiner, *The Making of Saudi Arabia 1916–1936: From Chieftaincy to Monarchical State,* New York and Oxford: Oxford University Press, 1993.
7. David Holden and Richard Johns, *The House of Saud: The Rise and Rule of the Most Powerful Dynasty in the Arab World,* New York: Holt, Rinehart and Winston, 1981, pp. 42, 101.
8. The solution was not always so simple. According to one report, Khalid bin Muhammad bin Abdul Rahman died in a mysterious hunting accident after Abdul Aziz's nephew had repeatedly attempted to have Abdul Aziz's son and the country's next King, Saud, assassinated. See Alexander Bligh, *From Prince to King: Royal Succession in the House of Saud in the Twentieth Century,* New York and London: New York University Press, 1984, pp. 32–33.
9. Abdallah bin Jiluwi ruled the province from 1913 to 1936, at which point his son Saud took over.

10. Holden, *op. cit.*, p. 203.

11. De Gaury, *op. cit.*, p. 95.

12. For a good recent introduction to the subject, see Simon Henderson, *After King Fahd: Succession in Saudi Arabia,* policy paper number 37, 2nd edition, Washington, D.C.: The Washington Institute for Near East Policy, 1995.

13. The choice of a non-Sudayri, Abdallah, was reported to have been a compromise born of a desire to limit the power faction of the Sudayris within the royal family. See Youssef M. Ibrahim, "Saudi King Issues Decrees to Revise Governing System," *The New York Times,* March 2, 1992, p. 1.

14. Abdallah was largely preoccupied with the internal affairs of the Kingdom until King Fahd's illness in 1996–1997 burdened the Heir Apparent with the monarch's myriad duties.

15. For a definitive study of the Al Rashid, see Madawi Al Rasheed, *Politics in an Arabian Oasis: The Rashidi Tribal Dynasty,* London and New York: I. B. Tauris & Co. Limited, 1991. See also A. Al Uthaymin, *Nashat Imarat al Rashid* [Accomplishments of the Al Rashid Emirate], Riyadh: n.p., 1981; and Bligh, *op. cit.*, p. 22.

16. Although highly critical of the Al Saud, Nasir Al-Said's tome on the family contains rich details on individual members, especially those originating in the Al Sudayri branch. See Nasir Al-Said, *Tarikh Al Saud* [History of the Al Saud], 2 volumes, Beirut: Al-Ittihad Press, 1985.

17. Khaled bin Sultan (with Patrick Seale), *Desert Warrior: A Personal View of the Gulf War by the Joint Forces Commander,* New York: HarperCollins Publishers, Inc., 1995.

18. "Prince Khaled's Departure is Unexplained," *Country Report Saudi Arabia 4–91,* London: The Economist Intelligence Unit, 1991, p. 12.

19. The two publications are the London-based Arabic-language daily *Al-Hayat* and weekly *Al-Wassat.*

20. F. Gregory Gause III, *Saudi-Yemeni Relations: Domestic Structures and Foreign Influence,* New York: Columbia University Press, 1990, pp. 150–162.

21. As was the case in the early 1960s, when the so-called free princes rallied behind King Saud as the fallen monarch struggled to overturn his initial deposition. See De Gaury, *op. cit.*, pp. 130–138, and Bligh, *op. cit.*, pp. 64–70.

22. For a theoretical discussion of succession, see Robbins Burling, *The Passage of Power: Studies in Political Succession,* New York: Academic Press, 1974; and Reinhard Bendix, *Kings or People: Power and the Mandate to Rule,* Berkeley and Los Angeles: University of California Press, 1978, 1980.

23. Christine Moss Helms, *The Cohesion of Saudi Arabia: Evolution of Saudi Arabia,* Baltimore and London: The Johns Hopkins University Press, 1981, p. 57. (Helms's discussion of "The Influence of the Tribal Segmentary System upon Political and Social Organization in Central Arabia," pp. 51–70, is extraordinarily analytical and informative.)

24. Noel J. Coulson, *A History of Islamic Law,* Edinburgh: Edinburgh University Press, 1964, pp. 9–20.

25. For a thorough discussion of the caliphate from both Sunni and Shia perspectives, see Henri Laoust, *Le Califat Dans La Doctrine de Ras[h]id Rida,* Paris: Librairie d'Amerique et d'Orient, 1986; and Abdulaziz Abdulhussein Sachedina,

The Just Ruler in Shi'ite Islam: The Comprehensive Authority of the Jurist in Imamite Jurisprudence, New York and London: Oxford University Press, 1988.

26. M. A. Shaban, *The Abbasid Revolution,* Cambridge: Cambridge University Press, 1970.

27. Marius Canard, "Fatimids," *Encyclopaedia of Islam,* new edition, volume 2, Leiden, the Netherlands: E. J. Brill, 1960– , pp. 850–862; and D. S. Richards, "Fatimid Dynasty," *The Oxford Encyclopaedia of the Modern Islamic World,* New York and Oxford: Oxford University Press, 1995, pp. 7–8.

28. Shaban, *op. cit.,* pp. 155–168.

29. H. A. R. Gibb, "Al-Mawardi's Theory of the Caliphate," in Stanford J. Shaw and William R. Polk (eds.), *Studies on the Civilization of Islam,* Princeton, New Jersey: Princeton University Press, 1982, pp. 151–165.

30. Bernard Lewis, "Politics and War," in Joseph Schacht with C. E. Bosworth (eds.), *The Legacy of Islam,* 2nd edition, Oxford: Clarendon Press, 1974, pp. 156–209.

31. Gary Samuel Samore, *Royal Family Politics in Saudi Arabia (1953–1982),* unpublished doctoral dissertation, Cambridge, Massachusetts: Harvard University, December 1983, pp. 9–10.

32. *Ibid.,* p. 10.

33. *Ibid.* See also Ira M. Lapidus, *A History of Islamic Societies,* Cambridge: Cambridge University Press, 1988, pp. 597–598.

34. Samore, *op. cit.,* pp. 11–12. See also Al Rasheed, *op. cit.,* especially, pp. 53–66.

35. Al Rasheed, *op. cit.,* p. 59.

36. *Ibid.,* p. 60.

37. *Ibid.,* pp. 63–64.

38. *Ibid.,* pp. 64–66.

39. David Howarth, *The Desert King: The Life of Ibn Saud,* London: Quartet Books, 1965, 1980, pp. 42–52.

40. Philby, *op. cit.,* pp. 265–291; see also Kostiner, *op. cit.,* pp. 10, 185–188.

41. On the 1744 alliance between the Al Saud and Al Shaykh families, see Ayman Al-Yassini, *Religion and State in the Kingdom of Saudi Arabia,* Boulder and London: Westview Press, 1985, pp. 21–37. See also Ahmad Abdul Ghafur, *Muhammad bin Abdul Wahhab,* Makkah: Muassasat Makkah Lil-Nashr, 1979; and Helms, *op. cit.,* pp. 76–126. The use of "unitarian," rather than "Wahhabism," throughout this study is not intended to equate the religious creed to its Christian namesake. On the contrary, the preference for "unitarian" is to avoid perpetuating any pejorative connotations associated with Wahhabism in some Western sources.

42. Abdul Saleh Al Uthaymin, *Tarikh al-Mamlakat Al-Arabiyah al-Sa'udiyah* [History of the Kingdom of Saudi Arabia], volume 1, Riyadh: n.p., 1984, 1995, pp. 105–113. See also Samore, *op. cit.,* p. 19.

43. Al Uthaymin, *ibid.,* 151–207.

44. *Ibid.,* pp. 219–224.

45. *Ibid.,* pp. 232–234.

46. The details of this particular change in leadership are rather complex because Faysal was away campaigning in Bahrain. In the event, his eventual return was "accelerated," perhaps by the British, who by then were fully aware of the need for stability in the area. See *ibid.,* pp. 237–241.

47. *Ibid.*, pp. 242–249.
48. Gary Troeller, *The Birth of Saudi Arabia: Britain and the Rise of the House of Sa'ud*, London: Frank Cass, 1976, pp. 15–19.
49. H. St. John Philby, *Sa'udi Arabia*, London: Ernest Benn Limited, 1955, pp. 160–168.
50. *Ibid.*, pp. 253–281; see also Al Rasheed, *op. cit.*, pp. 150–158; and Samore, *op. cit.*, pp. 26–28.
51. This study is based on specific interviews conducted during the past few years to clarify how current and future Saudi leaders perceive authority. Appendix 1 lists interviews conducted for this as well as for the author's companion volume under preparation, *The National Security of Saudi Arabia.*
52. See for example Mordechai Abir, *Saudi Arabia in the Oil Era: Regime and Elites; Conflict and Collaboration*, Boulder, Colorado: Westview Press, 1988, pp. 63–68, 108–120, 178–188; see also F. Gregory Gause III, *Oil Monarchies: Domestic and Security Challenges in the Arab Gulf States*, New York: Council on Foreign Relations Press, 1994, pp. 78–118.
53. Henderson, *op. cit.* Henderson writes frequently on this subject for *The Financial Times* of London, where he covers Saudi Arabia and the Gulf states.
54. Majid Khadduri, *Arab Contemporaries: The Role of Personalities in Politics*, Baltimore: Johns Hopkins, 1973. See also idem, *Arab Personalities in Politics*, Washington, D.C.: The Middle East Institute, 1981.
55. Lawrence I. Conrad (ed.), *The Formation and Perception of the Modern Arab World: Studies by Marwan R. Buheiry*, Princeton, New Jersey: The Darwin Press, Inc., 1989.
56. Biographies of key grandsons of King Abdul Aziz bin Saud Al Saud were compiled to separate the wheat from the chaff. Special attention was devoted to education, background, family contacts, marriages (if any), and special skills. In addition, how outsiders saw these key princes was also discussed. To better answer many of the questions raised here, a comprehensive research effort was undertaken to prepare the analytical construct presented throughout this volume. Toward that end, an effort was made to canvass the available literature on a number of Saudi officials, including what family trees, educational records, and specialized newsletters revealed. Moreover, Saudi opposition sources, which compiled a good deal of data on a number of junior officials, were also consulted—but the information was used only when it could be independently corroborated. Compiling biographies was not easy, and few scholars have ventured into the field given logistical difficulties associated with such endeavors. Finally, identifying key young princes' views on secularism, religious questions, and political participation was also difficult, since inferences from such assessments would help clarify the rise of alliances within the family. What were new generation leaders' outlooks on the behavior of the family, and how well did they think they were doing, both as a family as well as individually, proved almost impossible to answer. Still, an effort was made to identify their base of support within the family, associations that revealed the nuclei of specific alliances, and the identity of potential leaders and backers.
57. In analyzing potential leaders' views of intrinsic security issues, the aim was to infer what was the criteria for the family to survive as a family in power. Who was more likely to place the interests of the family above their own? What types

of alliances were most likely to ensure the unity of the ruling family in 2005 and beyond? And how did key young princes see the evolution of family politics? In this instance as well an effort was made to identify key princes' perspectives on working with other family members to form stronger units. This effort proved to be the most difficult in the entire study. Any inferences regarding the survival of the family, for example, necessitated a sound understanding of how senior and junior Saudi officials interacted at present and were likely to interact in the future. More important, the effort required a careful reading of potential alliances that could form within the Al Saud ruling family, to better ascertain how future leaders would ensure their authority.

58. Appendix 1 lists the interviews conducted for this study and, more important, the level of confidence earned throughout the region. While few Gulf officials allow one to take notes, jotting down major points immediately after each interview proved an effective and workable method. In no case did I submit a written list of questions, since I was far more interested in immediate responses than processed answers. Conversely, informal interviews were preferred, to put interlocutors at ease and draw more substance than polite responses.

Chapter 1

1. For a good discussion of the Al Saud ruling family see David Holden and Richard Johns, *The House of Saud: The Rise and Rule of the Most Powerful Dynasty in the Arab World,* New York: Holt, Rinehart and Winston, 1981.

2. King Abdul Aziz bin Abdul Rahman fathered at least 36 sons and perhaps an equal number of daughters. He accomplished this feat with 17 known wives, although he was always married to only 4 at any given time, even if several stood out as his "favorites." Given cultural and religious sensitivities regarding wives, and in the absence of a Saudi source clarifying this subject, the most authoritative genealogical reference book is by a former British military attaché in the Kingdom. See Brian Lees, *A Handbook of the Al Saud Family of Saudi Arabia,* London: Royal Genealogies, 1980. An equally useful scholarly source, with several additions and clarifications, is Alexander Bligh, *From Prince to King: Royal Succession in the House of Saud in the Twentieth Century,* New York and London: New York University Press, 1984.

3. The Saud Al-Kabir, Araif, and Jiluwi succession bids around the turn of the century were soundly rejected by Abdul Aziz bin Abdul Rahman, either through battle, marital connections, and/or co-option. When his cousins, the sons of Saud, opposed him—they were responsible for a serious uprising among the Ajman and Hazazina tribes in 1908—Abdul Aziz harnessed the power of his Ikhwan troops to end the revolt. In one episode, he gathered 19 of the captured leaders together at the town of Laila and conducted an impressive public execution. After 18 had fallen under the sword, the victor pardoned the 19th and "bade him to go free and tell what he had seen of the just vengeance of Ibn Saud." This example of stern justice immensely expanded Abdul Aziz's prestige with the tribesmen, who increasingly supported him. See Harold C. Armstrong, *Lord of Arabia: Ibn Saud, An Intimate Study of a King,* London: Arthur Barker, Ltd., 1934, p. 97. By relying on force, the founder established his impeccable credentials, even if his actions crystallized family rivalries. For further details on

this issue, see Gary Samuel Samore, *Royal Family Politics in Saudi Arabia (1953–1982)*, doctoral dissertation, Cambridge, Massachusetts: Harvard University, 1983, pp. 36–47.

4. David Howarth, *The Desert King: The Life of Ibn Saud*, London: Quartet Books, 1965, 1980. See also Muhammad Jalal Kishk, *Al-Saudiyyun Wal-Hal Al-Islami* [The Saudis and the Islamic Solution], Jeddah: The Saudi Publishing and Distribution House, 1982, especially, pp. 19–55.

5. Saud and Faysal were appointed viceroys of Najd and Hijaz, respectively, in 1926. They held these posts until 1933, when Saud was designated Heir Apparent and Faysal was elevated to the presidency of the Hijaz Council of Deputies. See Sarah Yizraeli, *The Remaking of Saudi Arabia: The Struggle Between King Sa'ud and Crown Prince Faysal, 1953–1962*, Tel Aviv, Israel: The Moshe Dayan Center for Middle Eastern and African Studies, 1997, pp. 32–33.

6. The so-called free princes included Talal, Badr, Nawwaf, Majid, and Fawwaz. In addition, both Bandar and Abdul Muhsin would join in, although their support was lukewarm. See Yizraeli, *ibid.*, pp. 85–96; see also Samore, *op. cit.*, pp. 139–154.

7. Benoist-Mechin, *Le Loup et le Leopard: Ibn-Seoud ou la naissance d'un royaume*, Paris: Albin Michel, 1955, pp. 467–485.

8. Madawi Al Rasheed, *Politics in an Arabian Oasis: The Rashidi Tribal Dynasty*, London and New York: I. B. Tauris & Co. Limited, 1991. See also A. Al Uthaymin, *Nashat Imarat al Rashid* [Accomplishments of the Al Rashid Emirate], Riyadh: n.p., 1981; Christine Moss Helms, *The Cohesion of Saudi Arabia: Evolution of Saudi Arabia*, Baltimore and London: The Johns Hopkins University Press, 1981, pp. 127–150; and John S. Habib, *Ibn Sa'ud's Warriors of Islam: The Ikhwan of Najd and Their Role in the Creation of the Sa'udi Kingdom, 1910–1930*, Leiden, the Netherlands: E. J. Brill, 1978, pp. 63–78.

9. These are Saad, Musaid, and Abdul Muhsin, born to Jauhara bint Saad Al Sudayri; and Badr, Abdul Illah, and Abdul Majid, born to Haiya bint Saad Al Sudayri.

10. Turki was appointed deputy minister of defense in 1969 but resigned in May 1979 after a marital scandal.

11. See chapter 2.

12. Another example of the reinforcement of the Fahd-Sultan alliance is the policy of arms purchases from Western sources, especially the United States, although the evidence to confirm this inference is anecdotal.

13. Abbas R. Kelidar, "The Problem of Succession in Saudi Arabia," *Asian Affairs* 9:1, February 1978, pp. 23–30.

14. Yizraeli, *op. cit.*, pp. 63–64.

15. William Powell, *Saudi Arabia and Its Royal Family*, Secaucus, New Jersey: Lyle Stuart, Inc., 1982, pp. 240–245.

16. This theme is developed in some detail in chapter 2 below. See also appendix 7.

17. For a more complete list of nominees, see H. St. John Philby, *Sa'udi Arabia*, London: Ernest Benn Limited, 1955, pp. 298–358; and Yizraeli, *op. cit.*, pp. 75–82.

18. Yizraeli, *op. cit.*, pp. 56–60.

19. Mordechai Abir, *Saudi Arabia in the Oil Era: Regime and Elites; Conflict and Collaboration*, Boulder, Colorado: Westview Press, 1988, pp. 135–139.

20. Holden, *op. cit.*, pp. 507, 512–513, 523.

21. The prominent role of Abdul Aziz's grandsons in the various armed forces of Saudi Arabia is striking. In addition to some of the sons of Faysal, Fahd, Abdallah, and Sultan, other grandsons serving in the armed forces include two sons of Nasir (air force officer Turki, army officer Muhammad) and one son of Salman (army officer Ahmad). Many others are unidentified, especially if they take their military careers more seriously than their family politics. Still, all "grandson" military officers represent a substantial power investment for their respective fathers, even if it is difficult to draw clear lines between their alliances.

22. Gerald De Gaury, *Faisal: King of Saudi Arabia*, New York: Frederick A. Praeger Publishers, 1966, p. 32. An account of the episode is also contained in a cable from J. Rives Childs, U.S. minister Jeddah, titled "Rivalry Between Saudi Arabian Princes," October 29, 1946, in Ibrahim Rashid (ed.), *Documents in the History of Saudi Arabia*, volume 5, Salisbury, North Carolina: Documentary Publications, 1980, p. 47.

23. Some members of the fourth generation (the great-grandsons) are also present as officers in the army and in high administrative posts. For example, Saud bin Abdallah bin Faysal bin Abdul Aziz is an army officer, and Muhammad bin Abdallah bin Faysal bin Abdul Aziz is undersecretary of state at the Ministry of Education. The total size of this group is not clear, but it is certain to grow larger and to increasingly play a more active political role in the future. Ghassan Salameh, *Al-Siyasat al-Kharijiyat al-Sa'udiyat Munzu 'am 1945* [Saudi Foreign Policy Since 1945], Beirut: Ma'had al-Anma' al-Arabi, 1980, pp. 45–50.

24. See appendices 6 and 7. It is, of course, next to impossible to know how many princesses survive.

25. For a detailed study on several of these families, see Philby, *op. cit.* See also Powell, *op. cit.,* pp. 201–221.

26. Samore, *op. cit.,* pp. 17–35.

27. Bligh, *op. cit.,* p. 107.

28. De Gaury, *op. cit.,* pp. 92–93. See also Bligh, *op. cit.,* pp. 29–34.

29. Musaid served as minister of the interior in the so-called reconciliation council from May 1958 to December 1960, and then as finance minister from March 1962 until 1975. See Yizraeli, *op. cit.,* pp. 205, 207.

30. David E. Long, *Saudi Arabia*, Beverly Hills and London: Sage Publications (for the Center for Strategic and International Studies, *The Washington Papers* 4:39), 1976, p. 28.

31. Holden, *op. cit.,* pp. 269, 461–462. See also Benoist-Mechin, *op. cit.,* pp. 305–310.

32. When the so-called collateral branches of the family are added to the total number claiming some kind of hereditary right in Saudi Arabia, the estimated total for the Al Saud crosses the 20,000 figure, which, without a doubt, is an unmanageable proposition for succession (as well as every other function). Still, several caveats must be made here to clarify these figures. First, although collateral branch members can and sometimes do describe themselves as princes, with the additional honorific of "His Highness" (HH), only direct male descendants of Abdul Aziz call themselves "His Royal Highness" (HRH). Consequently, there are less than 300 HRHs, but a few thousand HHs. Second, many Saudi tribal leaders can and sometimes do also use the title "prince," even if they

cannot and do not use HH or HRH. Third, and except for a few "senior" collateral branch families, the vast majority of such members are retinues and, naturally, not contenders.

33. Lees, *op. cit.*, p. 64.
34. Kamal Adham was King Faysal's brother-in-law (Queen Iffat's younger sibling) and, more than any other member of collateral branches, may be said to have played a disproportionately influential role in family affairs because the monarch trusted him. Although King Faysal relied on him for various "confidential" missions, Adham was not without controversy, as he was involved in various oil concession and arms purchase schemes—probably with the ruler's full knowledge—which, naturally, drew the ire of puritan members of the family. He was dismissed from his post as royal adviser on January 19, 1979, following the Camp David Accords (Adham was responsible for the entente between Saudi Arabia and Egypt), but remained a close confidant of King Fahd before and after the latter acceded to the throne. He died in 1999. See Holden, *op. cit.*, pp. 203, 217, 228, 364–365, 495.
35. Holden, *op. cit.*, p. 477.
36. *Ibid.*, p. 107. See also Philby, *op. cit.*, pp. 268–269.
37. Holden, *op. cit.*, pp. 525.
38. Philby, *op. cit.*, pp. 228–236.
39. Bligh, *op. cit.*, p. 17.
40. For a discussion of the Al Shaykh, see Ayman Al-Yassini, *Religion and State in the Kingdom of Saudi Arabia*, Boulder and London: Westview Press, 1985, pp. 22–32.
41. Ulama is the plural of *'alim.*
42. *The Saudi Arabia Report*, number 33, London: Middle East Economic Digest, 1999, p. 2.
43. Philby, *op. cit.*, pp. 179–200, 213.
44. Lees, *op. cit.*, p. 36.
45. *Ibid.*, p. 44.
46. *Ibid.*, pp. 43 and 48.
47. *Ibid.*, p. 40.
48. *Ibid.*, p. 42.
49. Bligh, *op. cit.*, pp. 106–107.
50. Powell, *op. cit.*, p. 230.
51. *The Saudi Arabia Report, op. cit.*, p. 2.
52. Although Prince Faysal was loyal to his King, he nevertheless sharply disagreed with his half brother, especially on financial matters and several foreign policy issues. See De Gaury, *op. cit.*, pp. 103–123; and Vincent Sheean, *Faisal: The King and His Kingdom*, Tavistock, England: University Press of Arabia, 1975, pp. 92–113.
53. Peter W. Wilson and Douglas F. Graham, *Saudi Arabia: The Coming Storm*, Armonk, New York: M. E. Sharpe, 1994, p. 59.
54. For a masterful analysis of the impact of modernization in the Kingdom, see the trilogy by Abdelrahman Munif: *Cities of Salt*, New York: Vintage International, 1989; *The Trench*, New York: Pantheon Books, 1991; and *Variations on Night and Day*, New York: Pantheon Books, 1993.

55. Little is actually known about the family council, reportedly headed by Prince Salman bin Abdul Aziz, the governor of Riyadh. See Said K. Aburish, *The Rise, Corruption and Coming Fall of the House of Saud,* London: Bloomsbury, 1994, p. 86.

56. King Saud's controversial rule cannot be adequately analyzed because so much of what actually occurred is either unknown or anecdotal. No reliable Saudi sources exist and most Western data are inadequate. This section aims to highlight key developments that emerged from this rule, focusing on succession, to better draw patterns. For a detailed assessment of Saud's rule, see Samore, *op. cit.,* pp. 74–229. See also Alexei Vassiliev, *The History of Saudi Arabia,* London: Saqi Books, 1998, pp. 354–368.

57. Dissatisfaction grew over wasteful expenditures, the lack of development of public projects and educational institutions, as well as the low wages for the growing labor force. See Helen Lackner, *A House Built on Sand: A Political Economy of Saudi Arabia,* London: Ithaca Press, 1978, pp. 57–68.

58. Powell, *op. cit.,* pp. 230–232.

59. Yizraeli, *op. cit.,* pp. 63–64.

60. *Ibid.,* p. 203.

61. *Ibid.,* p. 204.

62. Wilson and Graham, *op. cit.,* pp. 48–51.

63. Talal, thus becoming the first member of the Al Saud family to write a public exposé, later felt that Saud was misrepresenting the country and its people and, eventually, fled to Cairo along with several air force officers. See Talal bin Abdul Aziz, *Risalah ilal-Muwatin* [A Letter to the Citizen], Cairo: n.p., 1962?

64. Although several Al Saud family members urged Faysal to take control of the government and the country, the Heir Apparent at first declined, citing a promise he had made to his father to support Saud. Instead of just taking over, Faysal became prime minister, named Khalid deputy prime minister, and formed a new government. He took command of the armed forces and quickly restored their loyalty and morale. This step proved to be a turning point, as later developments proved. See De Gaury, *op. cit.,* pp. 93–94.

65. Yizraeli, *op. cit.,* p. 207.

66. De Gaury, *op. cit.,* p. 100.

67. For the full text of the ten-point program, see De Gaury, *op. cit.,* pp. 147–151.

68. Importantly, Faysal himself flew to Jeddah on the 14th, to conduct business as usual. His main concern was to let the ulama and the senior princes reach an independent decision. See Samore, *op. cit.,* p. 185.

69. *Ibid.,* pp. 186–187.

70. *Ibid.,* pp. 194–195.

71. Moreover, the interesting part of Faysal, which contributes to the modern-day succession dilemma, was his dedication to religious ideals, which he had learned from his maternal grandfather, a direct descendent of Abdul Wahhab. He was encouraged by his mother to embrace and develop values consistent with tribal leadership. For him, political administration was a religious act that demanded thoughtfulness, dignity, and integrity.

72. Summer Scott Huyette, *Political Adaptation in Saudi Arabia: A Study of the Council of Ministers,* Boulder and London: Westview Press, 1985, pp. 57–77.

73. Prince Fahd, who would later become King, pressed for King Saud's abdication. See Holden, *op. cit.*, p. 201.

74. Aburish, *op. cit.*, p. 68 and passim.

75. Holden, *op. cit.*, pp. 249–252.

76. *Ibid.*, p. 237. See also Bligh, *op. cit.*, pp. 86–87.

77. King Faysal provided for his deposed half brother's substantial expenses, although hard data are unavailable. He was quoted to have said: "Saud is our brother and we shall do our best to ensure his comfort." See Holden, *op. cit.*, p. 240.

78. Though many of these reports were clearly hostile to Saudi Arabia—especially in the Egyptian press—the consistency of several rumors was striking. For example, Egyptian sources reported throughout 1966 and 1967 that Interior Minister Fahd, supported by his full brothers Salman (governor of Riyadh) and Sultan (defense minister), intended to replace Abdallah as commander of the National Guard but was opposed by both Faysal and Heir Apparent Khalid. Even if exaggerated, it is interesting to note that factions and tensions currently ascribed to family politics may be traced to the Faysal period.

79. David E. Long, *The United States and Saudi Arabia: Ambivalent Allies,* Boulder and London: Westview Press, 1985, pp. 134–145; see also Parker T. Hart, *Saudi Arabia and the United States: Birth of a Security Partnership,* Bloomington and Indianapolis: Indiana University Press, 1998, pp. 237–247.

80. Holden, *op. cit.*, pp. 377–379. See also Henderson, *op. cit.*, pp. 12–13.

81. Aburish, *op. cit.*, pp. 51–54. See also Wilson and Graham, *op. cit.*, pp. 60–61.

82. Khalid had open-heart surgery in 1972 while he was Heir Apparent, two operations on his left hip in 1977, and a heart bypass operation in 1978. See Henderson, *op. cit.*, p. 13.

83. Ghassan Salameh, "Political Power and the Saudi State," *MERIP Reports,* number 91, October 1981, p. 8.

84. Samore, *op. cit.*, pp. 367–382.

85. Samore, *op. cit.*, p. 334.

86. Bligh, *op. cit.*, p. 91.

87. Fouad Al-Farsy, *Modernity and Tradition: The Saudi Equation,* London and New York: Kegan Paul International, 1999, pp. 145–171.

88. *Ibid.*, p. 147.

89. Samore, *op. cit.*, pp. 347–350.

90. Jeffrey Robinson, *Yamani: The Inside Story,* New York: The Atlantic Monthly Press, 1988, pp. 52–55.

91. Samore, *op. cit.*, p. 348.

92. Huyette, *op. cit.*, pp. 90–102.

93. Samore, *op. cit.*, pp. 351–355.

94. Huyette, *op. cit.*, pp. 92–94.

95. Saud bin Faysal emerged as an independent figure—emphasizing the bipartisan nature of his foreign policy responsibilities—but eventually joined the Khalid/Abdallah political alliance. Although he began as a Fahd protégé, he married into Prince Abdallah bin Abdul Rahman's family. See Colin Legum (ed.), *Middle East Contemporary Survey 1, 1976–1977,* New York and London: Holmes & Meier Publishers, Inc., 1978, p. 569. See also Lees, *op. cit.*, p. 60.

96. Turki bin Abdul Aziz's resignation may have been a consequence of changes in family politics following the Camp David agreements, but other explanations include his alleged implication in a business scandal at the Ministry of Defense, the failure of military intelligence to detect gunrunning into Saudi Arabia, and personal reasons. See Holden, *op. cit.,* p. 497.

97. Holden, *op. cit.,* p. 523. See also Powell, *op. cit.,* pp. 326–327.

98. Samore, *op. cit.,* pp. 461–465.

99. This phenomenon was repeated in the aftermath of the Iraqi invasion of Kuwait and the resulting 1991 war to liberate the shaykhdom that polarized the entire region.

100. Bligh, *op. cit.,* p. 97. See also Geoff Simons, *Saudi Arabia: The Shape of a Client Feudalism,* New York: St. Martin's Press, 1998, pp. 304–306.

101. Holden, *op. cit.,* pp. 422–424, 506–508.

102. Sandra Mackey, *The Saudis: Inside the Desert Kingdom,* Boston: Houghton Mifflin Company, 1987, pp. 325–328.

103. Arnaud de Borchgrave, "Undercutting Fahd," *Newsweek,* April 23, 1979, pp. 51–52.

104. Tewfik Mislhawi, "A New Direction," *The Middle East Magazine,* number 55, May 1979, pp. 25–28.

105. *Foreign Broadcast Information Service* [FBIS], March 26, 1979.

106. *The Washington Post,* April 8 and 15, 1979.

107. *FBIS,* April 2, 1979.

108. Jacob Golberg, "The Saudi Arabian Kingdom," in Colin Legum (ed.), *Middle East Contemporary Survey, Volume 3, 1978–1979,* New York and London: Holmes & Meier Publishers, Inc., 1980, p. 738.

109. Samore, *op. cit.,* pp. 469–480.

110. "Fahd Proclaimed King," *FBIS-MEA-V-82-114,* June 14, 1982, p. C1.

111. Steven Rattner, "Khalid is Dead; Fahd Succeeds in Saudi Arabia," *The New York Times,* June 14, 1982, p. A1.

112. For the text of Heir Apparent Abdallah's speech, see *FBIS,* June 15, 1982, pp. C2-C3.

113. Wilson and Graham, *op. cit.,* pp. 102–106.

114. Graham and Wilson report that staffers at the American embassy in Riyadh told them that the recall was likely tied to Horan's meeting with the King concerning the Saudi purchase of Chinese missiles. "When Horan protested, Fahd reportedly told him that every country had a right to defend itself. Later in the conversation, Fahd asked for American assurances that Israel would not attack its rockets. Horan infuriated the King by then repeating Fahd's own words that every country including Israel had a right to defend itself." See Graham and Wilson, *op. cit.,* pp. 106, 137 (footnote 43).

115. Mark N. Katz, "External Powers and the Yemeni Civil War," in Jamal S. al-Suwaidi (ed.), *The Yemeni War of 1994: Causes and Consequences,* London: Saqi Books for the Emirates Center for Strategic Studies and Research, 1995, pp. 81–93; see also Long, *The United States and Saudi Arabia, op. cit.,* pp. 44–48.

116. *The New York Times,* February 17, 1980. See also R. Hrair Dekmejian, "Saudi Arabia's Consultative Council," *The Middle East Journal* 52:2, spring 1998, pp. 204–218.

117. As later developments would confirm, delays in drafting a Basic Law for the Kingdom indeed centered on this key question. See *FBIS*, May 19, 1981. See also the interview with Prince Talal bin Abdul Aziz in "Change Is Inevitable in Saudi Arabia," *Al-Quds Al-Arabi*, April 16, 1998, reproduced in *Mideast Mirror*, April 17, 1998.

118. The so-called liberal and conservative challenges were manifested in public petitions calling for dramatic changes. See chapter 3 below.

119. Bligh, *op. cit.*, p. 22. See also Powell, *op. cit.*, pp. 60–68; and Al Rasheed, *op cit*.

120. Although Heir Apparent Abdallah does not have full brothers, his two sisters, Noof and Sita, played important roles behind the scenes. For example, it was Princess Noof who "arranged" the marriage of Jauhara bint Abdallah bin Abdul Rahman to Foreign Minister Saud bin Faysal.

121. Abdallah fathered six sons (Khalid, Mit'ab, Turki, Faysal, Abdul Aziz, and Mish'al) and seven daughters (Fahda, Aliya, Noof, Adilah, Sita, Abiyir, and Sara). Mit'ab, Turki, and Mish'al are in the National Guard.

122. Anwar Abdul Majid Al Jabariti, "Al Amir Abdallah Wal-Suq" [Prince Abdallah and the Market], *Al-Hayat*, number 13378, October 24, 1999, p. 23.

123. Faiza Saleh Ambah, "Crown Prince Popular With Saudis," *The Associated Press*, July 31, 1999.

124. Hassan al-Husseini as quoted in *ibid*.

125. The quote is attributed to Waheed Hashem, associate professor of political science at King Abdul Aziz University in Jeddah, in Ambah, *op. cit.*

126. Richard Engel, "Saudi Succession Unresolved," *The Washington Times*, April 22, 1998.

127. *Ibid.*

128. Hassa bint Ahmad Al Sudayri gave birth to seven sons (Fahd, Sultan, Abdul Rahman, Nayif, Turki, Salman, and Ahmad) and perhaps eight daughters, although the names of only three (Jauhara, Latifa, Lu'lua) appear on the family tree.

129. "And Prince Bandar Calls for Institutional Reform," *Country Report Saudi Arabia 1–1997*, London: The Economist Intelligence Unit, 1997, p. 12 (hereafter *CR-SA*).

130. Youssef M. Ibrahim, "Saudi Crown Prince to Take Over While King Rests," *The New York Times*, January 2, 1996, p. A3. See also "King Fahd's Poor Health Could Bring Forward the Crown Prince's Accession," *CR-SA 1–97*, p. 6.

131. Anonymous interview source; Washington, D.C.

132. The choice of a non-Sudayri, Abdallah, was reported to have been a compromise born of a desire to limit the power faction of the Sudayri within the ruling family. See Youssef M. Ibrahim, "Saudi King Issues Decrees to Revise Governing System," *The New York Times*, March 2, 1992, p. 1. For a thorough discussion of the decree and its implications, see John Bulloch, *Reforms of the Saudi Arabian Constitution*, London: Gulf Center for Strategic Studies, April 1992. See also chapter 2.

133. See appendix 8.

Chapter 2

1. Quoted in Richard Engel, "Saudi Succession Unresolved," *The Washington Times*, April 22, 1998. Earlier, Prince Talal had called for "real and authentic

elections" in Saudi Arabia. See "Politics This Week," *The Economist* 346:8058, March 7, 1998, p. 4.

2. For the texts of the speech, as well as the three documents, see appendices 13–16.

3. Simon Henderson, *After King Fahd: Succession in Saudi Arabia*, Washington, D.C.: The Washington Institute for Near East Policy, 1994, 1995, p. 21.

4. Basic Law of Government, Article 5, section (b). See appendix 14.

5. Basic Law of Government, Article 5, section (c). See appendix 14.

6. Henderson, *op. cit.*, p. 22.

7. *Ibid.*, p. 22, footnote 2.

8. Of the 19 successions in the Al Saud reign to date, a monarch's rule has gone to the son seven times, and to a cousin four times. The total for brother-to-brother succession stands at 8.

9. Gary Samuel Samore, *Royal Family Politics in Saudi Arabia (1953–1982)*, doctoral dissertation, Cambridge, Massachusetts: Harvard University, 1983, p. 483.

10. Of course, the process was completed in 1993 when the monarch appointed members of the Majlis al-Shura and, in a fundamental departure from past practices, limited the tenure of most cabinet officers to four-year terms—a decision that was periodically "updated" to allow senior Al Saud members to retain critical portfolios.

11. Samore, *op. cit.*, p. 486.

12. *Ibid.*

13. *Ibid.*, p. 487.

14. These ten individuals were chosen for two specific reasons: (1) all are encouraged by their powerful fathers to assume leadership responsibilities, and (2) all are ambitious enough to accept the challenges ahead. In addition to the ten listed in Chart 1, the following individuals are also rising stars, although not necessarily in the top list: Faysal bin Bandar (governor of Qasim), Turki bin Nasir (RSAF general); Fahd bin Sultan (governor of Tabuk); Faysal bin Muhammad Al Saud Al-Kabir (RSAF general); Saud bin Fahd (General Intelligence Directorate); Fahd bin Salman (deputy governor of the Eastern Province); Turki bin Sultan (Ministry of Information); Khaled bin Faysal (governor of Abha); Mansour bin Bandar (commander Jeddah Air Base); Saud bin Nayif (vice-governor of Riyadh].

15. The purpose of these short biographical descriptions is to introduce some of the key princes in the Kingdom. No attempt is made to be exhaustive.

16. According to Said Aburish, "In May 1981, Muhammad obtained his father's approval and claimed a share of Petromin Oil on the pretext of selling it to a Japanese company by the name of Petromonde. On the surface, this looked like a straightforward commission transaction similar to what members of the House of Saud do every day and which was meant to produce a huge, one-off profit—like those that Muhammad got from many of the commercial deals in which he had been involved. In reality, the purchaser did not exist and a close investigation by *The Wall Street Journal* revealed that Petromonde was part of Al-Bilad, an international corporation owned by none other than Prince Muhammad himself. His Highness was not content with the commission; he also wanted to control the resale of the oil to make more money, and it was estimated that his income from the deal amounted to $11 million a month for over a year." See

Said Aburish, *The Rise, Corruption and Coming Fall of the House of Saud,* London: Bloomsbury Publishing, 1994, p. 298.

17. *Ibid.,* p. 60.

18. For a full discussion of various military uprisings, see chapter 3, in Joseph A. Kechichian and Theodore W. Karasik, *The National Security of Saudi Arabia,* forthcoming.

19. Opposition forces in Britain maintain that his dismissal was the result of an unauthorized speech—declaring the doubling of the size of the Saudi armed forces—allegedly delivered without the King's approval.

20. *Al-Hayat* was a Lebanese newspaper whose credibility and diligence as protector of the freedom of speech cost its owner, Kamel Mroueh, his life in Beirut in 1966. Khaled first rented the name *Al-Hayat* but soon bought it after realizing it could be a useful tool. He turned the newspaper, a symbol of freedom of the press and democracy, into his personal podium. Along with *Al-Sharq Al-Awsat,* another London-based Saudi-owned daily, *Al-Hayat* covers the Middle East from the Kingdom's perspective. Other newspapers, magazines, and television networks complement the Al Saud's media portfolio.

21. Khaled bin Sultan (with Patrick Seale), *Desert Warrior: A Personal View of the Gulf War by the Joint Forces Commander,* New York: HarperCollins Publishers, Inc., 1995.

22. Alexander Bligh, *From Prince to King: Royal Succession in the House of Saud in the Twentieth Century,* New York and London: New York University Press, 1984, p. 90.

23. Interview with Prince Sultan bin Salman, Riyadh, January 18, 1997. The *New York Times* article was published on November 24, 1990, immediately after Washington announced that it was doubling the size of its Desert Shield deployment.

24. Interview with Prince Faysal bin Salman, London, March 2, 1997.

25. Albert Hourani, *A History of the Arab Peoples,* Cambridge, Massachusetts: The Belknap Press of Harvard University Press, 1991, pp. 315–332, 351–365.

26. Because the province was also home to some of the richest families in Saudi Arabia outside of the country's own royal family, it became pivotal as a trading center. For the better part of the past century, key entrepreneurs derived their wealth from trade, and, naturally, families endowed with such wealth also constituted a potential counterelite within the Kingdom. This was a haute bourgeoisie that needed to be co-opted if the Al Saud were to continue to rule in an unchallenged manner.

27. See appendix 8.

28. The ideological attack would come in the form of a claim that the unitarian school of Abdul Wahhab clearly was not holy enough to prevent the defiling of the holy sites. How then could the Al Saud claim that they were more suited to rule over the area in which these holy sites were located? This argument was further supported by the fact that no Quranic justifications existed for a monarchy to claim that it is an ideal form of government for an Islamic state. It was for this reason that Saudis have been so sensitive to Iranian-instigated disturbances in Makkah and Madinah since the early 1980s.

29. Judith Miller, *God Has Ninety-Nine Names: Reporting from a Militant Middle East,* New York: Simon & Schuster, 1996, pp. 84–127, 181, 468.

30. In addition to the favoritism displayed through appointments, as monarch, King Fahd is firstly responsible for the financial well-being of his large family, many of whom draw monthly salaries averaging $35,000 (senior princes can draw up to $100 million per year, not counting commissions earned from corporations doing business in the Kingdom). With close to 8,000 royals (both male and female), the financial burden is not negligible, and managing senior portfolios, even more difficult. How much is doled out is directly tied to the level of support that a senior member may garner from hundreds of junior princes whose duty is to praise the generous benefactor.

31. Although Chart 2 attempts to classify key members of the ruling family in first, second-, and third-line alliances, and despite existing solid support levels, it must be emphasized that these alliances are flexible. Depending on the primary succession issue—that is, after Abdallah assumes the throne—the necessity for alternative alliances may exist as well.

32. David Holden and Richard Johns, *The House of Saud: The Rise and Rule of the Most Powerful Dynasty in the Arab World,* New York: Holt, Rinehart and Winston, 1981, pp. 42, 101.

33. The solution was not always so simple. Khalid bin Muhammad bin Abdul Rahman died in a mysterious hunting accident after Abdul Aziz's nephew had repeatedly attempted to have Abdul Aziz's son and the country's next king, Saud, assassinated. See Bligh, *op. cit.,* pp. 32–33.

Chapter 3

1. H. St. John Philby, *Saudi Arabia,* London: Ernest Benn Ltd., 1955, p. 297.

2. John S. Habib, *Ibn Sa'ud's Warriors of Islam: The Ikhwan of Najd and Their Role in the Creation of the Sa'udi Kingdom, 1910–1930,* Leiden, the Netherlands: E. J. Brill, 1978, pp. 136–142.

3. David Holden and Richard Johns, *The House of Saud: The Rise and Rule of the Most Powerful Dynasty in the Arab World,* New York: Holt, Rinehart and Winston, 1981, pp. 55–79.

4. Nadav Safran, *Saudi Arabia: The Ceaseless Quest for Security,* Boston: Harvard University Press, 1985, p. 74.

5. The 1962 crisis in Yemen presented yet another dilemma to the ruling family. It forced the leadership to turn over, once again, additional powers to the Heir Apparent. Talal bin Abdul Aziz, certainly influenced by Nasser's Arab nationalist fervor, lambasted the Al Saud in the Beirut press. Prince Talal demanded that the rulers work within a democratic and constitutional framework. Shortly after these vitriolic reports were published, he flew to Cairo, where he was joined by three other princes—Badr bin Abdul Aziz, Fawwaz bin Abdul Aziz, and Saad bin Fahd—forming the Committee of Free Princes. For more on the Talal affair, see William Powell, *Saudi Arabia and Its Royal Family,* Secaucus, New Jersey: Lyle Stuart, 1982, pp. 242–244; see also Avi Plascov, *Security in the Persian Gulf: Modernization, Political Development and Stability,* Totowa, New Jersey: Allanheld, Osmun & Company, 1982, pp. 95–96.

6. This was done over strong objections voiced by the ulama, who had blocked the introduction of television in 1959. See Mordechai Abir, *Saudi Arabia in the Oil*

Era: Regime and Elites; Conflict and Collaboration, Boulder, Colorado: Westview Press, 1988, p. 89.

7. Safran, *op. cit.,* p. 100.

8. Powell, *op. cit.,* p. 249.

9. Abir, *op. cit.,* p. 136.

10. David Holden, "A Family Affair," *The New York Times Magazine,* July 6, 1975, pp. 8–9, 26–27.

11. Abir, *op. cit.,* pp. 143–144.

12. Safran, *op. cit.,* p. 218.

13. For two thorough studies on Aramco and the myriad developments associated with the giant company, see Irvine H. Anderson, *Aramco, the United States, and Saudi Arabia: A Study of the Dynamics of Foreign Oil Policy, 1933–1950,* Princeton, New Jersey: Princeton University Press, 1981; and Anthony Cave Brown, *Oil, God, and Gold: The Story of Aramco and the Saudi Kings,* Boston: Houghton Mifflin Company, 1999.

14. Abir, *op. cit.,* p. 73.

15. *Al-Dustur* (London), January 29-February 4, 1979, pp. 8–10, in "U.S. Presence Seen Troublesome For Country," *Joint Publications Research Service Report 73157, Near East and North Africa,* number 1937, April 5, 1979, p. 25 (hereafter JPRS). See also Fikri Abd Al-Muttalib, "Clandestine Opposition Movements in Saudi Arabia," *Al-Yaqzah Al-Arabiyah* (Cairo), December 1987, pp. 27–39, in "Russian Author Traces Opposition in Saudi Arabia," *JPRS-NEA-88–011,* February 26, 1988, p. 15.

16. Powell, *op cit.,* p. 340.

17. Al-Muttalib, *op. cit.,* p. 16.

18. Safran, *op. cit.,* p. 81.

19. Holden, *op. cit.,* pp. 271–282. See also Steven Emerson, *The American House of Saud: The Secret Petrodollar Connection,* New York: Franklin Watts, 1985, pp. 223–228 and 233–235.

20. In January 1979, Muhammad Ahmed Suwayli, commander of the Haradh garrison, rebelled, and 37 soldiers joined him and defected to Iraq. He had rejected orders to fire on striking foreign workers. See *Der Spiegel,* August 20, 1979, pp. 108–121, in "Saudi Strength, Problems Discussed," *JPRS-Near East/North Africa Report,* number 2020, September 20, 1979, p. 46; see also "Crisis in Ruling Family, U.S. Relations Noted," *Al-Safir* (Beirut), February 10, 1979, pp. 1, 12, in *JPRS-Near East and North Africa,* number 1956, May 7, 1979, pp. 50–51.

21. Abir, *op. cit.,* pp. 156–157.

22. For instance, in 1988, four Saudi Shias detonated bombs at a petrochemical plant in Jubail. A detailed announcement by the Saudi interior minister after the four were executed suggested that the rebels had been trained in Iran. In addition, an alleged Iranian plan to murder Saudis abroad was uncovered; see "Riyadh and Teheran try to mend fences despite conflicting undercurrents and an assassination in Ankara," *Country Report for Saudi Arabia 4–1988,* London: The Economist Intelligence Unit, 1988, pp. 6–7 (hereafter *CR-SA*); see also Douglas F. Graham, *Saudi Arabia Unveiled,* Dubuque, Iowa: Kendall/Hunt, 1991, p. 36.

23. *Al-Quds Al-Arabi* (London), November 1, 1993, p. 1, in "Government in 'Secret Talks' with Shiites," *FBIS-NES-93–212,* November 4, 1993, pp. 25–26; see also

Youssef M. Ibrahim, "Saudi Officials Reporting Accord with Shiite Foes," *The New York Times,* October 29, 1993, p. 6.

24. Joseph A. Kechichian, "The Role of the Ulama in the Politics of an Islamic State: The Case of Saudi Arabia," *International Journal of Middle East Studies* 18:1, February 1986, pp. 53–71.

25. The Al-Mushtarin sect broke away from unitarian doctrine in the late 1920s.

26. Plascov, *ibid.,* p. 20.

27. Fikri Abd Al-Muttalib, *op. cit.,* p. 17.

28. Problems between Prince Abdallah and Prince Sultan came to a confrontation in April 1979, when a clash occurred between units of the National Guard and the army. The most violent exchange of fire between regular soldiers and National Guard units since the creation of the state resulted in 16 dead and about 30 wounded. This incident led Prince Abdallah to strengthen the role of the National Guard and to concentrate its units around the entrances of the city, while the regular army was kept outside Riyadh. See "Differences Still Seen Within Ruling Family," *Al-Nida Al-Usbu* (Beirut), May 27, 1979, p. 1.

29. David Tinnin, "Saudis Recognize Their Vulnerability," *Fortune,* March 10, 1980, p. 48.

30. James Dorsey, "After Mecca, Saudi Rulers Provide a Channel for Dissent," *The Christian Science Monitor,* March 14, 1980, p. 7.

31. Plascov, *op. cit.,* p. 21.

32. Pierre Heim, "After the Shock," *Remarques Arabo-Africaines* (Brussels), number 527, 1980, pp. 10–12; see also Joseph A. Kechichian, "Islamic Revivalism and Change in Saudi Arabia: Juhayman Al Utaybi's 'Letters' to the Saudi People," *The Muslim World* 70:1, January 1990, pp. 1–16.

33. R. Hrair Dekmejian, *Islam in Revolution: Fundamentalism in the Arab World,* Syracuse, New York: Syracuse University Press, 1985, pp. 137–148. See also Plascov, *op. cit.,* p. 19.

34. "Government in 'Secret Talks' with Shiites," *Al-Quds Al-Arabi,* November 1, 1993, *op. cit.,* p. 1.

35. "Crackdown on Opposition Feared After Alleged Attack," *Al-Quds Al-Arabi,* September 17, 1993, p. 1. See also R. Hrair Dekmejian, "The Rise of Political Islamism in Saudi Arabia," *The Middle East Journal* 48:4, autumn 1994, pp. 627–643.

36. "Introduction to CDLR," *CDLR Yearbook '94-'95,* London: The Committee for the Defense of Legitimate Rights, November 1994, pp. xiii-xv.

37. "Seeds on Stony Ground," *The Economist,* June 12, 1993, p. 53; see also Caryle Murphy, "Saudi Arabia Bans Rights Group," *The Washington Post,* May 14, 1993, p. 35.

38. "Al-Salafiyah Opposition Training Camp Found," *Al-Ahd* (Beirut), October 29, 1993, p. 16.

39. Abir, *op. cit.,* p. 77.

40. Safran, *op. cit.,* p. 81.

41. Safran, *ibid.,* p. 104.

42. Abir, *op. cit.,* pp. 83–84.

43. Gause, *op. cit.,* p. 60.

44. Mordechai Abir, *Oil, Power and Politics,* London: Frank Cass, 1974, pp. 53–54.

45. Powell, *op. cit.,* pp. 247–248.

46. Avi Plascov maintains that about 300 officers were arrested in 1969. See Plascov, *op. cit.,* p. 96. J. B. Kelley, on the other hand, argues that 135 soldiers (officers and enlisted men in the army and air force) were sentenced to death and 305 to life imprisonment. Another 752 officers, soldiers, and civilians received sentences ranging from 10 to 15 years imprisonment. See J. B. Kelley, *Arabia, the Gulf and the West,* New York: Basic Books, 1980, p. 271. Finally, William Powell asserts that the whole plot was uncovered when Saudi special security forces infiltrated the organizations, thereby touching off numerous arrests throughout Saudi Arabia and as far away as England. See Powell, *op. cit.,* pp. 349–350. See also Abir, *op. cit.,* p. 116.

47. Taysir Khalid, "The Situation in Saudi Arabia and the Horizons for Development: Agencies, Political Decision-making, and the Special Role," *Al-Safir* (Beirut), February 1, 1981, p. 15.

48. Abir, *op. cit.,* p. 119.

49. *Ibid.,* pp. 119–120.

50. Kelley, *op. cit.,* p. 271.

51. Abir, *op. cit.,* p. 144.

52. "Saudis Welcome U.S. Troops to Stop Saddam," *Reuters Library Report,* August 29, 1990.

53. "Saudi King Fahd Shares Bush Peace 'Instinct'," *Reuters Library Report,* January 6, 1991.

54. For a thorough analysis, see Fred Frostic, *Air Campaign Against the Iraqi Army in the Kuwaiti Theater of Operations,* MR-357-AF, Santa Monica, California: RAND, 1994.

55. "King Fahd Bin Abdul Aziz Al Saud on the Occasion of Eid Al-Fitr," April 15, 1991, in "King Fahd Speaks on War Outcome, Government," *FBIS-NEA-91–073,* April 16, 1991, p. 11.

56. "Conscription ruled out again," *CR-SA,* no. 3, 1991, pp. 12–13.

57. "Prince Sultan is playing a prominent role—in contrast to Crown Prince Abdallah," *CR-SA,* no. 1, 1992, p. 9.

58. *Al-Quds Al-Arabi,* September 17, 1993, p. 1, in "Crackdown on Opposition Feared After Alleged Attack," *FBIS-NES-93–184,* September 24, 1993, p. 10.

59. Geoff Simons, *Saudi Arabia: The Shape of a Client Feudalism,* New York: St. Martin's Press, 1998, pp. 328–335.

60. Joseph A. Kechichian, "Trends in Saudi National Security," *The Middle East Journal* 53:2, spring 1999, pp. 232–253.

61. "Memorandum Presented to King Fahd of Saudi Arabia by Religious Scholars, Judges, and University Professors" (in Arabic), n.p., n.d., (in author's hands). A version of this letter, although not identical, was published by the Egyptian daily *Al-Sha'b;* see "Intellectuals Demand Reforms in Letter to King," *FBIS-NES-91–100,* May 23, 1991, pp. 21–22. This letter carried 52 signatures. See appendix 12.

62. "A Memorandum to the King" (in Arabic), n.p., September 1992, four pages (in author's hands).

63. Dekmejian, "The Rise of Political Islamism," pp. 638–643.

64. Interview with Shaykh Saleh Al-Lihaydan, president, Higher Justice Council, Riyadh, January 12, 1997. Shaykh Al-Lihaydan was explicit in his remarks. First, he insisted that there was a congruity of political views between the ulama and

the Al Saud. Second, he underlined that al-Awdah and al-Hawali were frauds and could not be taken seriously (a disputed view to say the least). Third, he posited that differences between junior and senior ulama were cosmetic and not substantive. Finally, and in a remarkable twist, the shaykh underlined the influence of the Supreme Council of Ulama. He clarified, for example, that it provided the "authorization" to the government to invite foreign forces into the Kingdom in 1990, further indicating that although the ulama supported the Al Saud, they were the latter's sole legitimizing force.

65. R. Hrair Dekmejian, "Saudi Arabia's Consultative Council," *The Middle East Journal* 52:2, spring 1998, pp. 204–218.

66. One observer of the region concludes that dynastic monarchies survive far better than generally credited. See Michael Herb, *All in the Family: Absolutism, Revolution, and Democracy in the Middle Eastern Monarchies,* Albany: State University of New York Press, 1999.

67. "Communiqué Number 3," *CDLR Yearbook '94-'95,* pp. 9–10.

68. It is important to note that the CDLR never portrayed itself as a "religious" organization, even if its founders were high-ranking religious figures. In fact, the CDLR must be considered a secular group (in the Saudi context), for two reasons: (1) because it presented itself as a nationalist organization bent on political reforms; and (2) because it distanced itself from the Kingdom's ulama.

69. More radical elements than the CDLR existed in Saudi Arabia. The Advice and Reformation Committee (ARC), for example, was headed by the wealthy businessman Usama bin Laden, who was the first Saudi to be stripped of his citizenship in February 1994. According to ARC director Khaled Al-Fawwaz, for years many Saudis "believed that individual petitions would accomplish desired objectives." "In the 1970s," he continued, "it was difficult to organize public gatherings and take collective actions. There was no need for the average Saudi to join an organized group because every Saudi had access to high ranking officials, including the King." In these public assemblies, an individual could petition the ruler, and even if no immediate action was taken, at least a promise was made to look after the particular grievance. In time, especially after the monarch's health deteriorated, this access was further curtailed.

70. Interview with Dr. Muhammad Al Masaari, spokesperson of the Committee for the Defense of Legitimate Rights, London, February 6, 1995.

71. Interview with Prince Turki bin Faysal, director, Directorate General of Intelligence, Riyadh, January 20, 1997.

72. Interview with Shaykh Abdulaziz Al-Tuwayjiri, deputy assistant commander, National Guard, Riyadh, January 12, 1997.

73. A palace coup would indeed be possible, especially if senior family members acquiesced. See chapter 4.

74. It was unclear whether Dr. Al Masaari had contacts with senior members of the ruling family to discuss his demands. What was known, however, was that his father—a prominent Islamic jurist—his son, and of course he himself were arrested, tried for sedition, and sentenced to prison terms (varying from three months to one year). Al Masaari served a full year in jail (and, according to his testimony, was tortured), and his son served eight months. His father received a more lenient sentence: six months and a loss of his practice (many of his "rare" books were also confiscated).

75. "The CDLR is a Persistent Critic of Prince Sultan—but is More Favorably Disposed Towards the Crown Prince," *CR-SA,* number 2, 1996, pp. 8–9.

76. See, for example, "Al-wada' al-mali yata'azam ta'wilat al-asrat 'asharat miliarat wa rusum jadidat ala al–hajaj" [The Financial Situation Necessitates Shifting 10 Billion and Imposing New Taxes on Pilgrims], *Al-Huquq,* number 39, March 15, 1995, p. 2. A variety of CDLR products were available for consultation. First, there was the weekly *Al-Huquq* newsletter, which often was published in four typeset pages. Periodically, these were translated into English in the *CDLR Monitor.* In addition, the CDLR published an irregular biographical sheet on its "Prince of the Month," which, not surprisingly, concentrated on the chosen individual's alleged corrupt activities. The CDLR also issued periodic "Bayans" (Communiqués) that were always numbered. Communiqué contents were precise and called for action and follow-up. Starting in early January 1995, their distribution was announced and monitored in the *Al-Huquq,* because of the sudden appearance of "counter-communiqués." These were also available on the CDLR home page on the World Wide Web.

77. Telephone interview with Dr. Al Masaari, February 8, 1997.

78. The most prominent Arab who called on dramatic policy changes toward Iraq was United Arab Emirates president Shaykh Zayed bin Sultan Al Nahyan. See Douglas Jehl, "Sheik Shares His Misgivings Over U.S. Policies," *The New York Times,* May 31, 1998, p. 5.

79. The British government was infuriated by the coverage that the London-based CDLR received throughout the 1990s. When Dr. Muhammad Al Masaari and Said Aburish, a Palestinian author who published a scathing volume on the Kingdom, attacked British Treasury Secretary Jonathan Aitken's business links with the Saudi ruling family on a television program, London was furious. This episode did not endear the CDLR to the British government, which faced its own scandals. To their credit, however, the British resisted the temptation to crack down on several opposition movements, for fear of exposing themselves to charges of violating human rights or, even worse, of not supporting "democratically inclined" alternatives to authoritarian rule. In late 1994, Muhammad Al Masaari was served with a deportation notice after the home office rejected his request for asylum, but this was quietly allowed to slide.

80. CDLR, "Nida' min-al qiyadat al-shar'iat li-tajdid Yawm al-tadamun ma' ulama al-Jazirat" [A Call From the Legitimate Leaders to Renew the Day of Solidarity with the Scholars of the Peninsula], *Bayan,* number 34, April 26, 1995, p. 1; see also CDLR, "Yawm al-tadamun ma' ulama al-Jazirat" [The Day of Solidarity with the Scholars of the Peninsula], *Bayan,* number 33, April 12, 1995, p. 1.

81. The cities and mosques identified in Communiqués numbers 33 and 34 were:

Riyadh	Abdul Wahhab Al Tuwayri Mosque
Jeddah	Shaykh Safar Al Hawaly Mosque
Al Qasim	Al Thiyab Mosque (in the suburb of Burayda)
Al Juf	Shaykh Faysal al-Mubarak Mosque
Al Ahsa	Al-Khalidiyyah Mosque
Eastern Province	Shaykh Ahmad Al-Ajmi'i Mosque
Khamis Mushayt	Al-Kabir Mosque
Al-Baha	Al-Kabir Mosque

It was important to note that these were very large mosques, each capable of handling several hundred worshippers simultaneously. The communiqués specifically called for sit-in protests for one hour after Friday prayers.

82. Interview with a high-ranking Al Saud family member conducted on a nonattribution basis.

83. *The Washington Post* reported in early May 1995 that 80 individuals had been sentenced to death in the Kingdom since the beginning of that year. Although most of these were for drug-related offenses, several were indeed CDLR sympathizers. This pattern has continued for the period since then, with over 100 annual executions, which, of course, draws the ire of international human rights organizations. See "Saudi Arabia Executes Man for Murder," *Reuters*, January 26, 2000.

84. Whether alleged supporters of Al Masaari and the CDLR turned the money spigot off is difficult to determine. Riyadh rumor mills posited that the Al Saud were taking credit for muzzling Dr. Al Masaari.

85. Khaled bin Sultan, *Desert Warrior: A Personal View of the Gulf War by the Joint Forces Commander.* New York: HarperCollins Publishers, 1995, p. 173.

86. George Bush and Brent Scowcroft, *A World Transformed.* New York: Alfred A. Knopf, Inc., 1998, p. 320.

87. *Ukaz,* August 29, 1990, pp. 6–7, in "News Conference by Saudi Joint Forces Commander," *FBIS-NES-90–174,* September 7, 1990, p. 13.

88. *Ibid.*

89. *Ibid.,* p. 14.

90. *Al-Madinah,* August 23, 1990, p. 6, in "Crown Prince Visits Front, Addresses Troops," *FBIS-NES-90–184,* September 21, 1990, p. 15.

91. *Ibid.*

92. *Ibid.,* p. 16.

93. "Foreign Minister Comments on Gulf Crisis," *FBIS-NES-90–174,* September 7, 1990, pp. 15–16.

94. "Defense Minister Addresses Peninsula Shield," *ibid.,* pp. 14–15.

95. *Ibid.*

96. *Der Spiegel,* October 15, 1990, pp. 190–191 in "Foreign Minister Discusses Gulf Crisis, Saddam," *FBIS-NES-90–201,* October 17, 1990, p. 25.

97. *Ibid.,* p. 26.

98. *Al-Sharq Al-Awsat,* October 25, 1990, p. 5, in "National Guard Leader Stresses War Readiness," *FBIS-NES-90–210,* October 30, 1990, p. 18.

99. "Commander Views Gulf Crisis," *FBIS-NES-90–211,* October 31, 1990, p. 28. See also "Prince Bandar Not Optimistic Saddam to Respond," *FBIS-NES-91–025,* February 6, 1991, p. 10.

100. "King Criticizes Saddam in Ramadan Address," *FBIS-NES-91–052,* March 18, 1991, p. 23.

101. Interview with Fahad bin Abdallah bin Mohammed Al Saud, assistant to the minister of defense and aviation, chairman of the Economic Offset Committee, Ministry of Defense and Aviation (in Jeddah), June 12, 1996.

102. "MEI's 53rd Annual Conference: Leadership for a New Century," *The Middle East Institute Newsletter* 50:6, November 1999, pp. 9, 11.

103. Importantly, Prince Faysal bin Salman noted that Saudi Arabia was aware of the suffering of the Iraqi people but feared that lifting sanctions would allow the

Iraqi strongman to rearm. He concluded his remarks to the Washington audience by clarifying that "a senior Saudi official once compared the dilemma facing Saudi Arabia to a plane being hijacked, and from the ground Saudi Arabia is attempting to rescue the people and capture the hijacker, Saddam Hussein." It should be noted that Prince Faysal spoke in his personal capacity, not as a Saudi official. *Ibid.*

104. Al-Khilewi made his comments to the *London Sunday Times,* July 31, 1994.

105. Khaled bin Sultan, *op. cit.,* pp. 142–145; 172–178.

106. Khaled bin Sultan, *op. cit.,* p. 109. See also "QNA: Saudi Foreign Minister Urges Shah to Remain in Iran," *FBIS-MEA-78–224,* November 20, 1978, p. C3.

107. "Crown Prince Expresses Support for Shah," *FBIS-MEA-79–005,* January 8, 1979, p. C1.

108. "Prince Abdallah Grants Interview to Gulf News Agency," *FBIS-MEA-79–081,* April 25, 1979, p. C2. See also "Further Interview," *FBIS-MEA-79–221,* November 14, 1979, p. C8.

109. "Defense Minister Grants Interview on Military Issues," *FBIS-MEA-79–218,* November 8, 1979, p. C2.

110. *Ar-Riyadh,* February 23, 1980, p. 3, in "Amir Fahd Discusses Domestic Situation, Mideast Events," *FBIS-MEA-80–041,* February 28, 1980, p. C7.

111. "King Khaled, Prince Fahd Congratulate Bani-Sadr," *FBIS-MEA-80–027,* p. C4.

112. Khaled bin Sultan, *op. cit.,* p. 143.

113. "Text of Foreign Minister's Speech to UN General Assembly," *FBIS-MEA-80–201,* October 15, 1980, p. C5.

114. "Prince Fahd on Gulf Security, Call for Jihad," *FBIS-MEA-81–015,* January 23, 1981, p. C1. In February 1992, or a decade after repeatedly calling for a cease-fire between Iran and Iraq, King Fahd revealed that he had warned President Saddam Hussein about fighting, but in the event, the Iraqi insisted that Iran be attacked while it was—allegedly—weakened by the revolution. See "King Fahd Cited on Foreign, Domestic Policy," *FBIS-NES-92–031,* February 14, 1992, p. 21.

115. "Kuwait's *As-Siyasah* Interviews Defense Minister," *FBIS-MEA-81–024,* November 5, 1981, p. C7.

116. The monarch provided the following details for the $25.7 billion: $5.84 billion in grant aid, $9.25 billion in concessional loans, $6.75 billion in oil aid, $3.74 billion in military and transport equipment, $95 million in development loans, $21.3 million in payment for asphalt-spreading tractors, $20.2 million in SABIC (Saudi Arabian Basic Industries Corporation) credits, and $16.7 million in industrial products to reconstruct Basra. See "King Fahd Sends Reply Letter to Saddam," *FBIS-NES-91–011,* January 16, 1991, pp. 11–13.

117. "Deputy Premier Interviewed on Arab Issues," *FBIS-MEA-81–242,* December 17, 1981, p. C6.

118. "Fahd on Iran-Iraq War, Iranian-Pilgrims," *FBIS-MEA-82–215,* November 5, 1982, p. C2.

119. "Crown Prince on Major Mideast Issues," *FBIS-MEA-83–199,* p. C4.

120. "King Fahd Discusses Arab Regional Issues," *FBIS-MEA-81–026,* February 7, 1984, p. C5.

121. "Prince Sultan Interviewed on Syria, Gulf War," *FBIS-MEA-83–093,* May 12, 1983, p. C2.

122. Khaled bin Sultan, *op. cit.,* p. 145.

123. "King Fahd on Arab Unity, OPEC, Gulf Market," *FBIS-MEA-87–097,* May 20, 1987, p. C3.

124. *Al-Ahram,* January 15, 1988, pp. 3, 7, in "King Fahd Interviewed on GCC, Arab Affairs," *FBIS-NES-88–012,* January 20, 1988, p. 22.

125. "King Fahd on Iran Ties, Hajj, Missiles, Hijack," *FBIS-NES-88–084,* May 2, 1988, p. 18.

126. *Ibid.*

127. *Ibid.*

128. "Foreign Minister Interviewed on Regional Problems," *FBIS-NES-88–214,* November 4, 1988, p. 21.

129. "Paper Cites Foreign Minister on Ties with Iran," *FBIS-NES-88–216,* November 8, 1988, p. 26.

130. "Kuwaiti Editors Interview King Fahd on Issues: On GCC, Iran," *FBIS-NES-88–219,* November 14, 1988, p. 24.

131. "Prince Sultan on Ties with Iran, Defense Spending," *FBIS-NES-88–222,* November 17, 1988, p. 16.

132. "Text of Agreement," *FBIS-NES-89–058,* March 28, 1989, p. 22.

133. "King Interviewed on Iraq, Arab Solidarity," *FBIS-NES-94–205,* October 24, 1994, p. 32. See also "King Fahd on Iraq, Boycott, Detainees, Egypt," *FBIS-NES-94–204,* October 21, 1994, p. 28.

134. "Prince Sultan Speaks at UN Session," *FBIS-NES-95–205,* October 24, 1995, p. 24.

135. "Prince Saud al-Faisal Addresses UN," *FBIS-NES-95–198,* October 13, 1995, p. 27.

136. *Ibid.,* pp. 28–29.

137. "Saudi Minister Sees Healthy Sign for Arab-Iran Relations," *FBIS—FTS1997121200044,* December 12, 1997.

138. *Ibid.*

139. Saeed Barzin, "Iran: Evolving New Axis?," *Middle East International,* number 600, May 21, 1999, pp. 13–14.

140. Jubin Goodarzi, "Behind Iran's Middle East Diplomacy," *Middle East International,* number 608, September 17, 1999, pp. 21–23.

141. Harvey Morris, "Saudi Arabia/Iran: Partnership," *Arabies Trends,* number 22, July-August 1999, pp. 14–15.

142. "Iran's Rafsanjani Visits HQ of Saudi National Guard," *FBIS—FTS19980-222000537,* February 22, 1998.

143. "Saudi Defense Minister Speaks in Tehran," *FBIS—FTS19990502000136,* May 2, 1999.

144. From a UAE perspective, President Khatami's charm necessitated skillful Arab persuasion to help settle the disputes over the occupied Abu Musa and Tunb islands. In the event, Riyadh accepted Teheran's pledge to help solve the conflict—but no more—further disappointing Shaykh Zayed bin Sultan Al Nahyan and distancing Saudi Arabia from one of its staunch GCC allies.

Chapter 4

1. Without implying similarities between that case and the current situation, the fact of the matter is that "corrective moves" are not new to the Kingdom and, under certain circumstances, could well occur again. Historically, intrafamily changes have been routine, often with sanguinary consequences. In King Saud's case, senior members of the ruling family agreed that the monarch was unfit to rule and, to save the day, called on Prince Faysal to assume the reigns of authority.

2. Given the supersensitive nature of this subject, any discussions that Al Saud family members entertained on its various permutations were strictly confidential. Few would venture to entertain the possibility that a member of the family would attempt a coup, although several honestly acknowledged that the Kingdom was not immune to such a threat. Most raised the theoretical possibility of a military coup in the United States in defending their views. While the comparison is theoretical (given the vast bureaucracy and myriad checks and balances in place in the United States), there is an element of truth to this interpretation. Where several erred was in comparing Saudi Arabia with the United States, two entirely different societies, where the loci of power are diametrically opposed: a parliamentary democracy versus an absolute monarchy. Still, such remarks could be interpreted as follows: first, a military coup can occur in Saudi Arabia (after all, several past attempts were well known to have occurred), and second, a successful military coup would require a member (or members) of the Al Saud family participating in it.

3. Arbitrarily choosing 3 million barrels per day, for example, would introduce a dramatic factor on price stability. The 3 mbpd figure was long believed the minimum level needed to sustain Riyadh's expenditures. Such an action would remove an estimated 5 million to 6 million barrels of oil per day from the world market, precipitating a worldwide financial mini-crisis.

Chapter 5

1. Majid Khadduri, *Arab Personalities in Politics,* Washington, D.C.: The Middle East Institute, 1981, p. 9. Khadduri's seminal work on Arab leaders emphasizes the role of personalities in Middle Eastern political life. Saudi leaders took into account the governance of a population but also of a large and complex family with multifaceted interests.

Bibliography

Master's Theses and Doctoral Dissertations

Samore, Gary Samuel. *Royal Family Politics in Saudi Arabia (1953–1982),* Cambridge, Massachusetts: Harvard University, December 1983.

Walt, Joseph William. *Saudi Arabia and the Americans: 1928–1951,* Evanston, Illinois: Northwestern University, 1960.

Books and Unpublished Manuscripts

bin Abdul Aziz, Talal. *Risalah ilal-Muwatin* [A Letter to the Citizen], Cairo?: n.p., 1962?

Abdul Ghafur, Ahmad. *Muhammad bin Abdul Wahhab,* Makkah: Muassasat Makkah Lil-Nashr, 1979.

Abdul-Hay Gazzaz, Hassan. *Al-Amn Allazi Na'ishuha* [The Security We Enjoy], 2 volumes, 3rd edition, Jeddah, Saudi Arabia: Dar Al-'Ilm Printing and Publishing Co., 1993. (A one-volume summary was published in English under the same title in 1992.)

Abir, Mordechai. *Oil, Power and Politics,* London: Frank Cass, 1974.

———. *Saudi Arabia in the Oil Era: Regime and Elites; Conflict and Collaboration,* Boulder, Colorado: Westview Press, 1988.

Aburish, Said K. *The Rise, Corruption and Coming Fall of the House of Saud,* London: Bloomsbury, 1994.

Ahrari, Mohammed E. *OPEC: The Falling Giant,* Lexington: The University Press of Kentucky, 1986.

Ali, Sheikh Rustum. *Saudi Arabia and Oil Diplomacy,* New York: Praeger Publishers, 1976.

Anderson, Irvine H. *Aramco, the United States, and Saudi Arabia: A Study of the Dynamics of Foreign Oil Policy, 1933–1950,* Princeton, New Jersey: Princeton University Press, 1981.

Armstrong, Harold C. *Lord of Arabia: Ibn Saud, An Intimate Study of a King,* London: Arthur Barker, Ltd., 1934.

Askari, Hossein. *Saudi Arabia's Economy: Oil and the Search for Economic Development,* Greenwich, Connecticut: JAI Press Inc., 1990.

Badeeb, Saeed M. *The Saudi-Egyptian Conflict Over North Yemen, 1962–1970,* Boulder, Colorado: Westview Press, 1986.

Beaver, Paul (ed). *Jane's Sentinel: The Unfair Advantage,* London: Jane's Information Group, 1994.

Bendix, Reinhard. *Kings or People: Power and the Mandate to Rule,* Berkeley and Los Angeles: University of California Press, 1978, 1980.

Benoist-Mechin, *Le Loup et le Leopard: Ibn-Seoud ou la naissance d'un royaume,* Paris: Albin Michel, 1955.

Bligh, Alexander. *From Prince to King: Royal Succession in the House of Saud in the Twentieth Century,* New York and London: New York University Press, 1984.

Brzezinski, Zbigniew. *Power and Principle: Memoirs of the National Security Adviser, 1977–1981,* New York: Farrar, Straus and Giroux, 1983.

Bulloch, John. *Reforms of the Saudi Arabian Constitution,* London: Gulf Center for Strategic Studies, April 1992.

Burling, Robbins. *The Passage of Power: Studies in Political Succession,* New York: Academic Press, 1974.

Bush, George, and Brent Scowcroft. *A World Transformed.* New York: Alfred A. Knopf, Inc., 1998.

Cave Brown, Anthony. *Oil, God, and Gold: The Story of Aramco and the Saudi Kings,* Boston: Houghton Mifflin Company, 1999.

CDLR Yearbook '94-'95, London: The Committee for the Defense of Legitimate Rights, November 1994.

Conrad, Lawrence I. (ed.). *The Formation and Perception of the Modern Arab World: Studies by Marwan R. Buheiry,* Princeton, New Jersey: The Darwin Press, Inc., 1989.

Cordesman, Anthony H. *Saudi Arabia: Guarding the Desert Kingdom,* Boulder, Colorado: Westview Press, 1997.

Coulson, Noel J. *A History of Islamic Law,* Edinburgh: Edinburgh University Press, 1964.

Darwish, Adel, and Gregory Alexander. *Unholy Babylon: The Secret History of Saddam's War,* New York: St. Martin's Press, 1991.

Dawisha, Adeed I. *Saudi Arabia's Search for Security,* London: The International Institute for Strategic Studies (Adelphi Paper Number 158), 1979.

Dekmejian, R. Hrair. *Islam in Revolution: Fundamentalism in the Arab World,* Syracuse, New York: Syracuse University Press, 1985, 1989.

Emerson, Steven. *The American House of Saud: The Secret Petrodollar Connection,* New York: Franklin Watts, 1985.

Fandy, Mamoun. *Saudi Arabia and the Politics of Dissent,* New York: St. Martin's Press, 1999.

Al-Farsy, Fouad. *Modernity and Tradition: The Saudi Equation,* London and New York: Kegan Paul International, 1994.

_____. *Saudi Arabia: A Case Study in Development,* New York: Routledge, Chapman & Hall Inc., 1986.

Field, Michael. *The Merchants: The Big Business Families of Saudi Arabia and the Gulf States,* Woodstock: The Overlook Press, 1985.

De Gaury, Gerald. *Faisal: King of Saudi Arabia,* New York: Frederick A. Praeger Publishers, 1967.

Gause, F. Gregory, III. *Oil Monarchies: Domestic and Security Challenges in the Arab Gulf States,* New York: Council on Foreign Relations Press, 1994.

_____. *Saudi-Yemeni Relations: Domestic Structures and Foreign Influence,* New York: Columbia University Press, 1990.

Graham, Douglas F. Saudi *Arabia Unveiled,* Dubuque, Iowa: Kendall/Hunt, 1991.

Habib, John S. *Ibn Sa'ud's Warriors of Islam: The Ikhwan of Najd and Their Role in the Creation of the Sa'udi Kingdom, 1910–1930,* Leiden, the Netherlands: E. J. Brill, 1978.

Hammed, Mazher A. *Arabia Imperilled: The Security Imperatives of the Arab Gulf States,* Washington, D.C.: Middle East Assessments Group, 1986.

Hart, Parker T. *Saudi Arabia and the United States: Birth of a Security Partnership,* Bloomington and Indianapolis: Indiana University Press, 1998.

Helms, Christine Moss. *The Cohesion of Saudi Arabia: Evolution of Saudi Arabia,* Baltimore and London: The Johns Hopkins University Press, 1981.

Henderson, Simon. *After King Fahd: Succession in Saudi Arabia,* policy paper number 37, 2nd edition, Washington, D.C.: The Washington Institute for Near East Policy, 1995.

Herb, Michael. *All in the Family: Absolutism, Revolution, and Democracy in the Middle Eastern Monarchies,* Albany: State University of New York Press, 1999.

Hiro, Dilip. *Desert Shield to Desert Storm: The Second Gulf War,* New York, Routledge, 1992.

Holden, David, and Richard Johns. *The House of Saud: The Rise and Rule of the Most Powerful Dynasty in the Arab World,* New York: Holt, Rinehart and Winston, 1981.

Howarth, David. *The Desert King: The Life of Ibn Saud,* London: Quartet Books, 1965, 1980.

Huyette, Summer Scott. *Political Adaptation in Saudi Arabia: A Study of the Council of Ministers,* Boulder and London: Westview Press, 1985.

Islami, A. Reza S., and Rostam Mehraban Kavoussi. *The Political Economy of Saudi Arabia,* Seattle: University of Washington Press, 1984.

Jerichow, Anders. *Saudi Arabia: Outside Global Law and Order-A Discussion Paper,* Surrey, United Kingdom: Curzon, 1997.

_____. *The Saudi File: People, Power, Politics,* New York: St. Martin's Press, 1998.

Katz, Mark N. *Russia and Arabia: Soviet Foreign Policy Toward the Arabian Peninsula,* Baltimore, Maryland: The Johns Hopkins University Press, 1986.

Kechichian, Joseph A. (ed.). *A Century in Thirty Years: Shaykh Zayed and the United Arab Emirates,* Washington, D.C.: The Middle East Policy Council, 2000.

_____. *Political Dynamics and Security in the Arabian Peninsula Through the 1990s,* MR-167-AF/A, Santa Monica, California: RAND, 1993.

_____. *Oman and the World: The Emergence of an Independent Foreign Policy,* MR 680-RC, Santa Monica, California: RAND, 1995.

Kelley, J. B. *Arabia, the Gulf and the West,* New York: Basic Books, 1980.

Khadduri, Majid. *Arab Contemporaries: The Role of Personalities in Politics,* Baltimore: Johns Hopkins, 1973.

_____. *Arab Personalities in Politics,* Washington, D.C.: The Middle East Institute, 1981.

Kishk, Muhammad Jalal. *Al-Saudiyyun Wal-Hal Al-Islami* [The Saudis and the Islamic Solution], Jeddah: The Saudi Publishing and Distribution House, 1982.

Kissinger, Henry. *Years of Upheaval,* Boston: Little, Brown and Company, 1982.

Knauerhause, Ramon. *The Saudi Arabian Economy,* New York: Praeger, 1975.

Korn, David A. *Stalemate: The War of Attrition and Great Power Diplomacy in the Middle East, 1967–1970,* Boulder, Colorado: Westview Press, 1992.

Kostiner, Joseph. *Middle East Monarchies: The Challenge of Modernity*, Boulder and London: Lynne Rienner Publishers, 2000.

Kostiner, Joseph. *The Making of Saudi Arabia 1916–1936: From Chieftaincy to Monarchical State*, New York and Oxford: Oxford University Press, 1993.

Koury, Enver M. *The Saudi Decision-Making Body: The House of Al-Saud*, Hyattsville, Maryland: Institute of Middle Eastern and North African Affairs, 1978.

Lackner, Helen. *A House Built on Sand: A Political Economy of Saudi Arabia*, London: Ithaca Press, 1978.

Laoust, Henri. *Le Califat Dans La Doctrine de Ras[h]id Rida*, Paris: Librairie d'Amerique et d'Orient, 1986.

Lapidus, Ira M. *A History of Islamic Societies*, Cambridge: Cambridge University Press, 1988.

Leatherdale, Clive. *Britain and Saudi Arabia, 1925–1939: The Imperial Oasis*, London: Frank Cass Publishers, 1983.

Lees, Brian. *A Handbook of the Al Saud Family of Saudi Arabia*, London: Royal Genealogies, 1980.

Legum, Colin (ed.). *Middle East Contemporary Survey 1, 1976–1977*, New York and London: Holmes & Meier Publishers, Inc., 1978.

Long, David E. *The Kingdom of Saudi Arabia*, Gainesville, Florida: University Press of Florida, 1997.

_____. *Saudi Arabia*, Beverly Hills and London: Sage Publications (for the Center for Strategic and International Studies, The Washington Papers 4:39), 1976.

_____. *The United States and Saudi Arabia: Ambivalent Allies*, Boulder and London: Westview Press, 1985.

Mackey, Sandra. *The Saudis: Inside the Desert Kingdom*, Boston: Houghton Mifflin Company, 1987.

McLoughlin, Leslie. *Ibn Saud: Founder of a Kingdom*, London: Macmillan Press, 1993.

Metz, Helen Chapin (ed.). *Saudi Arabia: A Country Study*, Washington, D.C.: Federal Research Division, U.S. Library of Congress, 1993.

Miller, Aaron David. *Search for Security: Saudi Arabian Oil and American Foreign Policy, 1939–1949*, Chapel Hill, North Carolina: The University of North Carolina Press, 1980.

Moore, John Norton. *Crisis in the Gulf: Enforcing the Rule of Law*, New York: Oceana Publications, Inc., 1992.

Mosely, Leonard. *Power Play: Oil in the Middle East*, Baltimore: Penguin Books, 1974.

Munif, Abdelrahman. *Cities of Salt*, New York: Vintage International, 1989.

_____. *The Trench*, New York: Pantheon Books, 1991.

_____. *Variations on Night and Day*, New York: Pantheon Books, 1993.

Plascov, Avi. *Security in the Persian Gulf: Modernization, Political Development and Stability*, Totowa, New Jersey: Allanheld, Osmun & Company, 1982.

Philby, H. St. John. *Saudi Arabia*, London: Ernest Benn Ltd., 1955.

Powell, William. *Saudi Arabia and Its Royal Family*, Secaucus, New Jersey: Lyle Stuart, Inc., 1982.

Pierre, Andrew J. *The Global Politics of Arms Sales*, Princeton, New Jersey: Princeton University Press, 1982.

Quandt, William B. *Saudi Arabia in the 1980s: Foreign Policy, Security, and Oil*, Washington, D.C.: The Brookings Institution, 1981.

Ramazani, R. K. *The Gulf Cooperation Council: Records and Analysis,* Charlottesville, Virginia: University Press of Virginia, 1988.

_____. *Revolutionary Iran: Challenge and Response in the Middle East,* Baltimore: The Johns Hopkins University Press, 1988.

Al Rasheed, Madawi. *Politics in an Arabian Oasis: The Rashidi Tribal Dynasty,* London and New York: I. B. Tauris & Co. Limited, 1991.

Rashid, Ibrahim (ed.). *Documents in the History of Saudi Arabia,* volumes 1–8, 1976-1985.

Rejai, Mostafa. *Comparative Political Ideologies,* New York: St. Martin's Press, 1984.

Robinson, Jeffrey. *Yamani: The Inside Story,* New York: The Atlantic Monthly Press, 1988.

Sachedina, Abdulaziz Abdulhussein. *The Just Ruler in Shi'ite Islam: The Comprehensive Authority of the Jurist in Imamite Jurisprudence,* New York and London: Oxford University Press, 1988.

Al-Said, Nasir. *Tarikh Al Saud* [History of the Al Saud], 2 volumes, Beirut: Al-Ittihad Press, 1985.

Safran, Nadav. *Saudi Arabia: The Ceaseless Quest for Security,* Boston, Massachusetts: Harvard University Press, 1985.

Salameh, Ghassan. *Al-Siyasat al-Kharijiyat al-Sa'udiyat munzu 'am 1945* [Saudi Foreign Policy Since 1945], Beirut: Ma'had al-anma' al-'arabi, 1980.

Salinger, Pierre, with Eric Laurent. *Secret Dossier: The Hidden Agenda Behind the Gulf War,* New York: Penguin Books, 1991.

Seymour, Ian. *OPEC: Instrument of Change,* New York: St. Martin's Press, 1981.

Shaban, M. A. *The Abbasid Revolution,* Cambridge: Cambridge University Press, 1970.

Sheean, Vincent. *Faisal: The King and His Kingdom,* Tavistock, England: University Press of Arabia, 1975.

Simons, Geoff. *Saudi Arabia: The Shape of a Client Feudalism,* New York: St. Martin's Press, 1998.

bin Sultan, Khaled (with Patrick Seale). *Desert Warrior: A Personal View of the Gulf War by the Joint Forces Commander,* New York: HarperCollins Publishers, Inc., 1995.

Tibi, Bassam. *Conflict and War in the Middle East, 1967–1991,* New York: St. Martin's Press, 1993.

Troeller, Gary. *The Birth of Saudi Arabia: Britain and the Rise of the House of Sa'ud,* London: Frank Cass Publishers, 1976.

Twitchell, K. S. *Saudi Arabia,* Princeton, New Jersey: Princeton University Press, 1953.

Al Uthaymin, Abdul Saleh. *Nashat Imarat al Rashid* [Accomplishments of the Al Rashid Emirate], Riyadh: n.p., 1981.

_____. *Tarikh al-Mamlakat Al-Arabiyah al-Sa'udiyah* [History of the Kingdom of Saudi Arabia], volume 1, Riyadh: n.p., 1984, 1995.

Vassiliev, Alexei. *The History of Saudi Arabia,* London: Saqi Books, 1998.

Abd al-Wahab, Muhammad. *Al-Usul Al-Thalatha wa Adillatuha* [The Three Principles and Their Proofs], Cairo: Dar Al-Tiba' Al-Yusufiyah, n.d.

Wilson, Peter W., and Douglas F. Graham. *Saudi Arabia: The Coming Storm,* Armonk, New York: M. E. Sharpe, 1994.

Woodward, Bob. *The Commanders,* New York: Simon & Schuster, 1991.

Yamani, Hani A. Z. *To Be A Saudi,* London: Janus Publishing Company, 1997.

Al-Yassini, Ayman. *Religion and State in the Kingdom of Saudi Arabia,* Boulder and London: Westview Press, 1985.

Yizraeli, Sarah. *The Remaking of Saudi Arabia: The Struggle Between King Saʿud and Crown Prince Faysal, 1953–1962,* Tel Aviv, Israel: The Moshe Dayan Center for Middle Eastern and African Studies, 1997.

Articles, Chapters, Monographs, and Pamphlets

Abd Al-Muttalib, Fikri. "Clandestine Opposition Movements in Saudi Arabia," *Al-Yaqzah Al-Arabiyah* (Cairo), December 1987, pp. 27–39.

Ambah, Faiza Saleh. "Crown Prince Popular With Saudis," The Associated Press, July 31, 1999.

Azydan, Hamad. "The Economic and Political Situation in Saudi Arabia and the Effect of the Iranian Revolution," *Al-Hurriyah* (Beirut), June 4, 1979, pp. 36–37.

Barzin, Saeed. "Iran: Evolving New Axis?" *Middle East International,* number 600, May 21, 1999, pp. 13–14.

Braibanti, Ralph, and Fouad Abdul-Salem Al-Farsy, "Saudi Arabia: A Developmental Perspective," *Journal of South Asian and Middle Eastern Studies* 1:1, fall 1977, pp. 3–43.

de Borchgrave, Arnaud. "Undercutting Fahd," *Newsweek,* April 23, 1979, pp. 51–52.

de Briganti, Giovanni. "Cash-Strapped Saudis Proceed on 3 French Contracts," *Defense News* 9:5, February 7–13, 1994, p. 36.

Canard, Marius. "Fatimids," *Encyclopaedia of Islam,* new edition, volume 2, Leiden, the Netherlands: E. J. Brill, 1960- , pp. 850–62.

"Change Is Inevitable in Saudi Arabia," *Al-Quds Al-Arabi,* April 16, 1998, reproduced in *Mideast Mirror,* April 17, 1998.

"Crackdown on Opposition Feared After Alleged Attack," *Al-Quds Al-Arabi,* September 17, 1993, p. 1.

Dakroub, Hussein. "Gulf States May Form Joint Military Unit," *The Washington Times,* December 22, 1993, p. 15.

Al-Darwis, Idris. "We Make Educated, Devout Fighters: Interview with Col. Mitab Bin Abdallah, Commander of the King Khalid Military Academy," *Al-Yamamah,* January 23, 1985, pp. 14–19.

Dawisha, Adeed I. "Internal Values and External Threats: The Making of Saudi Foreign Policy," *Orbis* 23:1, spring 1979.

Dekmejian, R. Hrair. "Saudi Arabia's Consultative Council," *The Middle East Journal* 52:2, spring 1998, pp. 204–218.

_____. "The Rise of Political Islamism in Saudi Arabia," *The Middle East Journal* 48:4, autumn 1994, pp. 627–643.

"Differences Still Seen Within Ruling Family," *Al-Nida Al-Usbu* (Beirut), May 27, 1979, p. 1.

Dorsey, James. "After Mecca, Saudi Rulers Provide a Channel for Dissent," *The Christian Science Monitor,* March 14, 1980, p. 7.

Engel, Richard. "Saudi Succession Unresolved," *The Washington Times,* April 22, 1998.

Feith, Douglas J. "The Oil Weapon De-Mystified," *Policy Review,* number 15, winter 1981, pp. 19–39.

Finnegan, Philip. "Iran Navy Buildup Stirs U.S.-Arab Response," *Defense News* 8:49, December 6–12, 1993, p. 28.

Gibb, H. A. R. "Al-Mawardi's Theory of the Caliphate," in Stanford J. Shaw and William R. Polk (eds.), *Studies on the Civilization of Islam,* Princeton, New Jersey: Princeton University Press, 1982, pp. 151–165.

Goodarzi, Jubin. "Behind Iran's Middle East Diplomacy, *Middle East International,* number 608, September 17, 1999, pp. 21–23.

"Growing Regional Influence of Kingdom Discussed," *Al-Majallah,* number 83, September 12–18, 1981, pp. 12–19.

Heim, Pierre. "After the Shock," *Remarques Arabo-Africaines* (Brussels), number 527, 1980, pp. 10–12.

Heisbourg, Francois. "France and the Gulf Crisis," in Nicole Gnesotto and John Roper (eds.), *Western Europe and the Gulf,* Paris: The Institute for Security Studies–Western European Union, 1992, pp. 17–38.

Holden, David. "A Family Affair," *The New York Times Magazine,* July 6, 1975, pp. 8–9, 26–27.

Ibrahim, Youssef M. "Saudi King Issues Decrees to Revise Governing System," *The New York Times,* March 2, 1992, p. 1.

"ICHR-GAP Lauds New Saudi Rights Group," *Arabia Monitor* 2:5, May 1993, pp. 1, 6.

Ignatius, David. "Royal Payoffs: Big Saudi Oil Deal With Italy Collapses After Fee Plan Is Bared," *The Wall Street Journal,* May 4, 1981, pp. 1, 21.

_____. "Some Saudi Princes Pressure Oil Firms For Secret Payments," *The Wall Street Journal,* May 1, 1981, p. 23.

"Interview with Minister of Petroleum and Mineral Resources Shaykh Ahmad Zaki Al-Yamani," *Al-Mustaqbal* (Paris), number 258, January 30, 1982, pp. 49–52.

"Iran 'Waiting for UAE' to Agree to Talks on Islands," *Mideast Mirror,* November 25, 1993, p. 17.

Al Jabariti, Anwar Abdul Majid. "Al Amir Abdallah Wal-Suq" [Prince Abdallah and the Market], *Al-Hayat,* number 13378, October 24, 1999, p. 23.

Jarrah, Najm. "Small Step Forward," *Middle East International,* number 457, August 28, 1993, pp. 12–13.

Jehl, Douglas. "Sheik Shares His Misgivings Over U.S. Policies," *The New York Times,* May 31, 1998, p. 5.

Karasik, Theodore. *Azerbaijan, Central Asia, and Future Persian Gulf Security,* N-3579-AF/A, Santa Monica, California: RAND, 1992.

Katz, Mark N. "External Powers and the Yemeni Civil War," in Jamal S. al-Suwaidi (ed.), *The Yemeni War of 1994: Causes and Consequences,* London: Saqi Books for the Emirates Center for Strategic Studies and Research, 1995, pp. 81–93.

"Kuwait Signs Defense Pact with Moscow," *Mideast Mirror,* November 30, 1993, p. 22.

Kechichian, Joseph A. "Islamic Revivalism and Change in Saudi Arabia: Juhayman Al-Utaybi's 'Letters' to the Saudi People," *The Muslim World* 70:1, January 1990, pp. 1–16.

_____. "Political Minefields in the Persian Gulf: The Succession Issue," *Energy Compass* 6:46, November 17, 1995, pp. 14–17.

_____. "The Role of the Ulama in the Politics of an Islamic State: The Case of Saudi Arabia," *International Journal of Middle East Studies* 18:1, February 1986, pp. 53–71.

_____. "Saudi Arabia's Will to Power," *Middle East Policy* 7:2, February 2000, pp. 47–60.

_____. "Sa'ud, Faysal Ibn 'Abd Al-'Aziz Al," *The Oxford Encyclopedia of the Modern Islamic World,* 1995, volume 4, pp. 3–4.

_____. "Saudi/US Partnership: The Ties that Bind," *Arabies Trends,* number 14, November 1998, p. 22–24.

_____. "Trends in Saudi National Security," *The Middle East Journal* 53:2, Spring 1999, pp. 232–53.

_____. "The United States and the Arab Gulf Monarchies," *Les Notes de l'IFRI,* number 8, Institut Francais des Relations Internationales, Paris, 1999, pp. 1–58.

Kelidar, Abbas R. "The Problem of Succession in Saudi Arabia," *Asian Affairs* 9:1, February 1978, pp. 23–30.

Khalid, Taysir. "The Situation in Saudi Arabia and the Horizons for Develpment: Agencies, Political Decisionmaking, and the Special Role," *Al-Safir* (Beirut), February 1, 1981, p. 15.

"King of Oil Surges Ahead," *Petroleum Economist* 58:12, December 1991, p. 7.

Knauerhase, Ramon. "Saudi Arabia: Our Conservative Muslim Ally," *Current History* 76:453, January 1980, pp. 35–37.

Lalevee, Thierry. "Teheran's New Allies in Africa," *World Press Review,* September 1993, p. 20.

Lewis, Bernard. "Politics and War," in Joseph Schacht with C. E. Bosworth (eds.), *The Legacy of Islam,* 2nd edition, Oxford: Clarendon Press, 1974, pp. 156–209.

Long, David E. "King Faisal's World View," in Willard A. Belling, *King Faisal and the Modernization of Saudi Arabia,* London and Boulder: Croom Helm and Westview Press, 1980, pp. 173–183.

_____. "Saudi Oil Policy," *The Wilson Quarterly,* winter 1979, p. 85.

Abd Al-Majid, Faruq. "The Saudi-Yugoslav Flirtation," *Al-Musawwar,* number 3118, July 13, 1984, pp. 35–38.

"Military College Graduates Include Palestinians," *Al-Madinah,* July 2, 1992, p. 3.

"Mitterrand to Press Saudis on Oil Threats," *The Financial Times,* October 15, 1993, p. 5.

Mishawi, Tawfik. "A New Direction," *The Middle East Magazine,* May 1979.

Morris, Harvey. "Saudi Arabia/Iran: Partnership," *Arabies Trends,* number 22, July-August 1999, pp. 14–15.

Al-Muqrin, Abd Al-Rahman, and Abdallah Al-Umayrah, "Prince Sultan: Feasibility Studies for Four Huge Military Factories," *Al-Riyadh,* April 27, 1987, p. 1.

Murphy, Caryle. "Saudi Arabia Bans Rights Group," *The Washington Post,* May 14, 1993, p. 35.

Al-Musaybah, Saud. "Acting for Al-Fahd, Crown Prince Observes Opening Ceremony Today at King Khalid Military College," *Al-Riyadh,* December 18, 1982, p. 4, in "Overview On King Khalid Military College," *JPRS-Near East/South Asia Report,* number 2730, April 1, 1983, p. 22.

Al-Muttalib, Fikri Abd. "Clandestine Opposition Movements in Saudi Arabia," *Al-Yaqzah Al-Arabiyah* (Cairo), December 1987, pp. 27–39, in "Russian Author Traces Opposition in Saudi Arabia," *JPRS-NEA-88–011,* February 26, 1988, p. 15.

Naaoush, Sabah. "A Catastrophic Financial Situtation," *Marches Tropicaux et Mediteranees,* May 29, 1992, pp. 1382–1384.

Nasrawi, Salah. "Saudi Prince Urges Changes," The Associated Press, June 6, 1999.

Nimr, Sulayman. "Saudi Arms: Diversified Sources and Modern Sites," *Al-Mustaqbal,* September 6, 1980, p. 18.

"No Change in Oil Policy Says Prince Nayif," *Middle East Economic Survey* 30:4, November 3, 1986, p. A5.

Podeh, Elie. "The Struggle Over Arab Hegemony After the Suez Crisis," *Middle Eastern Studies* 29:1, January 1993, pp. 91–110.

Pipes, Daniel, and Patrick Clawson. "Ambitious Iran, Troubled Neighbors," *Foreign Affairs* 72:1, America and the World 1992–1993, pp. 124–141.

"The Party Isn't Over," *The Economist* 327:7817, June 26, 1993, p. 57.

"18 Preachers Banned in Riyadh," *Arabia Monitor* 2:2, February 1993, p. 7.

"Prince Nayif Backs Gulf Rapid Deployment Force," *Al-Yawn* (Ad-Damman), February 23, 1982, p. 1.

"Prince Turki Discusses Saudi Role in Sudanese Crisis," *Al-Ashiqqa* (Khartoum), May 31, 1988, pp. 17–22.

Quandt, William B. "U.S. Energy Policy and the Arab-Israeli Conflict," in Naiem A. Sherbiny and Mark A. Tessler (eds.), *Arab Oil: Impact on the Arab Countries and Global Implications,* New York: Praeger Publishers, 1976.

Al-Rashid, Mashal. "Al-Jazirah Explores Opinions of Officials at King Abdulaziz War College on College's Educational Message," *Al-Jazirah,* May 15, 1984, p. 11.

Rattner, Steven. "Khalid is Dead; Fahd Succeeds in Saudi Arabia," *The New York Times,* June 14, 1982.

Richards, D. S. "Fatimid Dynasty," *The Oxford Encyclopaedia of the Modern Islamic World,* New York and Oxford: Oxford University Press, 1995, pp. 7–8.

Al-Rifa, Ahmad Sharif. "The King and Responsibility, Part Seven: Oil and Politics: As a Result of Fahd's Great Stand, the World Was Spared an Explosion that Would Have Led to Disaster," *Al-Madinah,* October 4, 1982, p. 9, in "King's Position on Oil Production, Pricing Reviewed," *JPRS-Near East-North Africa,* number 2661, November 17, 1982, p. 130.

"Royal Saudi Air Force: Safeguarding Peace and Stability," *Saudi Arabia* 8:1, spring 1991, p. 7.

Rusinov, Colonel R. "Saudi Arabia's Armed Forces" [in Russian] *Zarubehshnoye voyennoye obzreniye,* January 1994, pp. 9–11.

"Al-Salafiyah Opposition Training Camp Found," *Al-Ahd* (Beirut), October 29, 1993, p. 16.

Salameh, Ghassan. "Political Power and the Saudi State, *MERIP Reports,* number 91, October 1981, p. 8.

Samore, Gary. "The Persian Gulf," in David A. Deese and Joseph S. Nye (eds.), *Energy and Security,* Cambridge: Ballinger Publishing Company, 1981.

"Saudi King Fahd Shares Bush Peace 'Instinct,'" *Reuters Library Report,* January 6, 1991.

"Saudi Oil Grant to Help Turkish Military," *Middle East Economic Survey* 35:1, October 7, 1991, p. A3.

"Saudis Cooperated with Reagan, Bush," *World Oil* 213:8, August 1992, p. 9.

"Saudis May Buy Subs to Protect Coasts," *The Journal of Commerce,* April 18, 1994, p. 7B.

"Saudis Welcome U.S. Troops to Stop Saddam," *Reuters Library Report,* August 29, 1990.

Sciolino, Elaine. "Iran's Durable Revolution," *Foreign Affairs* 61:4, spring 1983, pp. 893–920.

"Seeds on Stony Ground," *The Economist* 327:7815, June 12, 1993, p. 53.

Standenmaier, William O. "Military Policy and Strategy in the Gulf War," *Parameters* 12:2, June 1982, pp. 25–35.

_____, and Shirin Tahir-Kheli, *The Saudi-Pakistani Military Relationship and its Implications for U.S. Strategy in Southwest Asia,* Carlisle Barracks, Pennsylvania: U.S. Army War College Strategic Studies Institute, October 1, 1981.

"Studies to Produce Military Hardware Conducted," *Al-Khalij,* May 17, 1992, p. 18.

"Sudur Al-Nizam Al-Jadid li-majlis Al-Wuzarat wa a'da' wa la-wa'ih majlis al-shura fil-Saudiyyah" [New Regulations for the Council of Ministers and Membership and By-laws of the Consultative Council in Saudi Arabia] *Al-Hayat,* number 11147, August 21, 1993, p. 6.

Sullivan, Robert R. "Saudi Arabia in International Politics," *Review of Politics* 32:4, October 1970, pp. 436–460.

Sultan, General Prince Khaled bin. "The Gulf War and Its Aftermath: A Personal Perspective," *RUSI Journal* 138:6, December 1993, pp. 1–5.

Tadjbakhsh, Shahrbanou. "The Bloody Path of Change: The Case of Post-Soviet Tajikistan," *The Harriman Institute Forum,* July 1993.

"Talal Ibn Abdulaziz Reveals the Secrets of the Base in Dhahran," *Al-Nahar Al-Arabi Wa Al-Duwali,* April 7–13, 1980, pp. 18–19.

"Telephone Interview with Saudi Ambassador to Sanna," *Ukaz,* April 21, 1992, p. 5.

Tinnin, David. "Saudis Recognize Their Vulnerability," *Fortune,* March 10, 1980, pp. 48–55.

Tucker, Robert W. "Further Reflections on Oil and Force," *Commentary,* March 1975, pp. 45–56.

_____. "Oil: The Issue of American Intervention," *Commentary,* January 1975, pp. 21–30.

Turner, Louis, and James Bedore. "Saudi Arabia: The Power of the Purse-Strings," *International Affairs* 54:3, July 1978.

Tusa, Francis. "LAV's in the Gulf: Saudi National Guard Hopes to Resume Modernization Plans," *Armed Forces Journal International* 131:10, May 1994, p. 39.

"U.K. Offers Submarine Lease," *Sentinel: The Gulf States* 1:7, April 1994, p. 1.

"When Saudi Arabia Says No to Storing Oil," *Al-Mustaqbal* (Paris), number 248, November 21, 1981, pp. 53–55.

Wylie, James. "Iran: Quest for Security and Influence," *Jane's Intelligence Review* 5:7, July 1993, p. 311.

Zanoyan, Vahan. *Saudi Arabia's Finances: Current Realities and Short-Term Prospects,* The Petroleum Finance Company, Washington, D.C., September 1993.

Newspapers and Periodicals

Arabies, Paris

Arabies Trends, Paris

The Christian Science Monitor

Country Report–Saudi Arabia, The Economist Intelligence Unit, London, 1990–2000.

FBIS-MEA-1980–1991

FBIS-NEA-1991–2000

The Financial Times

Foreign Report, 1989–1996

Gulf States Newsletter, London

Al-Hayat (Arabic daily), London

The International Herald Tribune
JPRS-NEA-1980–1996.
The Los Angeles Times
Middle East Economic Digest (MEED), London
The New York Times
Oil & Gas Journal
Saudi Arabia Quarterly Report, Middle East Economic Digest, London
The Washington Post

Index